Engaging Young People in Civic Life

Engaging Young People in Civic Life

Edited by James Youniss and Peter Levine

Foreword by Lee Hamilton

Vanderbilt University Press

Nashville

13 12 11 10 09   1 2 3 4 5

This book is printed on acid-free paper
made from 30% post-consumer recycled content.
Manufactured in the United States of America

Cover design: Gary Gore
Text design: Dariel Mayer

Library of Congress Cataloging-in-Publication Data

Engaging young people in civic life / edited by James
Youniss and Peter Levine ; foreword by Lee Hamilton.
p. cm.
Includes bibliographical references and index.
ISBN 978-0-8265-1650-3 (cloth : alk. paper)
ISBN 978-0-8265-1651-0 (pbk. : alk. paper)
1. Youth—Political activity. 2. Political participation.
I. Youniss, James. II. Levine, Peter, 1967–
HQ799.2.P6E54 2009
323'.0420835—dc22
2008037313

Contents

PART II.
POLITICAL ENVIRONMENTS: NEIGHBORHOODS AND CITIES

PART III: POLICY MODELS FROM OTHER NATIONS

Foreword

Lee Hamilton

I can think of no task more important for the future of American democracy than teaching young people about our system of government and encouraging them to get involved in politics and community service. This has been a passion of mine for a long time—during the 34 years I served in Congress, and continuing since I retired from the House in 1999 and established the Center on Congress at Indiana University.

When we fail to educate our children about our history and our system of representative government, we miss an opportunity to enrich their lives, and we miss an opportunity to enrich our country through their involvement. Civic education helps people reach their full potential. It challenges a young person to develop an idea, ask a question, take a stand, speak in public. Civic education can foster positive social interaction within schools and communities, teaching the skills, dispositions, and traits of character that encourage people from varied backgrounds and with different views to listen and to seek common ground. Civic education is the surest antidote to cynicism and apathy, because it shows a young person that he or she can, indeed, make a difference.

America faces challenges today that are so serious they can be downright frightening. A financial crisis, two wars, the threat of terror, and global warming are piled on top of our traditional struggles with economic inequality, access to health care and quality education, racial division, and crime. The more challenging our problems become, the more we need our younger generation to be able to work together to solve them. Human beings don't automatically obtain the skills and knowledge they need to address serious public problems. We must learn to be active citizens, and that takes guidance and experience.

Engaging Young People in Civic Life shows that civic education is much more than the traditional high school class about how a bill becomes a law—important as that may be. It includes all the ways that we prepare young Americans to address our great national challenges. It means moderated discussions of controversial issues in classrooms, which can teach youth to deliberate civilly and responsibly about serious matters. It means young people taking part in student governments and scholastic news media; becoming involved in city governments or working with the police to prevent crime; serving their country at home and abroad; and participating in politics as campaign workers, canvassers, and voters.

These opportunities are far from luxuries. They are essential to the preservation and development of our democracy. As Benjamin Rush, a signer of the Declaration of Independence and one of the first advocates for public education in America, argued, "There is but one method of rendering a republican form of government durable, and that is by disseminating the seeds of virtue and knowledge through education."

Rush might be concerned about the durability of our republic today. In the 2006 National Assessment of Education Progress, two-thirds of students scored below proficiency in civics. Not even a third of eighth graders surveyed could identify the historical purpose of the Declaration of Independence. Less than a fifth of high school seniors could explain how citizen participation benefits democracy.

These statistics are averages. They conceal very serious disparities in civic education, as Joseph Kahne and Ellen Middaugh show in their important chapter in this book. It is not much of an exaggeration to say that we reserve civic education for successful students in high-scoring schools. The very teenagers who most need opportunities for civic learning—those who will not attend college and who live in our most stressed communities—tend never to be included in current-events discussions, service projects, and other experiences that would develop their civic skills.

We invest billions of public dollars in the further education of college students, which often includes opportunities to develop their civic skills, knowledge, and confidence. But those Americans who do not or cannot attend college are eligible for almost no civic education beyond the little they received in high school. No wonder there are stark gaps between youth who attended college and those who did not in almost every form of civic engagement, including voter turnout, volunteering, and group membership.

One of the damaging myths about civic education and civic engagement is that young people don't care. Stereotypes about youth as apathetic or irresponsible are demonstrably false, and they contribute to an educational system that is much too narrowly focused on preventing kids from dropping out or getting in trouble with the police. Many young Americans want opportunities to contribute, lead, and address serious problems. When we give them such opportunities, they thrive. When we deny them the chance to contribute, we alienate them and waste their human gifts.

To provide good opportunities requires more than skillful teachers, well-designed textbooks, and enriching experiences (such as competitions, simulations, and online materials). It also requires changing our public policies so that civic education becomes a much higher priority for schools and other institutions. I am proud to join retired Supreme Court Justice Sandra Day O'Connor and former Colorado Governor Roy Romer in co-chairing the National Advisory Council of the Campaign for the Civic Mission of Schools, a nonpartisan advocacy effort that is working to change policies in Washington and the 50 states. This book will inform the campaign's efforts and should influence other citizens who care about democracy.

Engaging Young People in Civic Life is tough-minded, data-driven, and unsentimental. It is full of concrete policy proposals for schools, municipalities, service programs, and political parties. It offers all the appropriate scholarly caveats and qualifications. But at its heart, it is a plea to revive American democracy by offering all our young people the civic opportunities they want and so richly deserve.

Lee H. Hamilton is Director of the Center on Congress at Indiana University.

Acknowledgments

This volume was developed in a series of meetings held at the Catholic University of America in Washington, DC. These meetings were supported by Carnegie Corporation of New York through its U.S. Democracy Program under the guidance of Cynthia Gibson, who was then a Carnegie program officer. At these meetings, researchers and policy makers met to assess the literature and to discuss ways to promote the civic engagement of youth through schools, youth organizations, community initiatives, and government programs. We thank the Corporation for its generous support and encouragement on this important problem facing our democracy. Youth do not become citizens by dint of having reached voting age. Citizenship is formed through the development of habits of democratic practices and the construction of self-defining identities. Hence policies for youth are policies for our democracy now and in the future.

We also thank the staff members of the Life Cycle Institute at the Catholic University who managed arrangements for the meetings, especially administrative assistants Woinishet Negash and Mary Anne Eley, the Institute's director, Steven Schneck, and our colleagues, Michael Foley, Lene Jensen, John White, and Hugh McIntosh, who participated in our discussions and helped in many other ways.

We also thank the staff of the Center for Information and Research in Civic Learning and Engagement (CIRCLE), which was then located at the University of Maryland. Demetria Sapienza, Dionne Williams, and Barbara Cronin were especially helpful in planning and managing the meetings.

We also thank Michael Ames and his able staff at Vanderbilt University Press for their support throughout the book publication process.

Engaging Young People in Civic Life

Introduction
Policy for Youth Civic Engagement

Peter Levine and James Youniss

This book went to press soon after young Americans voted at extraordinarily high rates in the presidential primaries of 2008. The turnout rate of citizens under the age of 30 almost doubled that of 2000, the most recent year when there were competitive primaries in both parties (Kirby et al., 2000). As we write, young people are visibly excited, idealistic, and hopeful, as their high rates of volunteering and community service also demonstrate. Yet the turnout increase was uneven: young adults who had never attended college voted at very low rates. The results were still not adequate: more than 80 percent of all young adults did *not* vote in the primaries. And the uptick may not last. This burst of democratic participation invites us to ask how we can institutionalize the role of youth.

After all, America needs young people to participate in our politics and civil society. Participation is good for them; it gives them a sense of purpose and meaning as well as valuable skills. In this volume, Daniel Hart and Ben Kirshner summarize powerful evidence that civic engagement promotes healthy and successful development. Youth participation is also good for the institutions and communities in which they live. Schools, municipal governments, and neighborhoods function better when they can tap the energy and knowledge of youth, instead of having to control deeply disaffected adolescents.

Civic engagement enhances political equality, too. As Joseph Kahne and Ellen Middaugh argue, people who participate politically receive much more attention from government than those who do not, and this gap reflects differences in resources and social status. To reduce the gap, we must invest in the civic engagement of relatively disadvantaged youth, because extensive evidence shows that the early years are formative.

And civic engagement is essential to sustaining our democracy, as youth learn the pragmatics of citizenship through participation. This form of socialization can occur in school, where students may acquire habits of civil discussion; in neighborhoods, where youth interact with government and civic institutions; and in municipalities, where young residents can contribute to local government.

Civic engagement is the responsibility of society as a whole. Schools are usually given this burden, but political parties must also invite youth to join in. The news and entertainment media must stop portraying youth as a profligate, lost generation and feature youth's actual accomplishments. In taking up this task, policy makers need not operate in the dark. In this volume, Henry Milner, David Kerr, and Marc Hooghe offer insights from Western Europe, Scandinavia, and Canada, which recognized this challenge some time ago and inaugurated programs that the United States might try to model.

This book brings together a coherent synthesis of current research and thinking about policies for enhancing civic and political engagement in America's youth. These strategies and recommendations are unusual in five respects: (1) They come from frontline researchers who have studied and understood youth within the contemporary political context. (2) They are based on the premise that recent generations of youth are not alienated, deficient in moral character, or lacking in responsibility, but are ready to take advantage of opportunities for participation. (3) They are oriented to the realistic educational, demographic, and political circumstances that necessarily shape the formation of youth's political identity. (4) They take account of fresh approaches to civic education and political socialization, both of which are needed as bases for effective and realistic policy in the current educational and political climate. (5) They move from the "best practices" that might be adopted by an individual teacher or youth worker to questions of policy. After all, unless we change large-scale investments and incentives, we will never seriously expand opportunities for the civic engagement of all youth.

This book had its origin in a series of small group meetings at which scholars, policy makers, political advocates, and representative of professional associations exchanged insights about current research findings and analyses of policies regarding youth engagement. Through lively debate and shared expertise, it was agreed that available empirical results could serve as a launching pad for new and constructive policy recommendations. The question then turned to ways in which evidence could be connected to specific recommendations and how best to place research and policy ideas before the public and decision makers with the power to influence strategies and programs. This book provides answers to these questions.

The participants for the present book were chosen for the constructive nature of their approaches to one of the major issues facing our nation's democracy: At this moment in history, how ought we to be preparing our youth for active citizenship? We know, from looking at former communist states that suddenly became democracies after 1989, that active citizenship does not arise spontaneously as people age, nor does it result from official pronouncements. We know also from the story of massive immigration that families moving into democratic societies must develop new political responsibilities and opportunities appropriate to their new contexts. Individuals must learn how to form voluntary associations and interest groups, address community problems, participate in political campaigns, lobby elected officials, persistently vote, make their views known to fellow citizens, and keep abreast of current affairs. Until individuals turn these basic elements into practices, democracy remains an idealized abstraction and citizenship is little more than formal rights and duties not properly exercised.

Increasingly, educators, foundation leaders, scholars, and even politicians are committed to reviving civic education, reshaping political socialization, and altering expectations of youth's capacities and willingness to participate. They are asking for soundly based arguments, workable solutions, and public education about youth's potential and older generations' responsibilities in sustaining our democratic traditions.

This was not the case only a decade or so ago as the nation and much of the West anticipated the coming of the new millennium. The dominant rhetoric at the time was focused not on solutions but on the problematic status of youth. More than three decades of wide-scale immigration was seen as changing the composition of Western societies and threatening their core values. Consumers of mass media deserted serious, politically relevant programs and publications in favor of light entertainment. Schools, which historically were charged with the task of making new citizens, were seen as failing to communicate basic academic skills, much less providing depth in history, government, or civics. Meanwhile, the rate of voting in the youth cohort, ages 18–24, was in a systematic decline from its high in 1972. A further signal of the problem was found in elite college-bound freshmen who, in contrast to their parents' generation, placed the acquisition of personal wealth and self-satisfaction above obligations to the community and support for the less fortunate.

The repetition of this array of facts shaped public perception into the belief that something fundamental had gone awry in recent generations. Critics on the political left wondered what had happened to the youthful fire-in-the-belly that had stoked civil rights, antiwar, and environmental movements among the young. All that remained of that era seemed to be antipathy toward politics and an insatiable urge to stoke the consumer culture. Critics on the political right worried that young people were losing respect for fundamental institutions and values and would no longer sacrifice for them. Meanwhile, the media found that emphasizing youth's foibles intrigued the audience of aging adults who were becoming ever more distant from the actual experiences of growing up in our changing society. Hence, the supposition arose that perhaps contemporary youth were not worth the investment needed to correct warps in their character and were not ready to turn their self-absorbed apathy into patriotic passion.

A close look at the data on American youths' attitudes, values, and beliefs reveals some troubling trends, such as a deep decline in self-reported interest in public affairs since the 1970s. It also reveals some areas of stability: for example, levels of political knowledge seem to have changed little over the decades. And it reveals some notable improvements, such as a rapid rise in the rate of volunteering among adolescents. The overall picture is mixed, and that itself may surprise some readers who expect a dismal story. In analyzing the downward trends, we doubt that it is helpful to look for causes inside adolescents' heads. For example, the decline in voter turnout *might* be a function of reduced political commitment and interest, but it is more likely a symptom of declining partisan competition in American electoral districts.

Research can counter the negative public image of youth and the general pessimism regarding this generation's ability and will to sustain our democracy. Researchers who have observed youth closely, interviewed them regularly, and tried to understand the daily stresses and strains surrounding them see their subjects in a different light. Instead of focusing on youth's supposed deficits, they have centered on youth's capacities, strengths, and future potential. They have seen that when given adequate material and cognitive resources, youth have responded by joining in civic and political action with enthusiasm and seriousness. This insight has allowed their work to rise above the din of despairing commentaries by providing analyses of the conditions that either impede or enhance the mobilization of young people's political potential.

The 2004 presidential election and the off-year elections of 2006 offered seminal examples. In 2000, only 34 percent of eligible youth (ages 18–24) bothered to vote in a lively contest between George W. Bush and Al Gore. Commentators were dismayed with this low voter turnout, which only reinforced lowered expectations for youth. However, in the 2004 election, there was a sharp increase to 47 percent. Why this jump in interest (which we also observed in the 2008 primaries)? Had the nature of youth changed in four short years? Had youth's character taken a sudden turn for the better? Had alienation miraculously given way to concern for the common good? Probably not. It is more likely that the conditions that influence youth participation in the political process were altered. According to scholars who studied the 2004 election carefully, political parties and nonprofit organizations that promote youth interests consciously focused on youth and used tactics to register them and bring them to the polls on election day. This concerted effort to mobilize youth voters produced positive results that could have occurred only if youth were not alienated from civic life but were amenable to these directed efforts (Shea and Green, 2007). The continued participation of youth voters in 2006 confirmed these facts and helped to solidify the view that participation is more a consequence of mobilization and less a matter of youth's inherent character.

There are more detailed data that support this viewpoint. For example, a closer look at the youth vote indicates that for decades there has been wide variation in turnout from state to state. For example, in 2004, more than two out of three eligible youth voted in some states (for example, Minnesota), whereas fewer than four out of ten youth voted in other states (for example, Texas). This differential from state to state is much too large to allow a broad characterization of youth's civic interest. A more plausible explanation is that specific campaign tactics and other programs to bring out the youth vote in the former states, but not in the latter, yielded positive results, suggesting again that youth are open to engagement when the proper incentives and resources are invested in them. Campus registration drives, political-entertainment rallies, website solicitations, and the like were aimed at youth, and youth responded positively.

Some political scientists who are aware of the power of mobilization have cautioned against the uncritical use of categories of voters—black, women, youth, and the like. They have instead urged us to think of people as ready to participate when they are provided with appropriate incentives, resources, and opportunities. This point has been demonstrated with historical shifts in rates of voting (Rosenstone and Hansen, 1993) as well as contemporaneous differences that can be traced to available institutional supports (Verba, Schlozman, and Brady, 1995). It has taken youth researchers time to catch up with these insights, but as several authors in the current book demonstrate, the payoff is well worth the wait. The key to their approach is the shift of focus from the question of "why don't youth get involved?" to the researchable issue of "which conditions encourage, promote, and sustain youth civic engagement?"

With results from this kind of research clearly in mind, the authors of the present volume have set out to specify policy whose purpose is not to diagnose youth's failings or to ignore them but to foster their greater participation, which is based on understanding them and the contemporary political context. We, the editors, have chosen these authors because they offer an array of policy measures that deal with the central dimensions of engagement and the chief conditions that affect participation. One group of authors was asked to look at schools, and they have responded by proposing strategies that teachers can use to raise students' interest and capitalize on the passion that only youth can bring to politics. It is well known that many teachers are cowed by the task of introducing political issues, which the media have framed in divisive terms. As a result, teachers tend either to shy away from these topics in order to avoid controversy or to present them in bland ways even though only debate and discussion would do justice to the material. For this reason alone, strategies for bringing politics back into civics courses are essential for encouraging the young to become part of the political process. Thus, in her chapter, Diana Hess will offer teachers of civics courses strategies for dealing honestly with complex political issues without taking on the role of advocacy, but assigning it properly to the now better informed students.

It is an established finding that civics education requires more than textbook assignments and classroom simulations. We now know that it is enhanced when it is complemented by programs and projects that give students actual civic experiences. The rationale for learning experientially was stated by John Stuart Mill in the mid-nineteenth century when he noted that one would never teach reading, swimming, or horseback riding from textbook instruction alone. If democratic citizenship is to be learned, the experiential component cannot be ignored. Today there are numerous experiential programs in and after school, but there is mixed evidence as to their efficacy. This is due in part to variation in their quality and a lack of philosophical clarity in their driving rationale. Thus Joseph Kahne and Ellen Middaugh will suggest policy that is grounded in Kahne's assessment of supplemental experiential civics-learning programs in several states covering a variety of urban and suburban public schools. Kahne and his colleagues are known for their critical view of such programs as well as for careful research, which has helped to distinguish between advocacy and evidence-based analysis.

It is generally understood that changes following the end of the cold war, coupled with the rising global economy, have altered the way we need to look at political socialization. As a recent reviewer (Sapiro, 2004) suggested, this is "Not Your Parents' Political Socialization," but one requiring new approaches that confront the political contexts and the complex issues that mark contemporary life. One example of this complexity is seen in roles played by global immigration in diffusing and complicating the attainment of national identity. As traditional theories seem not up to the task, it is necessary to plot new lines of inquiry that retain basic fundamentals while incorporating fresh insights.

One of the stable findings with regard to youth voting is its relationship to socioeconomic status and educational attainment. For example, according to federal census data, youth with some college experience are twice as likely to register and vote as their age peers without college experience. Obviously, educational attainment is associated with a host of other factors, including socioeconomic status, which in itself may determine competence as well as opportunity to be civically engaged. Daniel Hart and Ben Kirshner have studied young people living in low-wealth communities in an effort to identify community-level factors that are crucial for participation. Among other things, they found that poverty is associated with a lack of social resources, a relative absence of adult mentors and models, and ethnic diversity, which may dampen tolerance. Hart and Kirshner's detailed observations of such neighborhoods lead to policy recommendations that emphasize the need for mediating institutions (e.g., 4-H, Boys and Girls Clubs, YMCA, etc.) that can provide opportunities for youth community service and youth organizing. These and other forms of participation are not unique to youth living in disadvantaged situations but apply to all young people. The question for policy is how to encourage institutions to step in and provide the requisite opportunities. The evidence reviewed by Hart and Kirshner shows that youth living in these circumstances have the potential for participation and growth because, when given resources, they accept responsibility and act as committed citizens.

James Gimpel and Shannon Pearson-Merkowitz have also studied variations across community contexts insofar as they affect political socialization. In Gimpel et al.'s recent study of schools and communities in the Baltimore–Washington, DC, corridor, they found little public discussion of political issues in communities with low levels of political competition (where long-serving candidates face little or no opposition in campaign after campaign). Youth in these communities reported that they had few discussions of political issues with adults, including teachers and parents. Some of these communities also had low median family incomes. Schools in such poor communities place diminished emphasis on the teaching of civics (and other data show that these schools are the least likely to have effective student governments, thus diminishing youth's sense of involvement). Overall, low- wealth communities, in comparison to ones that are better off, are less conducive to public debate of political matters and, perhaps as a consequence, shunt civic life to the background. This parsing of low-wealth areas into identifiable factors that impinge on political socialization is a major step toward forming fresh policy. We know that poverty alone is not an impediment to political activism; for example, during the 1950s and 1960s, youth in the South were readily mobilized in the service of the civil rights movement. From a policy perspective, then, the goal is to specify ways in which to enliven public civic life so as to provide youth with an environment that stimulates their political engagement and integrates it into their lives as a matter of course.

A third chapter dealing with context will be focused on structures that municipalities can build for encouraging and sustaining youth engagement.

Carmen Sirianni has studied this topic by surveying cities around the United States and studying the ways in which they involve youth in their governance. He has used the data to systematize types of programs that are now operative and to theorize as to the factors that account for success. In his chapter for this book with Diana Marginean Schor, focus will be on Hampton, Virginia, which has been developing youth involvement in local government since 1990, and San Francisco, which more recently initiated a similar initiative. They look at the ways that police, school boards, and planning commissions have come to include youth as fully functioning participants in their work. They also propose policy for expanding these efforts to other communities, discussing the impediments that have to be overcome as well as the gains that municipal officials believe they have made by bringing in youth as partners and fellow citizens.

Daniel Shea has studied the ways that political parties either ignore or focus on youth as campaign workers and voters. His work with John Green (Pew Survey Research Center) has been seminal in revealing that most Democratic and Republican county chairpersons have consciously neglected youth voters, favoring instead the elderly. But they also report that some chairpersons have mobilized the youth vote with great effect. Shea will build on this work to focus on policy initiatives that the parties can take to increase youth participation in their everyday activities. Probably no one is better situated with data to propose policy measures for this outcome (see Shea and Green, 2007).

Even if our main interest is in reforming American institutions, an international, comparative perspective is important. Some trends in youth engagement are evident in all the industrialized democracies; they probably arise from common features in the political economy of the current era. Other trends vary by country; they may result from particular institutions or policy changes. Henry Milner is an expert on the differences in civic knowledge among democracies. He will compare youth civic participation and knowledge in several countries, including Canada and the Nordic democracies. The latter nations have attempted to enhance youth participation by initiating programs that range from increasing voting to giving youth a voice in policy at local and federal levels.

The United Kingdom has been officially engaged in reform of civics education since the early 1990s. Much of the impetus for reform came from the problems produced by massive immigration, which altered the nature of schooling and created political concern about, for example, the inclusion of Muslims and other citizens. A national commission was established to assess the extent of the problem of youth disengagement and to propose revision of the civics curriculum. Through a succession of panels, the United Kingdom has produced a national program that involves teacher reeducation, curriculum reform, out-of-classroom experiences, and the like. David Kerr has been responsible for evaluating some of these initiatives and has been collecting longitudinal data that measure their outcome in terms of civic knowledge and involvement of youth. His chapter will report major findings and address the results of policy initiatives. These findings ought to provide leads that can be pursued in the United States, which is several years behind the United Kingdom in this regard.

Marc Hooghe reports on recently collected data regarding youth from several Western European countries. His work is focused on youth participation in nations experiencing high levels of immigration and, at the same time, incorporation into the entity of the Pan-European Union. These dual forces add complications to youth's task of becoming citizens while forming a clear civic identity. Hooghe describes countries wrestling in different ways with unavoidable challenges. For example, to require a course in civics risks isolating political and social discussion in one small part of the curriculum and letting all other teachers ignore such issues. On the other hand, requiring that civics be infused throughout the curriculum risks losing it entirely.

The concluding chapter is by the editors, who bring backgrounds in research on civic development, political philosophy, and education policy to this work. Peter Levine directs the Center for Information and Research on Civic Learning and Engagement (CIRCLE), which has stimulated research and national public discussion of civics education. James Youniss has studied youth civic engagement for two decades and has several publications that have helped to generate research on this relatively neglected topic. We distill the recommendations of the various chapters into an overall program for reform.

References

Kirby, E., Barrios Marcelo, K., Gillerman, J., and Linkins, S. (2008). The youth vote in the 2008 primaries and caucuses. CIRCLE, Medford, MA. Available at *www.civicyouth.org.*

Rosenstone, S. J., and Hansen, J. M. (1993). *Mobilization, participation, and democracy in America.* New York: Macmillan.

Sapiro, V. (2004). Not your parents' political socialization: Introduction for a new generation. *Annual Review of Political Science, 7,* 1–23.

Shea, D. M., and Green, J. C. (2007). *Fountain of youth: Strategies and tactics for mobilizing America's young voters.* Lanham, MD: Rowman and Littlefield.

Verba, S., Schlozman, K. L., and Brady, H. E. (1995). *Voice and equality: Civic voluntarism in American politics.* Cambridge: Harvard University Press.

PART I

Youth and Schools

1

A "Younger Americans Act"

An Old Idea for a New Era

James Youniss and Peter Levine

In 2001, a bill called the Younger Americans Act was introduced in Congress. It was modeled after the Older Americans Act, passed 20 years earlier, and was designed, like its predecessor, to take focus off of youth's problems and to allocate resources for building on their available capacities. Following the passage of the Older Americans Act, the income and health of the nation's elderly improved significantly. For example, previously the rate of poverty among the elderly was higher than that among children. Today, the rates have been reversed, and there are more children than elderly living in poverty.

The Younger Americans Act never made it out of committee because its sponsors were hard pressed to explain to their colleagues how strengthening young people's capacities would lead to a reduction in their problems. This outcome is not surprising, given that for the preceding four decades the main rationale for funding was to redress youth's problems of delinquency, pregnancy, drug abuse, violence, dropping out of school, gang behavior, and the like. Not only were billions of dollars allocated to these problems, but the media made sure each of them was well publicized. As a result, the term "youth" had come to be associated with difficulties. Youth were troubled and, worse, were troubling for society.

It is time once again to reintroduce the Younger Americans Act. The climate has changed, as it is no longer justifiable to view youth in a stilted negative fashion. School achievement has not plunged downward but has edged up slightly and risen significantly for minority youth. Teenage pregnancy and childbearing have declined to a low level matching that last observed in 1940. Teenage use of illegal substances is moderate by any account and is lower than the level of their parents when they were teenagers. Teenage violence, which in 1990 was predicted to erupt into an epidemic, has actually receded to its pre-1985 level; it is still unacceptable, but not indicative of a whole cohort of youth gone wild.

The evidence for these statements can be found on websites maintained by federal agencies that pride themselves on careful collection of national statistics. These findings cannot be ignored if there is to be a reasoned discussion of the civic status of contemporary youth, their needs, and their prospects. Fortunately, academic researchers have taken these statistics to heart, and their recent work has caused a revolution in thinking about youth. Whereas much research was previously focused on documenting youth's problems and finding remedies for them, a major effort is being made today to identify youth's capacities for growth and finding ways to foster them. This shift in focus can be found in the literature under a variety of headings from "positive psychology" to "youth as assets" and "positive youth development."

This is no small matter either for scholars or for the public, which must now revisit its unexamined beliefs about young people. Already foundations, nonprofit organizations, and youth-serving agencies have reoriented their focus to provision of resources that are designed to promote youth development. The landscape has changed, for example, as after- and out-of-school programs have been structured to provide academic tutoring, disciplined recreation, community service, and even opportunities for direct political engagement. In a recent overview of research of these several and diverse programs, Eccles and Gootman (2002) state that meta-analyses of research have identified two factors that account for success, defined in terms of youth's positive development: forming relationships with helpful mentors and having opportunities to do community service. One can immediately see the contrast between the "troubled and troubling" image that dominated public discourse in the 1980s and 1990s, and the current portrait of youth who can be energized to perform constructively at high levels.

We assume this movement will continue to be propelled forward as programs that operationalize this positive outlook on youth continue to produce persuasive examples and evidence. The aim of the present chapter is to advance this perspective by orienting it specifically to policy pertaining to youth's engagement in civic life and political processes. It might be the case that constructive psychological development lays the groundwork on which civic and political engagement build. For example, healthy personalities or a positive orientation to society may serve as preconditions for subsequent mature citizenship. Easton and Dennis raised this possibility in 1969. They argued, however, that psychological underpinning is not adequate to explain political functioning. An effective citizen does not merely hold positive attitudes about the community and understand how it works. Citizens need more than sociality plus cognitive competence. Political participation requires having concrete interests or purposes, being able to express them publicly, and having the ability to deal with other competitive interests and viewpoints in a disciplined way. Political socialization, or development into an effective political actor, must be geared to the real political system.

To the best of our knowledge, no developmental theories that have been brought into the study of political socialization deal explicitly with these operations which are needed to function in our democratic system. In the main, developmental theories do not address interests beyond broad motives pertaining to self-protection of self-enhancement. Economic interest, interest in promoting one's ethnic group, and concern for political issues are not topics of much research. (For a recent exception, see Junn and Masuoka, 2008.) Further, most theories do not explicitly deal with the public side of politics, where interests are expressed overtly and clash competitively with different and opposing views. Few developmental theories speak about collective interests and collective behavior that is fundamental to the expression and advancement of interests. And only rarely do developmental theories deal with organizational behavior or momentary coalitions that introduce novices to principles of negotiation, persuasion, comprise, and recovering from defeat.

We suggest that in order to change the focus of political socialization toward these operations that define active citizenship, it might be helpful, and perhaps necessary, first to clarify the terms in which contemporary youth are discussed and have come to be known. To this end, we will analyze five myths that block a fresh and constructive understanding of contemporary youth.

Myth 1: Youth or Particular Generations Are Meaningful Categories

It has become popular to identify each cohort of youth with a catchy label that gives a distinctive tone to attitudes and behavior that constitute "youth." Familiar terms include Baby Boomers, Gen-Xers, Generation Y, and the Millennials. Survey evidence can be provided that shows differences among average members of these successive generations. Nevertheless, naming cohorts is more a product of the marketing world than of scholarly research. No effort is made to explain why one cohort differs from another, and hence the origin of each peculiar cohort is rather mysterious. This kind of thinking has caught on in part because the grouping of people into categories provides a ready shortcut to several ends. In the case of marketing, it matters more that teenagers prefer brand A over B than why they do so. The aim is to catch the mood and capitalize on it quickly. When the goal is to satisfy consumers, one need know only preferences; their roots are less important.

This form of thinking has harmed policy for the development of civic engagement greatly. Shea (2004) has provided strong evidence of these ill effects with respect to the relationship between the two major political parties and contemporary youth. Shea surveyed a representative sample of Republican and Democratic county chairpersons, asking them about their efforts to mobilize youth registrants and voters. He found that only a small minority of chairpersons allocated funds to youth, with the majority focusing their resources on the elderly and other target groups of adults. The stated and implied rationale was that youth do not vote, whereas the elderly appear at the polls regularly in large numbers.

It is true that relatively few youth between 18 and 24 bothered to vote in elections from 1988 through 2000. It is estimated that only one out of every three eligible youth voted in the presidential contest of 2000. However, the youth turnout rate varied widely by year and by state. The proportion of eligible under-25s who voted was about 36 percent in 2000, 19 percent in 2002, and 46 percent in 2004. In 2004, 69 percent of eligible voters under 25 turned out in Minnesota, compared with 36 percent in Arkansas: almost a two-to-one ratio (CIRCLE, n.d.). It should be obvious that categorizing these data into a "youth vote" is not helpful. The average percentage hardly characterizes all youth, and it misses two essential questions: Why do almost twice as many youth in some states versus others bother to vote? And why did significantly more youth vote in 2004 than in 2000?

Such variation is not new in the study of voting. For example, when confronted with similar disparities, Rosenstone and Hansen (1993) argued that results called for a theory of resource mobilization. Rather than drawing distinctions among citizens by race, educational attainment, or gender, these authors saw all voters as potentially likely to vote if given the proper incentives, resources, and opportunities. Rosenstone and Hansen made their case by following certain categories of potential voters—for example, African Americans—over a span of history and showing that there was significant variation within the category. They showed further that variation was associated with opportunity and resource availability. For example, voting swelled during the Reconstruction era, waned during the early twentieth century, then surged again following the civil rights era and passage of the Civil Rights Act in the mid-1960s.

We need to move from treating youth as a problematic category to making sure they have the incentives to participate. The problem shifts from changing the inherent character of a generation to mobilizing youth's capacities by directing them to the political process. To wit, the studies assembled by Shea and Green (2007) provide specific examples of ways in which political parties and nonprofit advocacy organizations mobilized youth to register and to vote in 2004. Using vehicles attractive to youth such as entertainment venues in which political issues were blended, organizers were able to energize young people and alert them to their interest in the impending election. It is not happenstance that the overall rate of youth voting increased by 14 percent from 2000 to 2004 or that youth came out in large numbers in those states where youth were sought after. A shift from viewing youth as a cohort with an inherent character to understanding youth as always having the potential for political engagement is fundamental to forging a constructive policy for this and any youth cohort.

Myth 2: Youth-Serving Institutions Are Untrustworthy; Hence It Is Unwise to Invest in Positive Opportunities for Youth

A Nation at Risk (National Commission on Excellence in Education, 1983) claimed that academic standards had fallen in American public schools, and as a consequence, the United States was becoming uncompetitive with Japan and Germany. The report famously stated, "If an unfriendly foreign power had attempted to impose on America the mediocre educational performance that exists today, we might well have viewed it as an act of war. As it stands, we have allowed this to happen to ourselves." *A Nation at Risk* was a short but complex statement that demanded a "strong public commitment to the equitable treatment of our diverse population," praised the nation's historical commitment to investing in education, asserted that "the natural abilities of the young . . . cry out to be developed," and proposed that the nation "develop the talents of all to their fullest." But the report was widely remembered for its portrait of public schools as devastating failures.

Conservatives could embrace that view because schools were funded and managed by the government and staffed (in many cases) by unionized workers. For conservatives, governments and unions were inherently problematic because they avoided market competition. Many liberals (including some prominent authors of *A Nation at Risk*) held equally negative views of public schools, which they saw as inequitable, regimented, and corrupt. Both sides increasingly demanded "standards and accountability," meaning limited, measurable outcomes with penalties for schools that failed to measure up. They differed as to the nature of the penalties: conservatives favored vouchers that would allow parents to exit failing schools, whereas liberals preferred to fire superintendents or take over failing school systems. But both sides were increasingly unwilling to trust schools by providing resources for particular kinds of positive opportunities, such as community service, arts programs, school newspapers, or student governments. Thus the No Child Left Behind Act of 2002—passed with strong support from Democrats and Republicans to reflect two decades of mainstream thought about education—provided no guaranteed opportunities; rather, it required that every school achieve "adequate yearly progress" toward 100 percent passing rates in reading and mathematics. It left educational methods and approaches up to schools, but held them accountable for results, defined in narrow ways.

It seems safe to say that if the act had provided funds and mandates for opportunities such as community service, conservatives would have worried that the money would be wasted or that these programs would teach immoral values, and liberals would have worried that the resources would be channeled to white, middle-class students. Neither side was completely wrong, but the act overlooked strong evidence that positive opportunities pay dividends. It also defined educational success without reference to civic engagement, moral and aesthetic development, or skills and habits of collaboration.

Besides, it cannot simply be the case that American schools are failed institutions. They are accountable to local parents, who, for the most part, find them satisfactory. In the annual survey of the nation's adults by the *Phi Delta Kappan* (e.g., Rose and Gallup, 2006), respondents are asked to give public schools grades from A to F. Year after year, respondents tend to assign schools in general grades of C or D, while they assign the schools their children attend A or B.

Schools are only one of several types of public institutions that serve—or at least influence—youth. In recent decades, federal policy has supported positive opportunities for youth development in some of these venues. For example, the Corporation for National and Community Service, created by federal law in 1993, funds community service programs. The Clinton administration used the $40 million Community Schools program to "provide expanded learning opportunities for children in a safe, drug-free, and supervised environment." Some of the funded opportunities included community service and arts projects. However, these modest initiatives should be set against deep cuts in the educational programs of prisons. Further, the move toward narrow outcome-measures has affected out-of-school programs as well as schools. In 2002, the Bush administration renamed the Community Schools program "21st Century Community Learning Centers," expanded its funding to $1 billion, but required that funds be devoted exclusively to "academic enrichment." State agencies were required to assess academic outcomes (Pittman, Wilson-Ahlstrom, and Yohalem, 2003, 2).

Myth 3: Youth Are Self-Absorbed and Unconcerned

During the 1990s, a number of critiques of youth began with the hypothesis that young people were averse to politics and civic engagement primarily because they were caught in a consumer dynamic driven by the implanted motive of pleasure-seeking or self-satisfaction (e.g., National Association of Secretaries of State, 1999). This viewpoint is supported by some social science evidence insofar as Inglehart (1997) has connected the general rise in affluence with erosion of traditional values. When clothes, food, multiple forms of entertainment, and so forth are made abundant and oriented to youth, is it unreasonable to believe that they would forego momentary personal pleasure for the sake of abstract values such as the community's well-being or maintaining democracy? Rahn and Transue (1998) have argued that an increase in materialistic values during the 1970s and 1980s has undermined general social trust. Although this hypothesis seems plausible, other evidence complicates it. One set of data comes from an annual survey of a representative national sample of college freshmen that has been taken yearly since the 1960s. Students were asked whether they had participated in civic affairs or community service during the school year and, if yes, whether they did so daily, weekly, monthly, or occasionally. If general affluence has risen during the period, and if affluence generates self-absorption, then civic participation should have declined accordingly over the past 40 years. The data do not support this hypothesis. Instead, the proportion of students doing any service has increased gradually over the past four decades and now exceeds 65 percent (Pryor et al., 2007).

One must be careful in discussing results regarding community service because it has caused a bit of controversy among researchers who study civic development in youth. For example, the authors of the aforementioned 1999 report from the secretaries of state are doubtful about service, which they see as distinct from political behavior itself, such as voting. They also see service as a personal act that helps the individual feel good but that fails to redress social problems at their political roots. Moreover, they surmise that youth do service because they can see its immediate impact, whereas political labor may not have visible payoff until some future date. This is a legitimate critique, but there are other ways to understand service that allow a different interpretation that is more amenable to political involvement.

In our work (e.g., McLellan and Youniss, 2003; Metz, McLellan, and Youniss, 2003) and the work of others (e.g., Raskoff and Sundeen, 1999), service by high school students is more frequently than not an organizational rather than an individual act. Youth typically do service in settings sponsored and managed by nonprofit organizations that advocate philosophical positions toward social problems. Familiar examples are the Salvation Army, which advocates self-determined religious conversion, and Habitat for Humanity, which advocates volunteerism for the common good. When youth serve within these sites, they are not only performing individually but also participating in a sponsor's philosophical framework. They are operationalizing that framework and taking on virtual if not actual membership (Youniss and Yates, 1997). From this perspective, community service is anything but a personal act without political significance. It acquires this significance insofar as the sponsoring organization itself takes a stance toward the political system and that organization consciously makes its position known to the volunteers (Allahyari, 2000).

Two conclusions may follow. It is inaccurate to mistake the palpable display of material consumption for an overwhelming drive toward self-satisfaction on the part of contemporary youth. A substantial portion of the youth have done and are still doing service in communities on a regular, and not a one-shot, basis. Second, for many youth who do service, this activity embeds them in major organizations that constitute civil society and in some cases leads them directly into the political system. It follows that youth could be socialized into civil society and politics if they were given opportunities to participate in existing organizations that have defined stances toward society and its problems, say, combating poverty or conserving the environment. Contemporary youth are not unconcerned about the society around them, and their readiness to become active in it may be mediated by existing organizations whose civic and political worth are well established.

Myth 4: Minority and Poor Youth Are Especially "At Risk"

One reason Americans disparage "schools," but not the schools they know through personal experience, is undoubtedly the changing demography of our schools' population. They are increasingly populated by a majority of nonwhite, poor, minority, and immigrant students who are known to score low on tests of academic achievement. Even though scores for these students have been on the rise over the past 30 years, they still lag behind scores of white Anglo youth (NAEP, 2004). It is not incidental that this negative perception is abetted by two other factors. Many youth from wealthy families attend private schools when this choice by parents can signal an implicit putdown of public schools. In addition, the youth problems listed at the outset of this discussion are known to be focused largely in the population of low-income minority youth, for instance, teen pregnancy and youth violence. For example, in a recent government study, 87 percent of the nation's 3,000 counties reported no youth homicides, and another 6 percent reported a single youth homicide. It follows that only 7 percent of all counties accounted for almost all youth homicides in the country. Not surprisingly, these counties include our major urban cities where the low-income minority youth live (Snyder, Sickmund, and Bilchick, 1999).

One can readily see the basis for a judgment that youth should not be given positive opportunities when they are prone to risky behavior and seem to lack the motivation to perform well in school. Although we have not seen or heard this logic expressed by elected officials, it has appeared in veiled phrasings in debates about school reform. Of course, with the media promoting images of youth deviating from traditional norms, especially committing crimes (Center of Juvenile and Criminal Justice, 2008), it is difficult to combat the view that minority youth need to get themselves together and take a heavy dose of self-discipline before society begins to support them.

How can this image be changed? One line of countervailing evidence pertains directly to the political interest and capacities for participation by minority youth. Since 2000 a number of descriptive studies have documented the success of programs in which these youth have been trained in and encouraged to take political action on issues important to them in their local settings. For example, Larson and Hanson (2005) reported that minority youth in Chicago were able to change school policy on discipline when they felt it inequitably singled them out. They polled their peers to determine how accurate their perception was. Once they verified this perception, they rallied their peers, who then figured out how best to lobby the superintendent's office and to bring about a change in policy. Sherman (2002) has reported virtually the same findings for minority youth in Oakland, California. These and other studies illustrate Easton and Dennis's 1969 analysis that if one wants politically competent individuals, the venue of importance for learning is the political system itself. As these data show, when mentored in tactics of political behavior and offered opportunities for collective action on meaningful issues, these youth were quite willing to take part in the political system using effective strategies any group would employ to advance their interest.

It is unfortunate that baggy pants, bare midriffs, and lurid lyrics with loud thumping bass have come to symbolize minority youth. In fact, it can be argued that many minority youth strongly adhere to traditional values and make constructive contributions to their schools and neighborhoods. To wit, a 2005 Current Population Survey of youth living below the poverty line yielded results worth emphasizing. Spring, Dietz, and Grimm (2006) have reported on the volunteer behavior of these youth, noting the proportion who volunteer, how many hours they contribute, and the organizations through which they do their community service. They found that 43 percent have volunteered, compared with 59 percent of their age peers who come from wealthier backgrounds. Like their wealthier age peers, they provide free labor for others, participate in music or art events, collect and distribute food, and partake in fund-raising for various causes. Whereas their wealthier age peers are most likely to volunteer through youth clubs and established nonprofit organizations such as 4-H, low-income youth are most likely to volunteer through churches.

This last point merits further consideration because it tells much more than meets the eye. Volunteering, a self-evident civic action, is best understood as the consequence of opportunities available in the surrounding environment. The major sources of opportunities are established civic organizations. It is clear from this survey and from other studies that youth from low-income neighborhoods have few such organizations with which to become affiliated, whereas youth from wealthier settings have an abundance of them. What the former youth do have, however, are churches, which instill religious beliefs that include personal responsibility to serve others in the community.

These data lead directly to another point about policy. Minority and low-income youth have been shown to be responsive to mentoring for political and civic action. Their lower rates of participation, compared with wealthier youth, can be understood as a result of fewer opportunities. In the case of volunteering, for example, there are simply fewer service organizations located in their neighborhoods. When organizations such as churches provide opportunities, youth utilize them to do the same kind of volunteering that their wealthier peers do. It follows that an infusion of these mediating organizations would be a priority in policy making, the hypothesis being that rates of participation could be raised by allocating organizational resources to the geographic areas where these youth live. It is not character that these youth lack, but mentors, opportunities, and organizational mediators (Pittman, Irby, and Ferber, 2000).

Myth 5: There Is a Generation Gap in Commitment to Social Justice

Since the 1960s, much has been written about the "generation gap" with emphasis on discontinuities in values between the older population and contemporary youth. The topic is too large and complex to give a full summary of the issues. Instead, we will focus on whether or not there has been a discontinuity in moral traditions and specifically the importance of social justice. This issue was selected because four decades ago morality had become a focal point of criticism aimed at youth's widespread use of drugs, the flaunting of sexual mores, and demonstrations against campus authorities. The belief that there has been a break in moral tradition still lingers for many of the reasons noted in the preceding discussions.

In light of this criticism of youth, it is important to skirt images of youth that are portrayed in the public media and to center on evidence from current studies of youth. First, there are concurring results which indicate that contemporary youth consider working for social justice a primary goal. Much has been made of the fact that recent generations of youth feel little commitment to institutional churches, be they mainline Protestant or Catholic (cf. Hoge, Johnson, and Luidens, 1994; Smith and Denton, 2005). This seeming deficit in traditional religiousness, however, distracts from the fact that many of the younger generation hold established religious beliefs and are not lacking in spiritual fervor. Moreover, when forced to describe the essentials of their faith, most Catholic youth, for example, put working for social justice at the top of the list. This finding might upset theological purists, but clearly counters the view that commitment to a more equitable economy, helping new immigrants, or providing adequate health care is of little interest to our overly pampered, self-aggrandizing youth.

This same kind of moral commitment can be seen on college campuses in the efforts of students to deal with moral issues outside of their direct personal domain. The moral impulse was initially recognized during the mid-1990s with a notable rise in the number of students who did volunteer community service. Whereas motives for service during high school might be attributed to résumé building for college entrance, service while in college seemed to indicate more clearly a commitment to helping others in need. Using data from their studies of several campuses across the country, Astin, Sax, and Avalos (1999) reported that 40 percent of the students who came into college having done service continue to volunteer while they are in college. Helping others was the most cited motivation. In the intervening years, new cohorts of students have kept up the pace; a 2005 estimate of volunteering by college students, for instance, indicates that 30 percent of enrolled students did service during the previous year.

It was next noticed that new student movements were appearing in the late 1990s and after 2000. Students across the nation's campuses took up the cause of workers' rights as they organized to prevent sales of goods that were produced through overseas "sweatshop" labor. The Nike and Coca-Cola Corporations became the focal points for protests. Nike, which offered athletic departments free attire, was challenged for its labor practices of low wages, unhealthy work conditions, and disinterest in reform. Coca-Cola was criticized for its anti-union practices in South America. Both of these corporations operated through exclusive rights contracts on campuses. On several campuses, students sought to ban their products and pressed administrators to add fair labor practices into their negotiations for on-campus sales (Ballinger, 2006). These efforts constituted a social justice movement insofar as various campuses were united through a loose network whose functioning was facilitated by organized labor, yet run by student volunteers.

While voluntary service and protests against sweatshops have remained signs of moral life on campuses, one can see a widening of the scope of student concerns and an expansion of facilitating organizations. For example, large public institutions such as the University of Michigan and the University of Arizona have offices that coordinate the many organizations, programs, and academic offerings that fall into the category of social justice. The topics of interest are broad in scope and range from child poverty in Africa to attempts to legally eliminate the death penalty. Poverty, environmental protection, equal rights, and education remain central, as they were to previous generations of youth activists. The term "social justice" has many denoted references on the nation's campuses, but the central unifying theme is steeped in tradition (Colby, Ehrlich, Beaumont, and Stephens, 2003).

The social justice movement is driven in part from the bottom up by students who come to campuses already aware of crucial issues and with the experience of volunteer service through advocacy organizations. The movement has most likely been helped by a simultaneous top-down change in many universities that have tried to forge new partnerships with their surrounding communities (Kenny et al., 2002). The reason for this orientation seems to be that higher education has come to acknowledge its historical role as promoting the civic realm through the training of society's leaders. This role was diminished or ignored for decades as scholars focused on the advancement of their respective academic disciplines to the neglect of concern for the meaning of their work for society. However, seeing the needs for such things as ethical reforms in business and government, and realizing that leaders in these realms were socialized on campuses, some college and university administrators have come to recognize their historic role and obligation once again (Colby et al., 2003).

The shift in focus on the part of administrators constitutes a major policy implication. Young people care about morality and are sensitive to issues of social justice. In both regards, they are not at odds with the older generation but are firmly traditional. Key institutions that touch the lives of millions of youth each year are community colleges, four-year colleges, and universities. It is they who are capable of mobilizing youth's moral impulse and orienting it to the civic realm. Insofar as higher education provides a socializing venue for tomorrow's citizen leaders, it can fulfill its civic role by preparing youth to use their knowledge not only for self-advancement but also for society's betterment.

Conclusion

One of the biggest difficulties in dealing with youth is to realize that the world they confront needs to be understood on its own terms rather than via beliefs and perceptions that fit our own and other preceding generations. In times of rapid change, younger and older generations will necessarily view society differently, even when they focus on the same object. "Political engagement," "democracy," and "citizenship" are such terms for which each generation needs to forge a definition that fits its history if these conceptual entities are to be preserved.

For the past two decades, much has been written about the coming crisis because youth seem unprepared and uninterested in carrying on our system of government, its underlying civic ethic, and the values that provide the glue of social cohesion. We have tried to show that this view of youth is not warranted by the facts. We reviewed evidence that contemporary youth from all social statuses are civically and morally competent. Moreover, they are ready to utilize resources and opportunities that allow them to partake in the political system for the very ends which our generation seeks.

We started this chapter calling for a new Younger Americans Act that would focus on youth's potential instead of their problems. The legislation of that name introduced in the 107th Congress (in March 2001) would have provided \$5.75 billion over five years for community-based organizations that provided youth development opportunities. Two new steering institutions would have been created: an Office for National Youth Policy and a Federal Council on Youth. They would have been charged with developing a national policy for youth. At the state and local levels, existing organizations would have been designated as "agencies on youth" and assigned federal funds to distribute as grants. Youth would have had a significant voice at the local, state, and federal levels. All young Americans would have been eligible to participate in the funded programs, but minimum proportions of the total pool would have been earmarked for disadvantaged youth.

Representative George Miller (D-CA), who was also a leading sponsor of No Child Left Behind, introduced the Younger Americans Act in the House, saying:

> Too often, we find that public programs for young people focus on the problems of youth and promote piecemeal policies that seek to redress negative behaviors like juvenile delinquency or teen pregnancy. But the evidence shows that the most promising approaches to helping young people are those that foster positive youth development, build social and emotional competence, and link young people with adult mentors. This is the future of youth social programs in the 21st century and it is an approach we seek to advance through this legislation.

Although the bill was novel and forward-looking, in some respects it resembled the programs created roughly a century ago during the Progressive Era (Levine, 2000). At the time, America was flooded by immigrants whose moral character was being questioned in a confusing stew of languages, cultures, and religions. In the face of this challenge, some political leaders sought to stiffen laws, tighten social discipline, and require homogeneity in outlooks. Others, however, advanced the strategy of providing public schooling, improving public health, and making room for citizen participation. Support of the latter agenda required faith that individuals would respond to opportunity by participating and, in the process, growing into democratic citizens. We suggest that this image ought to be recalled today as we support young people with programs that challenge them to take up active citizenship. Our hypothesis, which is grounded in history as well as recent studies, is that youth will respond and grow up to our expectations as they always have (Levine, 2007).

References

Allahyari, R. A. (2000). *Visions of charity: Volunteer workers and moral community.* Berkeley: University of California Press.

Astin, A. W., Sax, L. J., and Avalos, J. (1999). The long-term effects of volunteerism during the undergraduate years. *Review of Higher Education, 21,* 187–202.

Ballinger, J. (2006). The other side of Nike and social responsibility. *Counterpunch.org,* February 8.

Center of Juvenile and Criminal Justice (2008). Myths and facts about youth and crime. Available at *www.cjcj.org/jjic/myths_facts.php*.

CIRCLE. (n.d.). State by state: Youth voter turnout and voter registration laws. Available at *www.civicyouth.org/Map.htm.*

Colby, A., Erhlich, T., Beaumont, E., and Stephens, J. (2003). *Educating citizens: Preparing America's undergraduates for lives of moral and civic responsibility.* San Francisco: Jossey-Bass.

Easton, D., and Dennis, J. (1969). *Children in the political system: Origins of political legitimacy.* New York: McGraw-Hill.

Eccles, J. S., and Gootman, J. A. (2002). *Community programs to promote youth development.* Washington, DC: National Academy Press.

Hoge, D., Johnson, B., and Luidens, D. A. (1994). *Vanishing boundaries: The religion of Mainline Protestant baby boomers.* Louisville, KY: Westminster / John Knox Press.

Inglehart, R. (1997). *Modernization and post-modernization: Cultural, economic, and political change in 43 societies.* Princeton, NJ: Princeton University Press.

Junn, J., and Masuoka, N. (2008). Identities in context: Politicized racial group consciousness among Asian American and Latino youth. *Applied Developmental Science, 12,* 93–101.

Kenny, M., et al. (2002). *Learning to serve: Promoting civil society through service learning.* Boston: Kluwer.

Larson, R., and Hansen, D. (2005). The development of strategic thinking: Learning to impact human system in a youth activism program. *Human Development, 48,* 327–49.

Levine, P. (2000). *The new progressive era: Toward a fair and deliberative democracy.* Lanham, MD: Rowman and Littlefield.

Levine, P. (2007). *The future of democracy: Developing the next generation of American citizens.* Lebanon, NH: University Press of New England.

McLellan, J. A., and Youniss, J. (2003). Two systems of service: Determinants of voluntary and required youth service. *Journal of Youth and Adolescence, 32,* 47–58.

Metz, E., McLellan, J. A., and Youniss, J. (2003). Types of voluntary service and adolescents' civic development. *Journal of Adolescent Research, 18,* 188–203.

National Assessment of Educational Progress. (2004). *Trends in academic progress: Three decades of student performance in reading and mathematics.* Center for Educational Statistics. Washington, DC: U.S. Department of Education.

National Association of Secretaries of State. (1999). The new millennium project. Part 1. American youth attitudes on politics, citizenship, government, and voting. Available at *www.stateofthevote.org/txtmediakit.*

National Commission on Excellence in Education. (1983). *A nation at risk.* Washington, DC: U.S. Department of Education

Pittman, K., Irby, M., and Ferber, T. (2000). *Unfinished business: Further reflections on a decade of promoting youth development.* Takoma Park, MD: Forum for Youth Investment.

Pittman, K., Wilson-Ahlstrom, A., and Yohalem, N. (2003). "Reflections on system building: Lessons from the after-school movement." Out of School-Time Policy Commentary #3, May. Available at *www.forumforyouthinvestment.org/files/OSTPC3.pdf.*

Pryor, J. H., et al. (2007). The American freshman: Forty year trends. Los Angeles: Cooperative Institutional Research Program, University of California at Los Angeles.

Rahn, W. M., and Transue, J. E. (1998). Social trust and value change: The decline of social capital in American youth, 1976–1995. *Political Psychology, 19,* 545–65.

Raskoff, S., and Sundeen, R. (1999). Community service programs in high schools. *Law and Contemporary Problems, 64,* 73–111.

Rose, L. C., and Gallup, A. M. (2006). The 38th annual PDK/Gallup poll of the public's attitudes toward public schools. *Phi Delta Kappan, 88,* 54–56.

Rosenstone, S. J., and Hansen, J. M. (1993). *Mobilization, participation, and democracy in America.* New York: Macmillan.

Shea, D. M. (2004). Throwing a better party: Local mobilizing institutions and the youth vote. CIRCLE Working Paper 13. College Park, MD: Center for Information and Research on Civic Learning and Engagement.

Shea, D. M., and Green, J. C. (2007). *Fountain of youth: Strategies and tactics for mobilizing young voters.* Lanham, MD: Rowman and Littlefield.

Sherman, R. F. (2002). Building young people's lives: One foundation's strategy. In B. Kirshner, J. L. O'Donoghue, and M. McLaughlin (Eds.), *Youth participation: Improving institutions and communities* (65–82). San Francisco: Jossey-Bass.

Smith, C., and Denton, M. L. (2005). *Soul searching: The religious and spiritual lives of American teenagers.* New York: Oxford University Press.

Snyder, H. N., Sickmund, M., and Bilchick, S. (1999). *Juvenile offenders and victims: 1999 national report.* Washington, DC: Office of Juvenile Justice and Delinquency Prevention.

Spring, K., Dietz, N., and Grimm, R. (2006). *Educating for active citizenship: Service-learning, school-based service, and youth civic engagement.* Washington, DC: Corporation for National and Community Service.

U.S. Congress. (2001). *Younger Americans act.* HR 17. 107th Cong.

Youniss, J., and Yates, M. (1997). *Community service and social responsibility in youth.* Chicago: University of Chicago Press.

2

Democracy for Some

The Civic Opportunity Gap in High School

Joseph Kahne and Ellen Middaugh

If Congress passed a law saying that those who earned less than $35,000 a year no longer had the right to vote or influence who gets elected to the U.S. Senate, most of us would be outraged. With such a law, some would ask, "Can we still call ourselves a democracy?" Unfortunately, according to recent research by Larry Bartels of Princeton University, such a law might not make a big difference. Indeed, after reading Bartels's findings, one might be tempted to ask, "Have we already passed this law?"

Bartels examined the way senators from all 50 states voted on key issues. He also looked at polling data from those states and assessed how well the preferences of these citizens predicted the votes of their senators on such high-profile issues as government spending, abortion, and civil rights laws. He found that the policy preferences of "constituents in the upper third of the income distribution received about 50 percent more weight than those in the middle third . . . while the views of constituents in the bottom third of the income distribution received no weight at all in the voting decisions of their senators" (2005, 5). In short, when it came to the votes of their U.S. senators, citizens in the bottom third of the income distribution had no identifiable political influence. These findings are reinforced in Gilens's 2005 separate study of the link between citizen policy preferences and actual policy outcomes from 1992 to 1998. He found that the relationship between policy preferences and policy outcomes was twice as strong for the wealthy (90th percentile) as for middle income (50th percentile) and more than twice as strong as for lower-income citizens (10th percentile).

Indeed, when it comes to political representation, inequality has been well documented. As the American Political Science Association Task Force on Inequality and American Democracy (2004) reported,

> The privileged participate more than others and are increasingly well organized to press their demands on government. Public officials, in turn, are much more responsive to the privileged than to average citizens and the least affluent. Citizens with low or moderate incomes speak with a whisper that is lost on the ears of inattentive government, while the advantaged roar with the clarity and consistency that policy makers readily heed.

Verba, Schlozman, and Brady (1995) found, for example, that family income was a strong predictor of voice in the political process. They found that 86 percent of those whose families were in the top 10 percent of the income distribution voted in presidential elections, while only 52 percent of those in the lowest 20 percent of the income distribution voted. These higher-income families were also

- four times as likely to be part of campaign work;
- three times as likely to do informal community work;
- twice as likely to contact elected officials;
- twice as likely to protest;
- six times as likely to sit on a board.

They were also fully nine times more likely to make campaign contributions—and one would assume that their contributions were far larger as well (190).

These inequalities are not only associated with income. As a recent study by the nonpartisan Public Policy Institute of California documents, "Those who are white, older, affluent, homeowners, and highly educated have a disproportionate say in California politics and representation in the civic life of the state" (Ramakrishnan and Baldassare, 2004). Although California is only 44 percent white (U.S. Census Bureau, 2007), whites made up 67 percent of registered voters in 2005 (DiCamillo, 2006). This is only one example of how significant inequality exists when it comes to political voice and broader civic participation. Moreover, these inequalities are not random. Factors such as race and class are structuring unequal political participation and influence. What can be done?

There are no simple answers to this complex problem. The elements of civic and political voice in a democracy are multidimensional, including everything from voting to participation in protests, community action organizations, and political campaigns. In addition to the right to participate, we must also be concerned with the capacity for effective engagement, as well as individual and group perception of inclusion in the political process (see Verba, 2003, for a review of these issues). Moreover, the factors that structure political inequality are numerous and deeply rooted in economic, social, and educational inequalities. We are especially interested in education because civic participation develops in childhood, schools can provide similar experiences to all young Americans, regardless of social class, and "civics" has a traditional place in American curricula. It is incumbent on us, as educators, to ask, "What can schools do to help?"

For the past two years we have been studying this question by surveying high school seniors throughout the state of California with support from the Constitutional Rights Foundation as part of Educating for Democracy: The California Campaign for the Civic Mission of Schools. In a series of surveys we have asked students about their exposure to specific school-based civic learning opportunities and, more generally, about their civic commitments and capacities. We have also examined a nationally representative data set focused on exposure to civic learning opportunities and outcomes. What we have found is troubling. Far from drawing on civic education as a potential tool for ameliorating civic and political inequality, schools are making matters worse. In a nutshell, the very individuals who have the least influence on political processes—the people whose voices schools most need to inform and support in order to promote democratic equality—often get fewer school-based opportunities to develop their civic capacities and commitments than other students. Given the evidence that these opportunities help promote effective civic engagement, these disparities in educational opportunities likely contribute to larger civic and political inequality.

In this chapter, we discuss these findings and their significance. We conclude by discussing strategies that policy makers, educators, foundation leaders, and others might employ to mount an effective response. We begin by discussing two related literatures. First, we examine studies of effective civic education practices in order to identify a set of learning opportunities on which to focus. Then we briefly review the extensive literature on curricular inequality and tracking and the very limited literature on curricular inequality related to civic learning opportunities. We then summarize our findings from three related studies of the distribution of civic learning opportunities. We conclude by discussing directions that policy makers and funders may wish to consider as they craft a response.

Civic Learning Opportunities That Make a Difference

Before working to provide equal civic learning opportunities or even studying whether such inequalities exist, we must ask whether civic learning opportunities make a difference. If they do not, why bother equalizing them? In fact, for many years scholars questioned whether civic learning opportunities were consequential. Studies failed to find that high school civics courses, for example, had a significant impact on student civic and political outcomes (Langton and Jennings, 1968). Over the course of the past decade, however, studies that looked at specific classroom practices have led to more promising findings. Specifically, Niemi and Junn's 1998 analysis of data from the National Assessment of Educational Progress revealed that some educational practices can increase students' civic and political knowledge, and Michael Delli Carpini and Scott Keeter (1996) have shown that such knowledge improves the quantity and quality of civic participation. In addition, large-scale studies such as the International Association for the Evaluation of Educational Achievement's (IEA) Civic Education Study of 14-year-olds in 28 countries found that certain curricular features were associated with such civic outcomes as interest in politics, the ability to apply knowledge accurately, and a range of civic and political commitments including youth willingness to vote (Torney-Purta, 2002; Torney-Purta, Amadeo, and Richardson, 2001). These largely correlational findings have been reinforced by a number of smaller but well controlled studies of particular curricular initiatives (Metz and Youniss, 2005; McDevitt and Kiousis, 2004; Kahne, Chi, and Middaugh, 2006). There are also well controlled longitudinal studies of participation with extracurricular activities which indicate that such activities support future civic engagement (Smith, 1999; McFarland and Thomas, 2006). In addition, we recently completed a study that found that classroom-based civic learning opportunities had a meaningful effect on Chicago high school students' commitment to civic participation and desire to vote. The impact of these opportunities was sizable even after controlling for prior civic commitments, demographic and academic factors, the degree to which youth talk with their parents about politics, and the levels of social capital in the student communities (Kahne and Sporte, 2008).

It is important to note that what constitutes "desirable" civic outcomes is a matter of some debate and necessarily includes a wide array of outcomes. In earlier work with Joel Westheimer, one of the authors has found that civic education programs vary considerably in the activities and values they promote depending on teachers' conception of what it means to be a good citizen (Westheimer and Kahne, 2004). For example, a teacher who views good citizenship as a matter of personal responsibility may design activities that engage students in activities that focus on individual acts of helping while a teacher who views good citizenship as promoting social justice might work to engage students in social analysis and related group action. While the relative merits of differing visions of good citizenship continue to be debated, research on the effectiveness of civic education must necessarily include a broad array of outcomes. In an attempt to synthesize the varying commitments, capacities, and activities valued by citizens and educators, the Carnegie Corporation and the Center for Information and Research on Civic Learning and Engagement (CIRCLE) consulted a group of over 50 scholars and practitioners in the field of civic education to arrive at a broad definition of competent and responsible citizenship that includes (1) being informed and thoughtful; (2) organized participation in communities, (3) political action, and (4) having moral and civic virtues (Gibson and Levine, 2003). These outcomes align with the forms of political engagement and influence that, as we noted above, are unequally distributed among adult Americans.

Based on these broad goals, specific evidence supporting what constitutes "best practice" is now emerging, highlighting strategies for students that include

- discussing current events;
- studying issues about which the student cares;
- experiencing an open climate for classroom discussions of social and political topics;
- studying government, history, and related social science;
- providing opportunities to interact with civic role models;
- engaging in after-school activities;
- learning about community problems and ways to respond;
- working on service-learning projects;
- engaging in simulations.[1]

Curricular Inequality

The release of Jeannie Oakes's seminal work, *Keeping Track: How Schools Structure Inequality*, focused attention on the fact that students placed in lower tracks generally experience lessened "expectations for achievement, access to subject matter and critical learning opportunities, instructional strategies, and resources (including teachers)." Studies have also found that students of low socioeconomic status and African American and Latino students are disproportionately placed in lower tracks (Oakes, 2005, 225).

While the research on tracking is extensive, little of it focuses on social studies instruction or on civic outcomes. As discussed above, those writing about civic and democratic education have instead tended to identify what constitutes high-quality curriculum and to focus on increasing the civic learning opportunities provided by schools. Differences in civic learning outcomes, what Meira Levinson (2007) has labeled "The Civic Achievement Gap," have been well documented, especially gaps related to civic knowledge and skills (see Hart and Atkins, 2002; National Center for Education Statistics, 2007; Levinson, 2007; Torney-Purta, Barber, and Wilkenfeld, 2006). Little attention, however, has been focused on whether equal civic learning opportunities are provided.

There are a few recent studies that focus on community service and service-learning. A study by the Corporation for National and Community Service (Spring, Dietz, and Grimm, 2007) found that youth from disadvantaged backgrounds were much less likely to report participation in school-based service or service-learning than other students (31 percent vs. 40 percent.) This result parallels findings by Atkins and Hart (2003) and Condon (2007). Examining the National Household Educational Survey of 1999, Condon also found that youth with better educated parents and higher household incomes were more likely to attend a school with a student government, to have given a speech in class, and to have debated in class. Highlighting a related theme, Daniel McFarland and Carlos Starmanns (2008) examined 278 school constitutions and found that the quality of opportunity afforded students was greater in well funded schools than in less well funded schools, potentially resulting in unequal opportunities for political socialization. Similarly, Torney-Purta, Barber, and Wilkenfeld (2007) find that differences between Latino and non-Latino civic outcomes are partially the result of school-level differences in the provision of an open classroom climate and time devoted to the study of political topics and democratic ideals.

And, of course, these inequalities are reinforced by broader social inequalities related to civic learning opportunities. Drawing on 448 face-to-face interviews with African Americans in Detroit, Cohen and Dawson (1993) show, for example, that African American residents who live in areas with high concentrations of poverty (>30 percent) are significantly less likely to belong to civic groups, including churches and community groups, and to have contact with political officials than African Americans who live in areas with either low or moderate levels of poverty (0–30 percent).

Thus the general educational literature on tracking as well as the limited data that have been collected related to civic learning opportunities in schools give us reason to believe that differences in civic learning opportunities may well exist. We have not, however, been able to find much systematic analysis of representative samples of students regarding the broad range of school-based civic learning opportunities that educators associate with best practice. In the discussion that follows, we respond to this need. Specifically, we examine three data sets and explore the distribution of civic learning opportunities in related but distinct ways. We discuss each study separately—highlighting the sample, the analysis, and the questions the analysis addresses. We then review these findings, their implications, and potential responses.

Before proceeding, we want to highlight one limitation to our approach. In an effort to focus on forms of inequality that can be clearly identified and universally applied, we are focusing on a widely accepted set of desired civic learning opportunities. While studies of civic learning opportunities have demonstrated their efficacy among differing student populations, research also indicates that there may be important variations within the United States related to the ways students from differing economic, racial, and ethnic backgrounds experience civic education and discussions of democratic institutions. For instance, our recent qualitative study of high school students in different social contexts in California suggests that youth from high-income, majority white communities are more likely to view political engagement as effective but less likely to view these activities as necessary or important compared with their counterparts from a primarily working-class Latino community. These differences in perception are likely important influences on how students perceive and make use of opportunities for civic education provided by the schools. Indeed, Rubin (2007) found, in her qualitative study of middle and high school students in New Jersey, that those from privileged, homogeneous environments were more likely to experience the ideals expressed in civic texts as congruous with their daily experiences compared with the urban youth of color. Thus, although the learning opportunities we describe and assess are likely desirable from the standpoint of promoting civic commitments and capacities, there is reason to believe that they are experienced differently by youth from different backgrounds. A more nuanced examination of the significance of these factors in relation to the impact of such opportunities on civic outcomes is clearly warranted.

Access to High-Impact School-Based Civic Learning Opportunities

In this section we detail findings from three studies. The first draws on survey data from high school seniors in California. It looks at the range of civic learning opportunities and then examines whether access to these opportunities was related to a student's racial and ethnic identity. In an effort to assess whether students on different academic trajectories received similar civic learning opportunities, we also examined whether students' plans for after high school (four-year college, two-year college, no college) were related to their exposure to civic learning opportunities while in high school.

The second study also examined students from a diverse set of California high schools. In addition, it was designed to assess whether the opportunities students received in AP government courses differed from those they received in College Prep government classes. The U.S. government course—the curricular requirement that most directly aligns with the preparation of citizens—is required of all students in California. AP and College Prep are two options.[2]

Both studies examined the experiences of students in relation to individual characteristics and school experiences. To strengthen our understanding of these relationships, we also wanted to know if the demographics of the classroom or, potentially, school was related to the volume of civic learning opportunities that students received. To address this issue, we draw on data from the IEA Civic Education Study. Because this study provides demographic data and information on classroom civic learning opportunities from entire classrooms of students from 124 schools throughout the country, we can examine the degree to which the demographic composition of classrooms may be related to a student's access to civic learning opportunities. These three studies, testing related dynamics in three different ways, all come to the same conclusion. Academically and socioeconomically privileged students, those who, on average, will have greater civic and political voice, also receive far more extensive access to the kinds of opportunities that educators have found to promote civic participation. The differences are sizable. Below, we discuss findings from each of these studies and then discuss related implications.

Study 1: The Relationship between Students' Demographic Characteristics and the Provision of Civic Learning Opportunities

Our first analysis of the equality of access to civic opportunities comes from our study of 2,366 California high school students. In this study we examined how frequently students experienced the kinds of opportunities that supported the development of committed, informed, and effective citizens. Students were drawn from 12 schools selected from across the state in order to create a sample that was diverse in race and ethnicity, socioeconomic status, and school achievement. (See Appendix A at the end of this chapter for a description of the sample.) We asked students to rate how frequently they had experienced opportunities identified as best practice in the 2003 Civic Mission of Schools Report (Gibson and Levine, 2003) and other studies in the civic education literature (see, e.g., Billig, 2005; Niemi and Junn, 1998; Smith, 1999; Kahne and Westheimer, 2003; Kahne, Chi, and Middaugh, 2006; Torney-Purta, Lehmann, Oswald, and Schulz, 2001; Verba, Schlozman, and Brady, 1995; Kahne and Sporte, 2008). We conducted a multiple linear regression and controlled for grade-point averages, mother's education, and gender. The findings suggest that access to these opportunities is uneven. Some opportunities are more common and some students are more likely than others to have experiences with those opportunities.

In Table 2.1, even with other controls in place, we see that students who identified as African Americans were significantly ($p < .05$) less likely than white students to report having civically oriented government courses, discussions of social problems and current events, student voice in decision making, and an open classroom climate.[3] They were also less likely than white students to report simulations of civic processes, although this relationship was approaching significant ($p < .10$). Students who identified as Asian, Filipino, or Pacific Islander reported more participation in extracurricular activities and more decision making in school than white students, but less open discussion in the classroom ($p < .05$). Latino students reported fewer opportunities for service, experiences with an open classroom climate, and experiences with role-playing and simulations than did white students ($p < .05$).

We also found that high school seniors who did not expect to take part in any form of post-secondary education reported significantly fewer opportunities to develop civic and political capacities and commitments than those with post-secondary plans. Indeed, the quantity of opportunities was strongly related to the amount of post-secondary education a student expected to receive. This held for all the opportunities measured ($p < .05$) (see Figure 2.1 and Table 2.1). For example, 25 percent of students who were planning to attend a four-year college reported that they had frequently been part of simulations in their classrooms; only 17 percent of students who planned on vocational education after high school could say the same. Only 10 percent of those with no post-secondary plans reported having such opportunities frequently in their classrooms. Moreover, since the survey was given toward the end of senior year, it does not include most high school dropouts. Students who dropped out before the 12th grade (in many schools a sizable percentage) got no high school U.S. government course at all, since it is typically offered during senior year. As a result, this group received far fewer civic learning opportunities during high school. Moreover, those dropping out are disproportionately low-income

Table 2.1: Relationship of demographic variables to experiences with civic opportunities

	Civically oriented government course	Discuss social problems and current events	Community service/ service-learning	Extra-curricular activities	Student voice/ decision making	Open classroom climate	Simulations of civic processes	Opportunities to practice civic skills
African American	–.079***	–.083***	–.007	.022	–.044*	–.104***	–.037†	–.001
Asian	–.016	–.043†	.004	.088***	.053*	–.103***	–.007	–.004
Latino	–.012	–.006	–.080**	–.015	.018	–.055*	–.059*	–.048
Other	–.046*	–.024	–.017	–.058**	–.033	–.053*	–.019	–.075*
GPA	.001	–.002	.082***	.128***	.006	.021	–.016	.119***
Mother's education	–.070**	–.040†	.044†	.073**	–.011	.012	.079***	.072*
Female	.076***	.105***	.115***	.167***	.040†	.104***	.027	.177***
Post–high school plans	.146***	.172***	.113***	.180***	.069**	.132***	.127***	.144***

Note: The demographic category "Native American" was not included because of the small number of students who chose that item only.

$^{*}p < .05$; $^{**}p < .01$; $^{***}p < .001$; $^{\dagger}p < .10$; all reported values above are standardized betas (β).

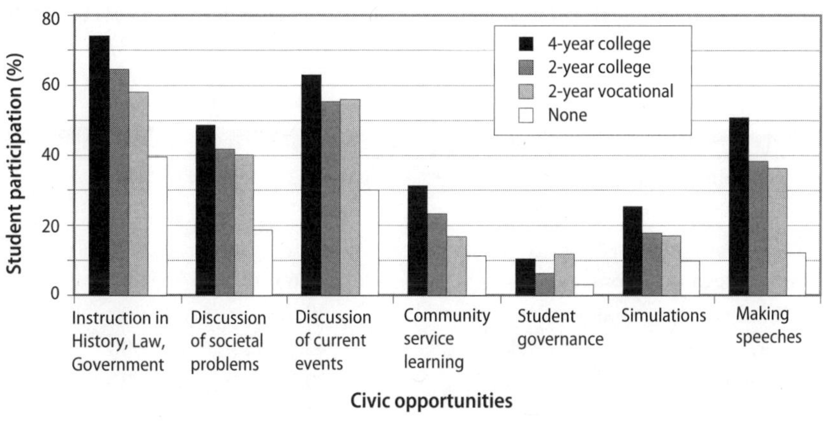

Figure 2.1: Civic opportunities and post-secondary education plans

students of color. Thus the civic opportunities gap that this study shows already exists would likely be even greater if students who dropped out of high school were part of our sample.

Study 2: The Relationship between a Student's Track and the Provision of Civic Learning Opportunities

In the following year (2005–2006 school year), we surveyed 898 seniors from across the state of California. In 6 of the 10 schools (371 students), we were able to clearly identify the track of the U.S. government course. Of these, 293 (79 percent) were enrolled in a College Prep U.S. government course and 78 (21 percent) were enrolled in an Advanced Placement (AP) U.S. government course. (See Appendix B at the end of this chapter for sample description.)

We used independent samples *t*-tests to examine whether there were statistically significant differences in the average level of opportunities experienced by students in College Prep vs. AP government classes. In Table 2.2 and Figure 2.2, we see that students in AP classes were significantly more likely to report experiences of all but one of the civic opportunities we measured. The largest differences between College Prep and AP classes were found in experiences with simulations of civic processes (mock trials, mock elections), community service, and open classroom climate. For example, 80 percent of students in the AP sample agreed that they had participated in simulations compared with 51

Table 2.2: Comparison of civic opportunities reported by California high school seniors in Advanced Placement vs. College Preparatory U.S. government classes ($n = 371$)

Civic opportunities	Mean difference[a] (AP–CP)	Significance
CMS6:[b] Simulations	1.22	.000
CMS4: Extracurricular activities	0.71	.000
CMS3: Community service	1.08	.000
CMS5: Open classroom	0.63	.000
CMS1: Instruction in government	0.62	.000
Opportunities to practice civic skills	0.56	.000
Media literacy	0.52	.000
CMS5: Student decision making	0.49	.003
CMS2: Debate and discussion of current events	0.38	.000
Experiences with diversity	0.32	.002
Experiences with role models	0.27	.042
Discuss immigration	0.08	ns

[a] Mean differences represent differences between average scores on a 5-point scale of "strongly disagree" to "strongly agree." For example, when asked about exposure to simulations, College Prep students on average answered 2.90, indicating answers falling between "slightly disagree" and 3 for "not sure," while AP students on average answered 4.12, indicating answers falling between "slightly agree" and "strongly agree."

[b] CMS refers to the *Civic Mission of Schools*, a report of six promising practices in civic education. CMS6 refers to Civic Mission of Schools recommendation #6: to engage students in simulations.

percent of College Prep students. Similarly 80 percent of students in the AP sample agreed that in their classes they were encouraged to make up their own minds about political or social issues and to discuss issues about which students have different opinions, compared with 57 percent of College Prep students.

Because of the potential that our findings were being driven by school-level differences between schools that had AP students and schools that did not, we also examined differences between AP and College Prep students' civic opportunities within the one school that had sufficient numbers of each to allow a comparison. In this school, as in the sample as a whole, AP students reported greater exposure to a number of civic opportunities than their counterparts in College Prep courses. Also, as was the case with the entire sample, the largest

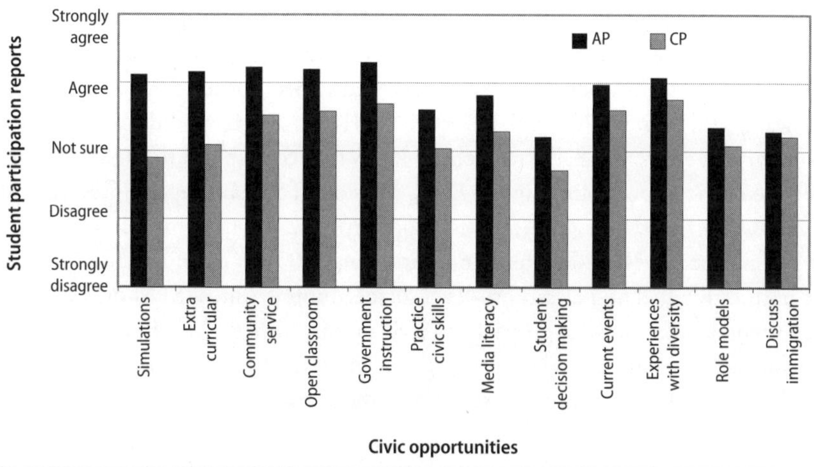

Figure 2.2: Comparison of civic opportunities reported by California high school seniors in Advanced Placement vs. College Preparatory U.S. government classes ($n = 371$)

differences were in reported experiences with simulations, community service, and an open classroom climate. For example, 38 percent of College Prep students agreed they had experiences with simulations, compared with 80 percent of AP students. Similarly, 43 percent of College Prep students reported experiences with community service, compared with 81 percent of AP students.

Within this particular school, there was no difference by track of student experiences with meeting and learning about civic role models or with student decision making. In contrast to the sample as a whole, College Prep students in this school were more likely than their AP counterparts to report having discussions about immigration (an important current event at the time of data collection).

Study 3: The Relationship between the Average SES of Students in a Classroom and the Provision of Civic Learning Opportunities

In our California samples, we focused solely on the characteristics of individual students because we did not have a sufficient number of schools to determine whether the demographic features of classrooms or school-level variables bore a statistically significant relationship to students' experiences with civic opportunities. Fortunately, our final analysis of equality of opportunity draws on the public release data provided by the IEA Civic Education Study, which includes a national sample of 2,811 9th-grade students from 124 schools across the nation (one classroom per school was surveyed). (See Torney-Purta, Lehmann, Oswald, and Schulz, 2001; Baldi et al., 2001.) In the Civic Education Study student survey, we were able to identify items that correspond to the six recommended civic opportunities in the Civic Mission of Schools report (Gibson and Levine, 2003) and one additional civic opportunity. We used multilevel modeling (described in Rabe-Hesketh and Skrondal, 2005) to examine the influence of both individual and classroom-level socioeconomic status (SES) on students' reported experiences with a variety of civic opportunities.[4] Multilevel modeling enables us to assess the relationship between civic learning opportunities and both individual socioeconomic status and the average SES of all students from the classroom.

As presented in Table 2.3, individual SES and school-level SES were related to how likely students were to report experiences with a number of civic opportunities. For example, students in classes with higher average SES levels (one standard deviation above the mean on parents' education) were

- 2.03 times more likely than students in classrooms with average scores on our SES indicator to report studying how laws are made;
- 1.89 times more likely to report participating in service activities;
- 1.42 times more likely to report having experiences with debates or panel discussions in their social studies classes.

At the same time, the socioeconomic status of individual students also plays a role in how likely they are to report some civic opportunities. As expected, this is particularly true for voluntary opportunities that are more likely to take place as extracurricular activities, such as community service or participation in clubs.

Summary of Findings

One clear and consistent set of relationships was observed in all three studies: students who are more academically successful and those with parents of higher socioeconomic status receive more classroom-based civic learning opportunities. For quite some time we have known that having well-educated parents and being successful in school are related to greater civic and political participation and influence in adulthood. Most studies of this phenomenon have emphasized the ways overall educational attainment and such family background elements as family income, parents' education, and political involvement foster participatory inequality across generations and between groups (see Verba, Burns, and Schlozman, 2003; Nie, Junn, and Stehlik-Barry, 1996). This study shows that these already privileged students also receive more classroom-based civic learning opportunities. Rather than helping to equalize the capacity and commitments needed for democratic participation, teachers appear to be exacerbating this inequality by providing more preparation for those who are already likely to attain a disproportionate amount of civic and political voice.

Policy Options

It is inevitable that students will have varying opportunities to develop a civic and political voice depending on the teachers they have for civic-related subjects. Schools, however, should not distribute these opportunities on the basis of race, class, or academic standing. Unfortunately, our California and national data indicate that this is occurring. Since a commitment to valuing the equal participation of all individuals is fundamental to a democracy, it is incumbent on policy makers, educators, and funders to respond. The discussion that follows is speculative, meant more as an early effort to consider possibilities than as a fully developed road map for action.

At the outset, it is important to highlight a fundamental tension that arises between policies promoting the quantity of civic education and those promoting equality of civic learning opportunities. A conflict between these two goals is not inevitable, but it can easily arise. The problem, simply put, is that if one focuses on promoting more civic education, those who already get the most will often get more and the civic opportunity gap will grow. This occurs because the teachers and schools with the most resources, flexibility, and interest in pursuing these goals are already doing more in this regard, and they will often be the ones who can best take advantage of new opportunities for civically oriented curricular and cocurricular activities. Thus, as we discuss ways to better emphasize civics within curricular frameworks, to provide professional development, and to foster more civically oriented extracurricular activities, particular emphasis is placed on structuring these efforts so as to augment equity at the same time that we aim to promote more civic learning opportunities for everyone. Generally speaking, we do this by developing initiatives that emphasize universal provision of civic learning opportunities or that emphasize supports for civic learning among those who currently receive the fewest such opportunities.

Table 2.3: Relationship between individual and classroom-level socioeconomic status (SES) and student-reported experiences with civic opportunities

	N	*Regression coefficient*	
	(L2, L1)	Classroom SES	Individual SES
Agree or disagree? In school I have learned to contribute to solving problems in the community.	(126, 1868)	ns[a]	ns[a]
CMS1—Knowledge Opportunities			
Over the past year, have you studied the U.S. Constitution?	(126, 1787)	1.75**[b]	1.15†[b]
Over the past year, have you studied the U.S. Congress?	(126, 1773)	1.96**[b]	ns[b]
Over the past year, have you studied the president and cabinet?	(126, 1737)	1.90**[b]	ns[b]
Over the past year, have you studied how laws are made?	(127, 1772)	2.03***[b]	ns[b]
Over the past year, have you studied the court system?	(127, 1751)	1.50**[b]	1.14*[b]
Over the past year, have you studied political parties, elections, and voting?	(126, 1756)	1.71**[b]	ns[b]
Over the past year, have you studied state and local government?	(127, 1730)	1.57**[b]	ns[b]
Over the past year, have you studied other countries' government?	(127, 1705)	ns[b]	ns[b]
Over the past year, have you studied international organizations?	(126, 1616)	ns[b]	ns[b]
CMS2			
Do you take part in debates or panel discussions when you study social studies?	(127, 1706)	1.58**[b]	ns[b]
Do you discuss current events when you study social studies?	(127, 1764)	ns[b]	ns[b]
CMS3			
Have you participated in a group conducting voluntary activities to help the community?	(127, 1787)	1.89***[b]	1.34***[b]
Have you participated in a charity collecting money for a social cause?	(127, 1996)	1.73***[b]	1.29***[b]

CMS4			
Think about the organizations listed above. How often do you attend meetings or activities for any or all these organizations?	(127, 1990)	.28***[a]	.20***[a]
CMS5			
Open classroom climate scale[c].	(127, 1787)	.16***[a]	.04*[a]
CMS6			
Do you take part in role-playing, mock trials, or dramas when you study social studies?	(127, 1787)	1.33*[b]	1.18**[b]

[a]Linear regression coefficient for a continuous outcome (estimated using random-intercept linear regression).

[b]Logistic regression coefficient for a dichotomous outcome (estimated using random-intercept logistic regression).

[c]Open classroom climate scale includes average of six items: students are encouraged to make up their own minds about issues; teachers respect our opinions and encourage us to express them during class; teachers present several sides of an issue when explaining it in class; students feel free to express opinions in class even when their opinions are different from most of the other students; students feel free to disagree openly with their teachers about political and social issues during class; teachers encourage us to discuss political or social issues about which people have different opinions.

* $p < .05$; **$p < .01$; ***$p < .001$; †$p < .10$; all reported values above are standardized betas (β).

Prevent Testing from Narrowing the Emphasis Placed on Civics

Research demonstrates that the range of civic learning opportunities discussed in this chapter support the development of civic commitments and capacities (McDevitt and Kiousis, 2004; Metz and Youniss, 2005; Torney-Purta, Amadeo, and Richardson, 2001; Kahne and Sporte, 2008; Kahne, Chi, and Middaugh, 2006; Gibson and Levine, 2003).

Unfortunately, there is evidence that the high stakes tests that focus on math and literacy and that are central to No Child Left Behind legislation can narrow the curriculum and make these civic learning opportunities less likely. For example, a recently completed study by the Center on Education Policy (2006) found that 71 percent of districts reported cutting back time on other subjects to make more space for reading and math instruction. Social studies was the part of the curriculum where these reductions generally occurred. Thus those who want more students to receive civic learning opportunities understandably want to broaden curricular goals to include an emphasis on civics.

This priority is also of great importance for those concerned with equity. Cutbacks in the emphasis placed on civics are more likely in schools facing sanctions by NCLB because civics is not tied to a high stakes test. Schools that easily meet NCLB standards are under less pressure to shift time and resources away from civics. Of course, civic learning opportunities can be provided in ways that are fully supportive of core academic skills. Indeed, linking government and other social studies course curricula to core academic skills and analytic abilities is desirable from all perspectives. Whether such changes are possible in the absence of changes to the testing environment, however, is uncertain.

Civics Tests?

While it may be clear that the current testing policy creates disincentives to focus on providing civic learning opportunities, how policy makers should respond is less obvious. One response would be to scale back current testing policies. If less emphasis were placed on these tests, perhaps more schools would choose to focus on civics. And since schools serving low-performing students, students of color, and students of low socioeconomic status are likely those most impacted by testing policies, schools serving these populations would be most likely to increase the civic learning opportunities they provide, thus narrowing the civic opportunity gap.

Alternatively, those promoting greater equity in civic learning opportunities might work to institute civics tests to complement tests in other subjects. The well-worn logic goes something like this: "What gets tested gets taught." If math, science, and literacy get tested but civics does not, few should be surprised that schools—and schools with low scoring students in particular—focus on math, science, and literacy. By creating a civics test, we might increase the incentives for schools to emphasize the provision of civic learning opportunities.

Although the pros and cons of civics tests are a worthy topic for discussion, considering how and why we might alter current testing policies is beyond the scope of this chapter. Rather than fully considering the desirability of various testing policies, the suggestions we make are more modest. We highlight three design principles related to tests and other civic assessments that we feel would promote greater quality and equality in access to civic learning opportunities for students. First, it is important to collect systematic data and to ensure that the focus of such data collection includes, but also extends beyond, the acquisition of civic knowledge. The relevance of civic knowledge for a high-functioning democracy is clear, but so is the need to develop civic skills, participatory commitments, democratic values, and the capacity for reasoned analysis of policy issues and political discussions (see Verba, Schlozman, and Brady, 1995; Delli Carpini and Keeter, 1996; Gibson and Levine, 2003).

Second, it is important that this data be used to assess the degree to which all students are accorded similar access to civic learning opportunities. Data collection must extend beyond outcomes to include assessments of the qualities and quantities of opportunities that students receive in schools and elsewhere. Indeed, it is quite problematic that many indicator-driven "report cards" dealing with youth civic and political outcomes focus only on outcomes and do not highlight learning opportunities at the same time. These indicators, while helpful, fail to focus attention on providing the learning opportunities that can advance desired goals. Moreover, there is some evidence that an emphasis on civic outcomes, especially civic knowledge, can actually diminish the provision of desired civic learning opportunities. For example, we found that Chicago's required civics tests that emphasized factual recall led teachers to focus on discrete facts and information and diminished students' exposure to high-quality civic learning such as opportunities to discuss or debate community issues or to work collaboratively with others (Kahne, Rodriguez, Smith, and Thiede, 2000). Thus pairing an emphasis on outcomes with one on learning opportunities is very important.

Third, findings from tests or surveys should be actively integrated into a reflective process in departments, schools, and districts in order to inform teacher development and professional practice. Given the enormous pressures that schools and students face, it is important that a testing policy in civics not become an additional unfunded mandate. In order for schools to fully benefit from testing and the data that result, educators will need time to work together and opportunities to learn from other successful teachers and curriculum specialists.

Professional Development and Curricular Support Are Needed

As discussed above, while indicators of civic learning opportunities will help focus attention on these priorities, professional and curricular development is also needed if educators are to thoughtfully engage civic content in a way that bolsters core academic skills and aligns with such best practices as introducing students to role models, simulations, and service-learning. As summarized in the Civic Mission of Schools consensus document, the 1998 National Assessment of Educational Progress found that more students had been asked to memorize material from social studies textbooks than to engage in a range of best practices, for example, role-playing exercises and mock trials, visits from those who are active in the community, or opportunities to help solve community problems. That study also found, consistent with the findings presented here, that students of color and those from low-education families were the least likely to experience these desired opportunities.

In response, one could imagine a professional development effort at the state or federal level modeled after the Teaching Traditional American History grants. This federal program provides funding to local education agencies and groups that have content expertise to develop, document, evaluate, and disseminate innovative and cohesive models of professional development. A similar program, funded at either the state or federal level, could focus on the civic and democratic aims of education. To help redress the inequality that currently exists, proposals that focused on serving high percentages of low SES students could be granted special consideration. Extra points might be awarded to proposals that were universal in focus (for example, by serving all social studies teachers or students) and did not enable students or teachers to "choose" to participate.

Finally, to help ensure systematic attention to issues of quality and equality, the grant requirements could stipulate that participating schools collect, analyze, and reflect upon survey data by asking: How does the reform impact the equality of student access to civic learning opportunities and associated civic outcomes? Support for survey administration and analysis from a state-funded entity would also be helpful.

Foster More Civically Oriented Extracurricular Activities

There is a great deal of evidence that extracurricular activities, particularly those that emphasize civic themes, can meaningfully support civic outcomes (see McFarland and Thomas, 2006; Otto, 1976; Smith, 1999). In response to this potential, Hart and Kirshner, in this volume, propose supporting the development of community-based organizations (CBOs) that provide these civic learning opportunities. Such initiatives might take the form of the new version of the Younger Americans Act that Youniss and Levine propose in this volume. Funds could be designated for CBOs that provide support for positive youth development as well as for organizations to work with schools to expand opportunities for civic and political engagement.

We like the idea of partnering schools and CBOs in this way. Many of these organizations have well developed curricular efforts that address the development of civic and political commitments and capacities. For example, Hart and Kirshner, in this volume, note the many examples in which adolescents in poor urban areas take an interest in civic and political participation. Particularly effective are programs where adults reach out and provide opportunities for engagement. They also find that activities that address "clear, present, and compelling issues" are more likely to engage young people than those that are abstract or removed from their daily concerns.

By pairing CBOs that have expertise in these areas with schools, it may be possible to achieve more universal access by taking advantage of the fact that schools serve a broad cross-section of young people. For example, mock trials could be incorporated into the social studies and U.S. government curriculum. Alternatively, schools could institute structures that engage all students in senior projects and perhaps also freshman projects where they were given support to identify and study a "clear, present, and compelling" civic or political issue. Ideally, students would consider various ways to respond to the issues they were studying and, where appropriate, they might act.

While we are fully supportive of such an initiative, we want to stress the need to structure such efforts to ensure that they diminish rather than expand inequality. Unfortunately, research indicates that the provision of extracurricular and voluntary activities often reinforces rather than diminishes inequality. Indeed, findings from the National Educational Longitudinal Survey indicates that students with greater interest, those who demonstrate greater academic ability, and those of greater SES are all more likely to participate in service clubs, student government, school newspapers, and yearbook clubs—all opportunities that commonly provide civically oriented leadership opportunities (McNeal, 1998). In addition, schools that are safer and have lower concentrations of students of color tend to provide more of these extracurricular opportunities (McNeal, 1999; Feldman and Matjasko, 2005). Finally, and not surprisingly, several studies have found that parent involvement in community activities is a strong predictor of adolescent involvement (see Feldman and Matjasko for a review). Thus, as a result of both self-selection and inequalities tied to socioeconomic factors, many of the after-school extracurricular opportunities that develop civic capacities and commitments are attended by those who already have more interest and more access to opportunities in classrooms. While these civic development opportunities are desirable in and of themselves, if they are not distributed equally, they exacerbate existing inequality.

We are not arguing that high performing or high SES students should be denied these opportunities. Rather, we are advocating that educators, funders, and policy makers work to identify ways to make such opportunities more universal and common in schools serving students who are currently receiving the fewest opportunities. The Younger Americans Act mentioned above could be structured in this way. Furthermore, we suggest that simply providing more opportunities, without specifically reaching out to those who are most likely to need them, is insufficient. Indeed Quiroz, Gonzales, and Frank (1996) found that increasing the number of available extracurricular opportunities in a school does not necessarily result in more equitable participation. Typically, a core group of students will take on multiple activities, becoming "hyper-networked," while a larger number of students than would be expected, based on available opportunities, will be excluded from extracurricular activities altogether. Thus, when civic opportunities are provided primarily through voluntary extracurricular activities, such as speech and debate clubs, mock trial clubs, elective leadership classes, student councils, and service clubs, we expect that inequalities will continue to be exacerbated.

A Reason to Act

Schools alone cannot solve this problem. Numerous forms of social, racial, and economic inequality influence the political and civic inequality we have identified in this chapter. That said, we have some indications that offering civic learning opportunities to low-income students could provide a valuable way to respond to broader inequalities.

Our longitudinal study in Chicago engaged 4,057 students. We found that the degree to which parents discussed politics and current events and the civic qualities of their neighborhood mattered. But we found that what happened in school could compensate in powerful ways for differences in these contexts.

Imagine for a moment a student defined as average in the sample with

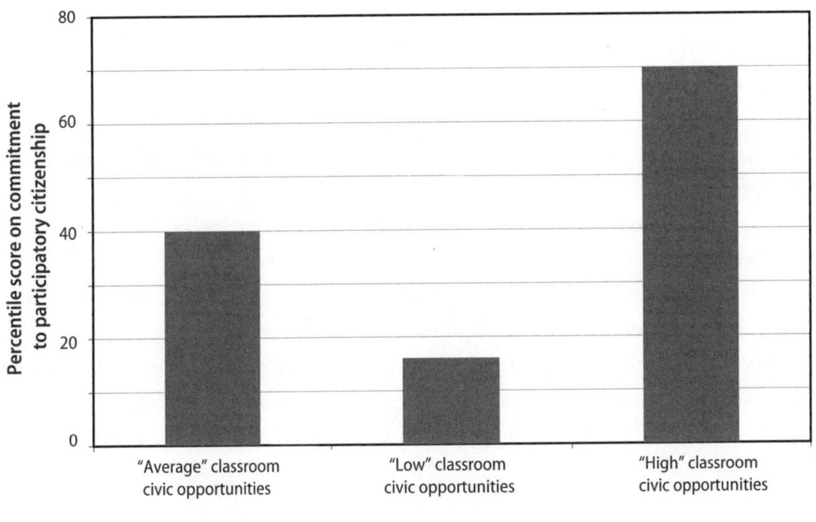

Figure 2.3: Comparison of participatory citizenship scores for students with few family and neighborhood civic learning opportunities, by amount of classroom civic opportunities

Note: In this figure, classroom civic opportunities are measured as "average" = sample mean, "low" = 1 SD below the sample mean, and "high" = 1 SD above the sample mean.

respect to demographics, schooling related to academic achievement, and after-school participation (see Figure 2.3). Imagine further that this student comes from a family where his or her parents rarely discuss politics or current events and from a neighborhood where there is little civically oriented social capital (i.e., that students do not see evidence that members of their community actively work to address their problems). Assume that this student is only in the 16th percentile for both of these variables (one standard deviation below the sample mean). If, in school, the student experienced opportunities to learn about civics (such as service-learning, an open classroom climate, exposure to role models, and discussion of problems in the society and ways to respond), that student's commitments to civic participation would be in the 39th percentile (see first column). If, instead of being average, the student received few civic learning opportunities in school, that student's commitments to civic participation would be at the 16th percentile (see second column). If, however, the student experienced many civic opportunities to learn, despite the lack of focus on these issues in the student's neighborhood and home, that same student would be expected to develop civic commitments that would place him or her well above average—the 68th percentile (see third column).[5]

In short, these findings indicate that educators can provide meaningful support for the development of commitments to civic and political participation among the relatively low-income students who attend public schools in Chicago. Policies that work to ensure that students in these contexts receive more equitable access to civic learning opportunities may well make a meaningful difference.

Thomas Jefferson wrote, "The qualifications for self-government in society are not innate. They are the result of habit and long training." Neither political equality nor a high-functioning democracy is guaranteed by the legal right to vote. The education and preparation of students to be informed and engaged citizens is essential and must be provided equitably. Democracy for some is not democracy at all.

Appendix A: Study 1 Sample Description

The total 12th-grade enrollment for California public schools during the 2004–2005 school year was 409,576. Our sample included 2,366 12th-grade students from 12 schools around the state. We evaluated the initial sample on three criteria of representation: (1) ethnic distribution, (2) socioeconomic distribution, and (3) schoolwide academic performance.

Because this sample differed considerably from the state profile of students, we created a subsample that balanced students in terms of school-level academic achievement and school-level SES and that came closer to the ethnic distribution of students across the state. This subsample consisted of 1,887 students from 10 schools. Among these students, 34 percent were from low SES schools, 32 percent from moderate SES schools, and 34 percent from high SES schools. Similarly, 35 percent were from low-performing schools, 33 percent from moderate-performing schools, and 33 percent from high-performing schools. The ethnic distribution of this state sample also bore a closer similarity to the ethnic distribution of the state population of 12th-grade students. The underrepresentation of Hispanic students and overrepresentation of Asian students was somewhat compensated for. White students remained underrepresented, although we suspect this happened in part by confusion over the use of the term "European American," with some white students opting for "other." We repeated our analyses using the balanced subsample and found no large differences. All analyses reported here are based on the original sample described in the tables above.

Appendix A. Table 1

Ethnicity	Population of graduating high school seniors in CA, 2004–2005 (%)	Survey sample, 2004–2005 (%)
Hispanic	36.5	30.5
White	39.6	24.9
Asian/Pacific Islander/Filipino	14.1	21.0
Asian	10.2	
Pacific Islander	0.7	
Filipino	3.2	
African American	7.5	7.5
American Indian	0.8	6.0
Other ethnicity		20.0

Note: Numbers add up to more than 100 percent because participants were allowed to choose more than one ethnicity.

Appendix A. Table 2

Group	Students qualifying for free/reduced lunch (%)	Schools in the survey sample
Low SES (bottom third)	45.5–100	3
Moderate SES (middle third)	18.2–45.4	4
High SES (top third)	0–18.1	5

Group	API rank	Schools in CMS sample
Low performing	1–3	3
Moderate performing	4–7	3
High performing	8–10	6

Appendix B: Study 2 Sample Description

We have been able to identify U.S. government course information from 371 of the 898 (41 percent) seniors who completed the survey. Of these, 293 (79 percent) reported being enrolled in a College Preparatory (CP) U.S. government course and 78 (21 percent) reported being enrolled in an Advanced Placement (AP) U.S. government course. These students were drawn from six schools.

Appendix B. Table 1

Ethnicity	Population of graduating high school seniors in CA, 2005–2006[a] (%)	Study sample, 12th grade ($N = 371$) (%)
Hispanic	35.7	17.4
White	39.7	34.5
Asian/Pacific Islander/Filipino	15.0	30.0
Asian	11.0	25.1
Pacific Islander	.7	1.1
Filipino	3.3	3.8
African American	7.3	8.4
American Indian	.8	4.1
Other/no response	1.6	5.8

[a]California Department of Education, 2007.

Appendix B. Table 2

School	Total responses for school	CP	AP	API	Free/reduced lunch (%)
School 2	20	0 (0%)	20 (100%)	2	65
School 3	98	98 (100%)	0 (0%)	2	43
School 4	143	107 (75%)	36 (25%)	6	39
School 5	78	68 (87%)	10 (13%)	10	6
School 6	13	1 (8%)	12 (92%)	3	23
School 11	19	19 (100%)	0 (0%)	7	30

Source: Chimerine, Panton, and Russo, 1993.

Notes

The authors wish to thank the staff of the Constitutional Rights Foundation and all participating students and schools. Chris Evans, Jim Youniss, Peter Levine, Judith Torney-Purta, Britt Wilkenfeld, and Gary Homana also provided very helpful feedback. In addition, we wish to thank the Carnegie Corporation of New York, the Annenberg Foundation, and the W. R. Hearst Foundation for their support of this research and the broader Educating for Democracy Project. The authors are solely responsible for any and all conclusions. Related research can be found at *www.civicsurvey.org.*

1. See Billig, 2000; Niemi and Junn, 1998; Smith, 1999; Kahne and Westheimer, 2003; Kahne, Chi, and Middaugh, 2006; Torney-Purta et al., 2001; Torney-Purta, 2002; Torney-Purta, Amadeo, and Richardson, 2001; Verba, Schlozman, and Brady, 1995; Kahne and Sporte, 2008; and Gibson and Levine, 2003.
2. Districts can use a variety of labels for U.S. government, including "regular" and "honors" as well as "College Prep" and "AP," but these were the two headings that were most prominent and clear for our analysis.
3. These are government courses where teachers emphasize the importance of individual citizens staying informed and acting on issues that are relevant to them.
4. The indicator used for SES was a standardized average of mother and father's level of education. In cases where students could not answer for both parents, the value available for either parent was used. Classroom-level SES represents the average score on this variable for each classroom. Individual SES represents each student's deviation from the classroom mean on this variable.
5. By "few" we mean one standard deviation below the mean, and by "many" we mean one standard deviation above the mean.

References

American Political Science Association Task Force on Inequality and American Democracy. (2004). American democracy in an age of rising inequality. *Perspectives on Politics, 2* (4), 651–89.

Atkins, R., and Hart, D. (2003). Neighborhoods, adults, and the development of civic identity in urban youth. *Applied Developmental Science, 7* (3), 156–64.

Baldi, S., Perle, M., Skidmore, D., Greenberg, E., Hahn, C., and Nelson, D. (2001). *What democracy means to ninth graders: U.S. results from the international IEA civic education study.* Washington, DC: Department of Education, Office of Educational Research and Improvement.

Bartels, L. M. (2005, August). Economic inequality and political representation. Available at *www.princeton.edu/~bartels/economic.pdf.*

Billig, S., Root, S., and Jesse, D. (2005). The impact of participation in service-learning on high school students' civic engagement. CIRCLE Working Paper 33. Washington DC: Center for Information and Research on Civic Learning and Engagement.

California Department of Education, Educational Demographics Office. (2007). (CBEDS, sifco5 4/28/08). Graduates by Ethnicity. State of California, 2004–2005 and 2005–2006. Accessed at *www.ed-data.k12.ca.us.*

Center on Education Policy. (2006). *From the capital to the classroom: Year four of the No Child Left Behind Act.* Washington, DC: Center on Education Policy.

Chimerine, C. B., Panton, K. L. M., and Russo, A. W. W. (1993). *The other 91 percent: Strategies to improve the quality of out-of-school experiences of Chapter 1 students.* Washington, DC: U.S. Department of Education.

Cohen, C. and Dawson, M. (1993). Neighborhood poverty and African American politics. *American Political Science Review, 87* (2), 286–303.

Condon, M. (2007). Practice makes participants: Developmental roots of political engagement. Paper presented at the Annual Meeting of the American Political Science Association, Chicago.

Delli Carpini, M. X., and Keeter, S. K. (1996). *What Americans know about politics and why it matters.* New Haven: Yale University Press.

DiCamillo, M. (2006). Special field poll presentation: Three California election megatrends and their implications in the 2006 gubernatorial election. Accessed at *www.field.com/fieldpollonline/subscribers/.*

Feldman, A. F., and Matjasko, J. L. (2005). The role of school-based extracurricular activities in adolescent development: A comprehensive review and future directions. *Review of Educational Research, 75,* 159–210.

Gibson, C. and Levine, P. (2003). *The civic mission of schools.* New York and Washington, DC: Carnegie Corporation of New York.

Gilens, M. (2005). Public opinion and democratic responsiveness: Who gets what they want from government? Presented at the annual meeting of inequality working groups sponsored by the Russell Sage Foundation, Berkeley, CA. Available at *www.russellsage.org/programs/main/inequality/workingpapers/050830.944626/download.*

Hart, D. and Atkins, R. (2002). Civic competence in urban youth. *Applied Developmental Science, 6* (4), 227–36.

IEA Civic Education Study. (n.d.). Available at *www.wam.umd.edu/~iea.*

Kahne, J., and Westheimer, J. (2003). Teaching democracy: What schools need to do. *Phi Delta Kappan, 85* (1), 34–40, 557–66.

Kahne, J., Chi, B., and Middaugh, E. (2006). Building social capital for civic and political engagement: The potential of high school government courses. *Canadian Journal of Education, 29* (2), 387–409.

Kahne, J. and Sporte, S. (2008). Developing citizens: The impact of civic learning opportunities on students' commitment to civic participation. *American Educational Research Journal, 45* (3), 738–66.

Kahne, J., Rodriguez, M., Smith, B., and Thiede, K. (2000). Developing citizens for democracy? Assessing opportunities to learn in Chicago's social studies classrooms. *Theory and Research in Social Studies Education, 28,* 311–38.

Langton, K. and Jennings, M. K. (1968). Political socialization and the high school civic curriculum in the United States. *American Political Science Review, 62,* 862–67.

Levinson, M. (2007). The civic achievement gap. CIRCLE Working Paper 51. Washington, DC: Center for Information and Research on Civic Learning and Engagement.

McDevitt, M. and Kiousis, S. (2004). Education for deliberative democracy: The long-term influence of kids voting. CIRCLE Working Paper 22. Washington, DC: Center for Information and Research on Civic Learning and Engagement.

McFarland, D. A., and Thomas, R. J. (2006). Bowling young: How youth voluntary associations influence adult political participation. *American Sociological Review, 71,* 401–25.

McFarland, D. A. and Starmanns, C. (2008, August). Inside student government. *Teachers College Record, 110* (August).

McNeal, R. B., Jr. (1998). High school extracurricular activities: Closed structures and stratifying patterns of participation. *Journal of Educational Research, 91,* 183–91.

McNeal, R. B., Jr. (1999). Participation in high school extracurricular activities: Investigating school level effects. *Social Science Quarterly, 80,* 291–309.

Metz, E. C., and Youniss, J. (2005). Longitudinal gains in civic development through school-based required service. *Political Psychology, 26* (3), 413–38.

National Center for Education Statistics. (2007). *The nation's report card: Civics 2006.* Washington, DC: Department of Education.

Nie, N., Junn, J., and Stehlik-Barry, K. (1996). *Education and democratic citizenship in America.* Chicago: University of Chicago Press.

Niemi, R., and Junn, J. (1998). *Civic education.* New Haven: Yale University Press.

Oakes, J. (2005). *Keeping track: How schools structure inequality.* New Haven: Yale University Press.

Otto, L. B. (1976). Social integration and the status attainment process. *American Journal of Sociology, 81,* 1360–83.

Quiroz, P.A., Gonzales, N. F., and Frank, K. A. (1996). Carving a niche in the high school social structure: Formal and informal constraints on participation in the extra curriculum. In A. Pallas, *Sociology of Education and Socialization*, vol. 11. London: JAI Press.

Rabe-Hesketh, S., and Skrondal, A. (2005). *Multilevel and longitudinal modeling using stata.* College Station, TX: Stata Press.

Ramakrishnan, S. K., and Baldassare, M. (2004). *The ties that bind: Changing demographics and civic engagement in California.* San Francisco: Public Policy Institute of California, 2004.

Rubin, B. C. (2007). "There's still not justice": Youth civic identity development amid distinct school and community contexts. *Teachers College Record, 109* (2), 449–81.

Smith, E. S. (1999). The effects of investment in the social capital of youth on political and civic behavior in young adulthood: A longitudinal analysis. *Political Psychology, 20,* 553–80.

Spring, K., Dietz, N, and Grimm, R. (2007). *Leveling the path to participation:*

Volunteering and civic engagement among youth from disadvantaged circumstances. Washington, DC: Corporation for National and Community Service.

Torney-Purta, J., Lehmann, R., Oswald, H., and Schulz, W. (2001). *Citizenship and education in 28 countries: Civic knowledge and engagement at age 14.* Amsterdam: International Association for the Evaluation of Educational Achievement (IEA).

Torney-Purta, J. (2002). The school's role in developing civic engagement: A study of adolescents in twenty-eight countries. *Applied Developmental Science, 6* (4), 203–12.

Torney-Purta J., Amadeo, J., and Richardson, W. K. (2001). Civic service among youth in Chile, Denmark, England, and the United States: A psychological perspective. In J. Torney-Purta, R. Lehmann, H. Oswald, and W. Schulz (Eds.) (2001), *Citizenship and education in 28 countries.* Amsterdam: International Association for the Evaluation of Educational Achievement (IEA).

Torney-Purta, J., Barber, C., and Wilkenfeld, B. (2006). Difference in the civic knowledge and attitudes of U.S. adolescents by immigrant status and Hispanic background. *Prospects: A UNESCO Journal, 36,* 343–54.

Torney-Purta, J., Barber, C., and Wilkenfeld, B. (2007). Latino adolescents' civic development in the United States: Research results from the IEA Civic Education Study. *Journal of Youth and Adolescents, 36,* 111–25.

U.S. Census Bureau. (2007). U.S. Census Bureau: State and county quickfacts. Accessed at *quickfacts.census.gov/qfd/states/06000.html.*

Verba, S. (2003). Would the dream of political equality turn out to be a nightmare? *Perspectives on Politics, 1* (4), 663–80.

Verba, S., Burns, N., and Schlozman, K. L. (2003). Unequal at the starting line: Creating participatory inequalities across generations and among groups. *American Sociologist, 34* (1–2), 45–69.

Verba, S., Schlozman, K. L., and Brady, H. E. (1995). *Voice and equality: Civic volunteerism in American politics.* Cambridge: Harvard University Press.

Westheimer, J. and Kahne, J. (2004). What kind of citizen? The politics of educating for democracy. *American Educational Research Journal. 41* (2), 237–69.

3

Principles That Promote Discussion of Controversial Political Issues in the Curriculum

Diana Hess

In the "Bong hits for Jesus" case (*Morse v. Frederick*, 2007), the U.S. Supreme Court justices wrestled with the question of whether their traditional, albeit muted, support for the free speech rights of students in public schools should be curtailed if the "speech" uttered by a student could be interpreted as promoting the use of illegal drugs. The Court's split decision in the case illustrates different views about the purposes of schools in a democratic society. Writing for the majority, Chief Justice Roberts said that when a school principal suspended a high school student for unfurling a banner proclaiming "Bong hits for Jesus," she was acting within the bounds of the Constitution because the speech could be interpreted as advocating illegal drug use. Justices Alito and Kennedy, while agreeing with Roberts, were careful to draw limits on a public school's ability to restrict the rights of students to speak on public issues. Conversely, Justice Thomas wrote that the very idea that students possess First Amendment speech rights in school was spurious: "In light of the history of American public education, it cannot seriously be suggested that the First Amendment 'freedom of speech' encompasses a student's right to speak in public schools. Early public schools gave total control to teachers, who expected obedience and respect from students." Notably, even on a Supreme Court that is considered quite conservative, Justice Thomas was unable to garner any support for his position.

I begin with the *Morse v. Frederick* case because even though the majority opinion did place some limitations on students' free speech rights in public schools that had not been articulated previously by the Court, both conservative and liberal justices, with the exception of Justice Thomas, went to great pains to stipulate that students *should and do* have a constitutionally enshrined right to speak about important political issues while they are in public schools. Extending some free speech rights to young people in schools is lauded—at least theoretically—by liberals and conservatives alike because of the intrinsic connection between the schools' traditional role of educating citizens for political participation and the goal of exposing young people to multiple and competing views about controversial issues. For example, in his dissent, Justice Stevens encourages schools to engage students in discussions of the wisdom of contemporary drug policy, likening current drug laws to prohibition, which was a hot topic when he attended secondary schools. He explicitly argues that silence about controversial issues, both in schools and in society, makes it more likely that bad policies will prevail.

While I disagree with the wisdom of the Court's decision in the *Morse v. Frederick* case because I am concerned that it sends a message to the lower courts that students' speech rights can be whittled away, I strongly support the position articulated by some of the justices that speech, schooling, and democracy are inextricably linked. Justice Thomas is wrong, I think, to so cavalierly ignore the reality that public schools *are* the government, and while suppressing student speech may well be a potent policy in a totalitarian state, surely it has no place in a democratic nation. However, the mere absence of the suppression of student speech in schools is an impotent policy if one of the primary purposes of schooling truly is to build democrats (note the small *d*). Instead, a more enlightened policy would purposely increase student speech by teaching all young people to engage in high-quality public discussions about controversial political issues. Ideally, this learning would occur throughout the young person's school career in multiple subject areas and in co- and extracurricular activities.

To clarify from the outset, by controversial political issues, I mean authentic questions about what kind of public policies should be adopted to address public problems. For example, glancing at recent newspapers I notice a plethora of issues embedded in many of the stories. Should the United States send more troops to Iraq? Or withdraw? Should people in the United States without legal documents be granted amnesty? Should my local community build a new school? What should my state do to make it more likely that all of its citizens will have access to health care? While these issues differ in numerous ways (for example, in who would be influenced by the decision), they are similar because they are authentic, and it is likely that they would generate multiple and competing answers. This is what makes them controversial.

It is important to define another term as well. While a formal written policy supporting the inclusion of controversial political issues in the school curriculum would be a helpful step toward ensuring that all students learn about such issues in school, it will not be enough. I am defining policy much more broadly—as a coherent and democratically developed set of principles and practical actions that are designed to create change in an institution—in this case, schools. Some of the principles I advocate are rooted in the theory and practice of deliberative democracy, most notably the need for inclusive discourse instead of talk among power elites. To achieve these principles, practical actions need to occur on many fronts, but those that will likely have the most positive impact must involve teachers. The barriers to achieving this goal are formidable. Consequently, a targeted, comprehensive, and well-resourced policy is the only way to ensure that it will be achieved.

In this chapter, I briefly explain the rationales for including controversial political issues in the curriculum and describe what we know from theory, research, and practice. I then turn to the barriers that prevent this core component of democratic education from taking hold in many schools. Next, I move to the policy front. Here I explain four principles—equity, quality, focus, and currency—that should be considered when crafting policy. Finally, I describe a few illustrative practical actions that, if actively promoted by policy, could enhance the quantity and quality of controversial political issues teaching and learning in schools.

Rationales

It may be helpful to begin by noting that teaching young people how to talk about highly controversial political issues in schools is not a new concept. For almost a century, many advocates of civic education, especially within the social studies, have called for the infusion of controversial issues into the curriculum. For example, in the early twentieth century, teachers were encouraged to focus on the "problems of democracy" through the analysis of authentic political issues.

Nor is the infusion of controversial political issues in the curriculum considered outside of mainstream conceptions of democratic education. In fact, evidence indicates that the advocacy for such an approach to democratic education has become more widespread. For example, the broadly disseminated Civic Mission of Schools report (Carnegie Corporation of New York and CIRCLE, 2003) makes only six research-based recommendations for improving civic education in the United States. One of these recommendations is to "incorporate discussion of current local, national, and international issues and events into the classroom, particularly those that young people view as important to their lives" (26–27).

The most frequently articulated reason to include controversial issues in the curriculum is the connection between learning how to deliberate controversial issues, especially those that focus on public problems, and participating effectively in a democratic society. This connection hinges on a definition of democracy that requires people to engage in high-quality public talk—what is often labeled a *deliberative* democracy. For example, Mansbridge (1991) posits that "Democracy involves public discussion of common problems, not just silent counting of individual hands" (122).

The axiom "talk is cheap" is turned on its head in this deliberative paradigm, with public talk instead becoming the "valued currency of public life" (Kettering Foundation, 1993, 2). Those who hold this view of democracy advocate the inclusion of controversial issues in the school curriculum as a form of authentic instruction to prepare young people to participate fully and competently in a form of political engagement that is important in "the world outside of school" (Newmann and Wehlage, 1995).

Another commonly advanced rationale for discussing issues presumes the very opposite in terms of authenticity. It is not unusual for scholars to note that few people engage in public talk of political issues and then to suggest that this is a problem that schools should be working to ameliorate. This "schooling for social betterment" thinking is not unique to the advocacy of issues discussions, but it is notable that a number of highly regarded scholars have documented low levels of adult political talk in recent years and urged the schools to work to change this trend. For example, in a groundbreaking study of Americans' beliefs about how government should work, political scientists John Hibbing and Elizabeth Theiss-Morse (2002) paint a depressing picture of a citizenry that does not care about most political issues and policies. Contrary to the views of some political socialization researchers who believe that people yearn for greater and more meaningful involvement in self-governance, their research suggests that the vast majority of Americans tend to avoid political participation and that many actually recoil from a system they perceive as driven by narrow self-interest and messy conflict.

Certainly, Hibbing and Theiss-Morse are not the only scholars documenting the low level of political engagement among citizens of the United States (e.g., Mutz, 2006; Conover, Searing, and Crewe, 2002). Their study is particularly compelling, however, because it pinpoints the fact that people in the United States generally like conflict and controversy (witness the addiction to viewing competitive sports), but dislike conflict and controversy related to politics, policy issues, and governance. The solution these scholars propose is to change the content of civic education. Specifically, they argue that "exposing students to a range of issue interests of people across the United States and simulations illustrating the challenges of coming to agreement in the face of divided opinion is what we need" (2002, 225). In short, they advocate a civic education program that does not ignore controversy but embraces it as a core element of democracy.

Regardless of whether one seeks to introduce young people into a society where such discussions occur or one hopes that the next generation will create a society where issues discussions are commonplace, advocates of deliberative democracy make strong claims about the need for more talk about issues in schools.

Other rationales for issues discussions promote them as *vehicles* for a host of outcomes, some of which are explicitly connected to democratic education. Examples in this category include the expectation that, via issues discussions, students will develop an understanding and commitment to democratic values, such as tolerance, equality, and diversity (Lockwood and Harris, 1985; Oliver and Shaver, 1966); enhance their sense of political efficacy (Gimpel, Lay, and Schuknecht, 2003); increase their interest in engaging in public life (Zukin et al., 2006); and learn how to break down historic divides in a community or nation and forge bonds between groups of people who are markedly different from one another (McCully, 2006). The Civic Mission of Schools report summarizes the civic power of controversial issues discussions in a clear and straightforward manner: "Studies that ask young people whether they had opportunities to discuss current issues in a classroom setting have consistently found that those who did participate in such discussions have a greater interest in politics, improved critical thinking and communications skills, more civic knowledge, and more interest in discussing public affairs out of school. Compared to other students, they also are more likely to say that they will vote and volunteer as adults" (Carnegie Corporation of New York and CIRCLE, 2003, 8).

Thus the advocacy for issues discussions in this important report represents another powerful rationale—the likely connection between this form of democratic education and the development of attitudes, knowledge, and skills linked to informed and engaged citizenship. Issues discussions are advocated also for reasons traditionally associated with schooling outcomes writ large, such as learning important content (Harris, 1996), improving critical thinking, or building more sophisticated interpersonal skills (Johnson and Johnson, 1995). It is clear from this list that an ambitious set of aims is attached to the use of controversial political issues discussions in democratic education.

Why Schools?

Schools are probably the most diverse environments that young people inhabit, notwithstanding the recent trend toward resegregation. Consequently, they are good sites for such discussions. Most schools contain gender diversity, religious diversity, ethnic diversity, and some degree of racial diversity. Moreover, even classes that appear to be homogeneous along a number of these dimensions likely encompass broader ideological diversity than students encounter in their own homes. The relative diversity of schools makes them particularly good places for controversial issues discussions because it enhances the likelihood that students will be exposed to views that differ from their own and that they will have to explain their own views. This kind of "cross-cutting political talk" (Mutz, 2006) is markedly different from talk that occurs in an "echo chamber" of similar views.

As a case in point, a study that I am directing examines the degree and impact of ideological diversity that exists in high school social studies courses.[1] Not surprisingly, we are finding that schools reflect the ideological diversity that exists within the communities to some extent; however, even classes that appear to be extremely homogeneous have a fair amount of ideological diversity. Our interviews with students consistently show that they are more likely to recognize and appreciate the ideological diversity in their midst if their teachers include discussions of controversial issues in the curriculum. Many students report that the range of opinions they hear in their classes is far wider than in their homes, partially because there are simply more participants in class discussions, which yields more diversity of viewpoints, but also because the elaborate mechanisms that teachers use are more likely to bring out differences of opinion.

The Prevalence of Controversial Issues in the School Curriculum

Given the research findings that show the impact of controversial issues discussions in schools, it is clearly the case that some students in some schools are engaging in this form of democratic education. However, it is exceptionally difficult to assess just how many students encounter issues discussions in schools, as well as whether those discussions are an occasional treat or a staple of the curricular diet. Some evidence indicates that the vast majority of teachers report an emphasis on controversial issues in their curricula. For example, Engel (1993) surveyed 337 secondary social studies and English teachers in eight counties in a midwestern state about their views on the examination of controversial issues in their classrooms, finding that 75 percent of the teachers reported spending up to 25 percent of class time examining controversial issues. Many students also report that their social studies classes include a focus on controversial issues. In an internet-based survey of more than 1,000 people ages 15–25, 69 percent report that they often (48.3 percent) or sometimes (28.7 percent) discussed political and social issues on which people have different opinions in their social studies classes (Andolina, Jenkins, Keeter, and Zukin, 2002). Similarly, in the 1999 International Association for the Evaluation of Educational Achievement (IEA) study of civic education (Torney-Purta, Lehmann, Oswald, and Schulz, 2001), 75 percent of the 2,811 9th graders from 124 nationally representative public and private schools in the United States reported that their social studies classes included the discussion of controversial issues.

However, in another survey given to 278 randomly selected public high school social studies teachers in Florida, Phillips (1997) reported that while 63 percent of the teachers said they experienced controversial issues instruction in their own precollegiate education, only 23 percent said they discussed controversial issues with their students more than 25 percent of the time. Moreover, in the first phase of the IEA study that involves the development of a detailed case study of civic education in the United States based on multiple data sources, researchers reported they did not find much evidence from their focus group interviews that this kind of teaching was occurring in classrooms (Hahn and Torney-Purta, 1999). Kahne and his colleagues (2000) made a similar report in their observations of 135 middle and high school social studies classes in the Chicago public schools, finding that controversial issues received scant attention. In over 80 percent of the classes observed there was no mention of a social problem, and even when problems were mentioned, there rarely was any discussion of possible solutions, connections to modern times, or action.

Until recently, there was little information about which students were provided with opportunities to engage in discussions of controversial political issues. Kahne, Chi, and Middaugh's 2006 analysis of civic learning opportunities in high schools shows students are much more likely to experience controversial issues discussions if they are academically successful and have wealthy parents (see Chapter 2, this volume). This finding is especially troubling because these relatively privileged young people are already likely to have more influence on the political system than those who are less privileged. So even while schools are especially good venues for issues discussions because of their diversity, it is also the case that they can perpetuate political inequality if the most powerful forms of civic education are more likely to be doled out to the very students who are already on the top of the political heap.

Skillful Teaching of Controversial Issues Discussions

Even though it is unclear how prevalent controversial issues are in classes, a number of recent studies investigate the beliefs and practices of teachers who do include controversial issues in the curriculum.[2] While it is clear that teaching students to discuss issues is an extremely complex enterprise that can be implemented successfully in a variety of ways, some similarities stand out among teachers who achieve this goal. First, they recognize that many of their students do not come into their classes already possessing the background knowledge, communicative skills, and deliberative dispositions necessary to participate effectively in thoughtful civic discussions of highly controversial issues. Consequently, simply providing students with the opportunity to engage in such discussions is not sufficient, especially if the goal is to reach all students as opposed to simply providing a forum for students who are already proficient discussants. Instead, teachers who are unusually good at this form of teaching carefully structure instruction to explicitly teach students the skills they need, such as how to ask clarifying questions, how to use different kinds of evidence, and how to use reasoning to back up or probe a claim.

Second, skillful issues discussion teachers are attentive to creating a classroom climate that encourages the airing of multiple and competing views and the participation of all students. Such teachers recognize that peer relations within a class are undoubtedly going to influence students' willingness to participate, as well as the nature and tone of the interaction. While there are many aspects of peer interactions that teachers cannot control, they can ensure that within-class grouping does not reify existing power hierarchies among students, that students learn and use one another's names, and that students are not allowed to engage in taunting or personal putdowns that unfortunately characterize some of the political talk we see in the world outside of school.

Third, skillful discussion teachers do not aim for spontaneous discussions, because they recognize those rarely occur, and when they do, participation is typically minimal. Instead, discussions are carefully planned, students learn background information so they feel that they know enough to participate, and a particular model or form of discussion is used that aligns with the teachers' goals. These discussions are not "free for alls" that generate more heat than light. While the best issues discussions are still lively and highly engaging, they are also organized and civil.

What Teachers Need to Know

In order for teachers to orchestrate the kind of instruction that leads to such discussions, they need much more than simply the desire to do so. Like other forms of especially challenging teaching, teachers must possess certain conceptual understandings and know how to translate these into pedagogical practice in their classrooms. With respect to issues discussions, two concepts are particularly important for teachers to understand—discussion and controversial political issues. These concepts are also ambiguous and contested. Teachers need to understand what constitutes discussion and how it differs from other forms of classroom talk, such as lectures punctuated by questions, recitations, and debate. With respect to issues, teachers need to understand the difference between a topic (such as immigration) and a specific issue about that topic that generates controversy (such as whether amnesty should be granted to people who are undocumented). This much is generally not contentious, nor is it particularly challenging to learn. But there is another definitional issue with respect to the concept of controversial political issues that generates considerably more angst and debate, which is how to determine whether a topic is a controversial political issue or a question for which there is a "right" answer.

Underpinning controversial issues discussions is an assumption that it is possible to make morally defensible decisions about what society (and therefore schools) should deem controversial and to teach those issues in such a way that what makes them controversial is honored. Michael Hand argues that there is quite a bit of agreement in the educational literature about what it means for a topic to be considered controversial:

> To teach something as controversial is to present it as a matter on which different views are or could be held, and to expound those different views as impartially as possible. It is to acknowledge and explore various possible answers to a question without endorsing any of them. The intended outcome of such teaching is, at least, that pupils should understand a range of views on a topic and arguments in their support, and at most, that they should hold and be able to defend considered views of their own; it is emphatically *not* that they should come to share the view favoured by the teacher. (Hand, 2008, 213)

The problem with this definition, as Hand rightly points out, is that it rests on a presumption that there is agreement about whether the different views that are or could be held are normatively in line with the larger purposes of education. In some cases, that agreement actually does exist. For example, it is generally not controversial in democratic societies for teachers to believe that it is important for young people to learn that racism is wrong. If the question of whether racism is wrong is even advanced in school, it is taught with an answer. Hand labels this "teaching as settled" as opposed to the "teaching as controversial" that would occur with a question for which a particular answer would not violate the larger normative purposes of schooling.

The more significant and challenging problem for teachers and curriculum developers in this field arises when there is real disagreement about whether a question should be presented as settled or controversial. Issues are not controversial by nature but are socially constructed in ways that cause them to be more or less controversial. This is why it is common for issues that are considered well settled in one nation or region to be controversial in others. For example, the question of whether evolution or other ideas about the origin of life should be taught in schools is a matter of bitter controversy in some parts of the United States, but the issue does not generate the same level of controversy in much of Europe. Similarly, in many parts of the world, health care is considered a basic human right that governments should provide their citizens, and thus the role of government vis-à-vis health care is a "settled" matter and is taught as such in the schools. In other nations, such as the United States, this question is controversial and is taught that way.

But just as issues are controversial in some venues and not in others, over time issues "tip" from controversial to settled, and vice versa. This tipping process is a major reason why one scholar deemed controversial issues teaching "a multi-risk business" (Cavet, 2007, 1). Much of the controversy that arises from the teaching of controversial issues in schools is rooted in disagreements about whether a teacher (or school or curriculum material) has made the right decision about which side of the "tip" to promote (Hess, 2004). For example, at one time the question of whether suffrage should be extended to women was controversial in many democratic nations, and now it is settled (though not in all nations). Although it would not be controversial in many nations for teachers now to teach about women's suffrage as a settled matter, imagine what it was like for teachers when society was "tipping" from viewing this issue as one that was controversial to one that was settled. The decision about whether to teach the issue as controversial is, by definition, a form of position-taking on the part of the school and the teacher, which accounts for why there are so many disagreements about what should be considered controversial.

What is unclear is what causes schools to lead or follow during the tipping process. In some cases, it may be that disputes about settled versus controversial are curricular "canaries in the mine," whose purpose is to provide early warning to society that an issue is ready to tip from being considered a matter of legitimate controversy to a settled question, or vice versa. In other cases, schools are expected to follow society and change the curriculum to reflect the consensus that has emerged about what was once a controversial issue.

It is often teachers who make the decision about whether an issue should be presented as settled or controversial in the first place, a decision undoubtedly influenced by their own political views. The research I have conducted that examines how and why teachers select controversial issues for the curriculum illustrates how this works in practice (Hess, 2002). In one study, a teacher argues that gay rights issues are not controversial. Instead, he characterizes them as human rights issues for which there are answers he wants his students to understand and believe. Other teachers make the same point with respect to other issues, suggesting that a threshold criterion that teachers use to select issues is based on their personal views of whether they think the issue is legitimately in the public square. The fact that teachers' political views inform their decision about what they consider an "open" or "settled" issue is not necessarily problematic. However, as I argue elsewhere (Hess, 2004), it is important for teachers to make these decisions in deliberation with other teachers so, at a minimum, they are aware of the criteria they are using to determine which questions are infused into their curricula as open issues.

Barriers

If the goal is to ensure that all students learn how to participate effectively in public discussions of political issues, then it is essential to address the numerous and significant barriers that currently prevent that from happening in many schools. Based on my experience as a teacher and researcher, three barriers are critical to address because they are widely shared and powerful. First, many teachers do not know how to teach students to engage in high-quality discussions of political issues and often do not feel they have support from administrators and parents to take on this form of democratic education. Second, the current emphasis in many districts and states on conceptualizing the acquisition of content knowledge that can be easily measured in multiple-choice assessments sends the message that this kind of in-depth and more difficult to assess learning is not valued. Third, it is difficult for many people to understand the key distinction between political indoctrination and the kind of political education that this form of teaching and learning entails. Parents, school administrators, teachers, and students do not want schools to be turned into ideological boot camps, and they often mistakenly believe that the purposeful insertion of highly contentious political issues into the school curriculum is a step in that direction. This is especially the case if there is a dispute about whether the issues inserted in the curricula are "open" or "settled."

Principles for Policy

Earlier I suggested that because of the complexity of this kind of teaching and the formidable barriers to its implementation that exist in many schools, a targeted, comprehensive, and well-resourced policy is likely the only way to ensure that the goal of teaching all students how to discuss controversial political issues will be achieved. It would be foolhardy to suggest a "model" policy that a school or district should implement to achieve this aim because so much variance exists in school contexts and in the challenges schools face. Instead, I propose a set of four principles that can guide policy making and a few practical actions that have worked well in other schools as illustrations of what such policies might promote.

These principles are equity, quality, focus, and currency. By equity, I mean crafting policy that works to ensure that all students—regardless of which academic track they are in, the wealth of their parents, or the degree to which their school is integrated—have access to quality instruction in controversial issues discussions.

Discussions about equal access to a superior curriculum are beginning to occur in other domains (most notably literacy and math), but tracking of the social studies courses that tend to focus on civic education appears to be increasing. This is potentially problematic for at least two reasons. First, when social studies classes are tracked, there is a tendency to lower the intellectual demands that are placed on students in the lower tracks. Given the difficulty of controversial issues discussions, they may be reserved only for students who are viewed as already capable of participating effectively. Moreover, the most skillful teachers are often placed with students in the upper track classes; given the amount of teacher skill required to orchestrate controversial issues discussions, it seems likely that there would be a strong positive correlation between the skill of the teacher and the prevalence of issues discussions. On the other hand, the trend toward creating Advanced Placement U.S. government courses in high schools may also work to deprive the upper-tracked students of exposure to controversial issues because teachers fear taking time out of the demanding content-driven curriculum that must be followed to align with the tests. Regardless of whether social studies courses are tracked or not, the principle remains the same: it is important to ensure that *all* students learn how to talk about controversial political issues.

By quality, I mainly focus on teachers' prowess and the intellectual integrity of the materials used to prepare students for discussion. It would be virtually impossible to overestimate the importance of skillful teaching to the enterprise of political discussions. The first study I conducted such discussions used a "models of wisdom" design to research the practice of middle and high school teachers who were unusually skillful in teaching their students how to participate effectively in such discussions (Hess, 2002). These "models of wisdom" studies are advocated when there is a sense that some commonalities may exist in practice and that if those were induced, made transparent, and thoroughly explicated, others could gain an understanding of what "good looks like."

The teachers I studied are undeniably skillful, and much of what I explained earlier about what strong teaching of controversial issues looks like emanates from the study of their practice. But I came away from the study with a sense that teachers did not have to be "classroom wizards," defined by Levy as the "great exception," the individual teachers who "overcome apparently insurmountable odds to succeed where others have failed" (1998, 3). Instead, what marks these teachers as skillful is the ability to put into practice well thought-out and thorough lesson plans on controversial political issues that are informed by a sophisticated understanding of the purpose of discussion and its link to democracy writ large.

Since that first study, I have conducted two others involving more than 25 teachers and 1,200 of their students (Hess and Posselt, 2002; Hess and Ganzler, 2007). Many of the teachers included controversial issues in their courses—some with demonstrably more success than others. From the second study I learned that students could improve at discussing such issues if they were expected to talk, received direct instruction on the skills they needed to participate, considered issues that had meaning to them, and then had multiple opportunities to engage in discussions. Again, teacher skill matters in significant ways, especially with respect to establishing classroom norms that promote participation, planning strong lessons, and providing quality materials.

The third study is ongoing with only preliminary findings, but it is probably most instructive because of the variance in approaches practiced by the teachers (Hess and Ganzler, 2007). Teachers who are unusually adept at leading controversial issues discussions are examined alongside teachers who use lectures as their primary style of pedagogy. The study includes both teachers who have students participate in issues debates once a week and others who engage their students in semester-long legislative simulations that are marked by almost daily discourse about issues. What seems apparent to us at this point in the analysis is that high quality and frequent experiences with discussing controversial political issues have more of an impact on students than courses that are only rarely punctuated by discussion.

Thus the third principle is focus, meaning that enough attention is given to this form of democratic education to enable students at various grade levels to learn how to participate effectively and to form a sense of themselves as someone whose political voice matters. Although I generally support secondary-level courses specifically dedicated to discussions of controversial issues, it is clear from the research that young children can deal successfully with ideas that are developmentally appropriate and highly scaffolded (Paley, 1992; Beck, 2003). I think it is a mistake for schools to wait until students are older to introduce these discussions. Ideally, by the time students get to high school, they will have had multiple opportunities throughout their elementary and middle school years to begin developing the skills and dispositions needed to discuss controversial issues topics.

Finally, by currency, I refer to avoiding the tendency to dodge controversy by only focusing on the tensions in the past—as if studying them alone prepares students for the real issues facing society now. Instead, contemporary issues must be included in the curriculum—not to the exclusion of historical controversies, but alongside them.

I have noticed a tendency among some teachers to conflate current events with contemporary issues (similar to the topic/issue definitional problem described earlier). This is problematic because many events are not issues, and many issues are not events. While it may be that a specific event has occurred that relates to a controversial political issue, and it is certainly the case that current events often serve to spark issues, just because an event is current does not make it an issue, nor does an issue lose that status because it is temporarily out of the news cycle. Moreover, yoking controversial issues to the day's news often leads to quick pseudo-discussions at the beginning of a class period, which become a weak substitute for the more thorough and in-depth discussions of issues that the best practice literature supports. This is not to suggest that students should not study current events in school—this is clearly important. However, students must also learn to wrestle with and discuss the contemporary issues that may be entwined with, but also reach deeper than, current events headlines.

With those principles in mind, let's turn to some concrete actions that can be promoted by broad-based and multifaceted controversial political issues discussion policy. Again, because context matters to such a degree when considering any kind of change in a school, I am not suggesting that these actions must be taken, or that others would not do the job equally well. These are described only as illustrations of actions used in some schools that seem aligned to the principles I advocate.

A written policy that explains the purpose of controversial political issues discussions and states explicitly that this form of democratic education is endorsed in the school can be extremely helpful. Not only does such a policy make clear that these types of discussions are encouraged (instead of merely tolerated). It can also establish specific guidelines that can serve as guideposts of practice. For example, one school district's policy calls for teachers to work to develop a classroom atmosphere in which pupils feel free to express opinions and to challenge ideas, to teach respect for the opinions of others and develop skills of critical thinking, and to choose suitable instructional materials presenting data on varying points of view (Board of Education, Madison Metropolitan School District, 2002).[3]

But formal written documents will probably have little impact on what happens in classrooms unless they are a piece of a much broader policy that is more specifically geared toward practice. For that reason, I highly recommend sustained professional development for teachers, beginning with those who teach courses where the "fit" with controversial issues is immediately apparent (such as a middle school civics class or a high school government course).

Since 1987, I have spent a considerable amount of time experimenting with various forms of professional development for teachers on controversial political issues, and I have carefully followed what others are doing in this regard. For example, there are a number of democratic education organizations that develop materials and professional development programs for teachers on controversial political issues, such as the National Issues Forum, the Choices for the 21st Century Project at Brown University, and the Deliberating in a Democracy project of the Constitutional Rights Foundation Chicago and Street Law, Inc.[4]

While these organizations and others each have their own approach to professional development, I have noticed many of them share some key features. First, they explicitly teach what discussion/deliberation is, especially as it compares with other forms of classroom discourse. The professional development programs often begin with a particular model of discussion that has attributes that distinguish it from other approaches and provide teachers with immersion experiences with the model. Second, they are all supported with high-quality materials that are created by professional writers with expertise in content and curriculum design. Third, there is some type of ongoing support given to teachers as they hone their skills in facilitating issues discussions.

While I think that the features these professional development programs share are powerful, I doubt that the principles I advocate will be realized in practice unless a school or school district takes seriously the charge to ensure that all students learn how to discuss political issues. A major concern is that typically only one teacher from a school comes to a workshop, institute, or course on issues discussions, and then that teacher returns to school as a "solo practitioner." In the best-case scenario, the teacher will do well with issues discussions—but only his/her students will benefit. In the worst-case scenario, the teacher needs more support and follow-up via ongoing professional development to become proficient with issues discussions. After a few failures and no easily accessibly support network from similarly trained colleagues, the teacher gives up, and issues discussions become just one more educational reform that did not work.

As an alternative, I would recommend tapping into the programs run by organizations with expertise in issues discussions, and then adding school-based professional development that provides ongoing follow-up and support to teachers. There are lots of models for how to do this, but I believe that the best are teacher study groups that convene regularly throughout the school year.

So far, I have talked about a formal policy and teacher professional development as practices that can be helpful in providing all students with controversial issues experiences in school. A third practice that has potential, but is rarely used, actively involves parents and other adults in the community in the school's mission to teach about controversial political issues. I studied controversial issues teaching and learning in one school that had developed an innovative parent discussion program as a companion to a course about controversial political issues, which was required for every 10th-grade student (Hess and Posselt, 2002). At least once during a semester, parents or other adults who were connected to the students in some way were invited to come to evening political discussions about the same issues that the students were studying in class. They were given background materials about the issue and then asked to participate in discussions facilitated by the teachers. Students participated in the discussions, too—though often not in the same group as the parent/adult he/she had invited. The discussions were lively, and I heard many of the adults say that they wished they had experienced such a course when they were in school.

Clearly, many aspects of this program would not work in all schools or for all parents. The program presumes that parents do not work at night (which is certainly not the case for many), and it is predicated on parents having a comfort level with school and with talking in public with strangers, comfort levels that many people simply do not have. As a result, this program might be criticized as reeking of privilege. However, in this program I think there is a nugget that is worth exploring, which is generating cross-generational issues discussions in order to further expand the diversity of perspectives and to provide an opportunity for different political generations to hear one another's views. An added benefit, I think, might be to generate support among adults in the community for the inclusion of controversial issues in the schools by involving them in the process.

Clearly, the inclusion of discussion of controversial issues in social studies classes is supported by numerous rationales and is advocated by many as a particularly potent approach in democratic education. Although it would be impossible to provide a specific formula for the best way to include controversial issues discussion in each and every school and classroom, a few key principles will help guide efforts to make those discussions an effective part of the curriculum, while still allowing for local adaptation. By developing a targeted, comprehensive, and well-resourced policy that focuses on the issues of equity, equality, focus, and currency, we can best ensure that we attain the goal of effective political talk among all of our students. This policy must be further supported by "on the ground" teacher training and support in fostering high-quality discussion of controversial issues, as well as consideration of tracking and other barriers that could prevent achievement of the ultimate goal. Such a goal might be considered lofty, given analyses such as that of Hibbing and Theiss-Morse's 2002 picture of a politically apathetic American citizenry. But in a democracy, the goal of creating a deliberative citizenry is both worthy and necessary.

Notes

The author thanks Sam Roecker and Shannon Murto for their helpful comments and editing of the chapter.

1. The study is focused on what impact controversial issues discussions in high school classes have on the political and civic engagement of young people after they leave high school. See Hess and Ganzler, 2007.
2. There is a rich case-study literature about controversial political issues discussions. See Rossi, 1995; Hess, 2002; and Hess and Posselt, 2002.
3. These are excerpts from the controversial issues policy of the Madison (WI) Metropolitan School District. Available at *www.madison.k12.wi.us/policies/3177.htm*.
4. For information about the National Issues Forum, go to *www.nifi.org/*; Choices for the 21st Century Program, go to *www.choices.edu*; Deliberating in Democracy, go to *www.deliberating.org/*.

References

Andolina, M. W., Jenkins, K., Keeter, S., and Zukin, C. (2002). Searching for the meaning of youth civic engagement: Notes from the field. *Applied Developmental Science, 6* (4), 189–95.

Board of Education, Madison Metropolitan School District. (2002). Madison Metropolitan School District Board of Education policies and procedures. Available at *www.madison.k12.wi.us/policies/3170.htm.*

Beck, T. (2003). If he murdered someone, he shouldn't get a lawyer: Engaging young children in civics deliberation. *Theory and Research in Social Education, 3* (3), 326–46.

Carnegie Corporation of New York and the Center for Information and Research on Civic Learning and Engagement (CIRCLE). (2003). *The civic mission of schools.* New York: Carnegie Corporation of New York.

Cavet, A. (2007). Teaching "controversial issues": A living, vital link between school and society? *Service de Veille Scientifique et Technologique.* Available at *www.inrp.fr/vst.*

Conover, P. J., Searing, D. D., and Crewe, I. M. (2002). The deliberation potential of political discussion. *British Journal of Political Science, 32,* 21–62.

Engel, S. L. (1993). *Attitudes of secondary social studies and English teachers toward the classroom examination and treatment of controversial issues.* PhD diss., University of Illinois at Urbana-Champaign. Available at ProQuest Digital Dissertations database (Publication No. AAT 9329022).

Gimpel, J., Lay, C., and Schuknecht, J. (2003) *Cultivating democracy: Civic environments and political socialization in America.* Washington, DC: Brookings Institution Press.

Hahn, C. L. and Torney-Purta, J. (1999). The IEA Civic Education Project: National and international perspectives. *Social Education, 63* (7), 425–31.

Hand, M. (2008). What should we teach as controversial? A defense of the epistemic criterion. *Educational Theory, 58* (2), 213–28.

Harris, D. (1996). Assessing discussion of public issues: A scoring guide. In R. W. Evans and D. W. Saxe (Eds.), *Handbook on teaching social issues* (289–97). Washington, DC: National Council for the Social Studies.

Hess, D. (2002). Teaching controversial public issue discussions: Learning from skilled teachers. *Theory and Research in Social Education, 3* (1), 10–41.

Hess, D. (2004). Controversies about controversial issues in democratic education. *PS: Political Science and Politics,* 37 (2), 253–55.

Hess, D., and Ganzler, L. (2007). Patriotism and ideological diversity in the classroom. In J. Westheimer (Ed.), *Pledging allegiance: The politics of patriotism in America's schools.* New York: Teachers College Press.

Hess, D., and Posselt, J. (2002). How high school students experience and learn from the discussion of controversial public issues in secondary social studies. *Journal of Curriculum and Supervision, 17* (4), 283–314.

Hibbing, J., and Theiss-Morse, E. (2002). *Stealth democracy: America's beliefs about how government should work.* New York: Cambridge University Press.

Johnson, D. W., and Johnson, R. (1995). *Creative controversy: Intellectual conflict in the classroom.* (3rd ed.). Edina, MN: Interaction.

Kahne, J., Chi, B., and Middaugh, E. (2006). Building social capital for civic and political engagement: The potential of high school civics courses. *Canadian Journal of Education, 29* (2), 387–409.

Kahne, J., Rodriguez, M., Smith, B., and Thiede, K. (2000). Developing citizens for democracy? Assessing opportunities to learn in Chicago's social studies classrooms. *Theory and Research in Social Education, 28* (3), 311–38.

Kettering Foundation. (1993). *Meaningful chaos: How people form relationships with public concerns.* Dayton, OH: Kettering Foundation.

Levy, T. (1998, November/December). Only a teacher: Break out of the stereotype. *Social Studies Professional, 148,* 3.

Lockwood, A. L., and Harris, D. E. (1985). *Reasoning with democratic values: Ethical problems in United States history.* New York: Cambridge University Press.

Mansbridge, J. (1991). Democracy, deliberation, and the experience of women. In B. Murchland (Ed.), *Higher education and the practice of democratic politics: A political education reader* (122–35). Dayton: Kettering Foundation. (ERIC Document No. 350909).

McCully, A. (2006). Practitioner perceptions of their role in facilitating the handling of controversial issues in contested societies: A Northern Irish experience. *Educational Review, 58* (1), 51–65.

Morse v. Frederick, 551 U.S. 1 (2007).

Mutz, D. C. (2006). *Hearing the other side: Deliberative versus participatory democracy.* New York: Cambridge University Press.

Newmann, F. M., and Wehlage, G. G. (1995). *Successful school restructuring: A report to the public and educators.* Madison: University of Wisconsin, Center on Effective Secondary Schools.

Oliver, D. W. and Shaver, J. P. (1966). *Teaching public issues in the high school.* Logan: Utah State University Press.

Paley, V. G. (1992). *You can't say you can't play.* Cambridge: Harvard University Press.

Phillips, J. P. (1997). Florida teachers' attitudes toward the study of controversial issues in public high school social studies classrooms. PhD diss., Florida State University, 1997. Available at ProQuest Digital Dissertations database. (Publication No. AAT 9813696).

Rossi, J. A. (1995). In-depth study in an issues-orientated social studies classroom. *Theory and Research in Social Education, 23* (2), 88–120.

Torney-Purta, J., Lehmann, R., Oswald, H., and Schulz, W. (2001). *Citizenship and education in 28 countries: Civic knowledge and engagement at age 14.* Amsterdam: International Association for the Evaluation of Educational Achievement.

Zukin, C., Keeter, S., Andolina, M., Jenkins, K., and Delli Carpini, M. X. (2006). *A new engagement? Political participation, civic life, and the changing American citizen.* Oxford: Oxford University Press.

PART II

Political Environments

Neighborhoods and Cities

4

Policies for Civic Engagement beyond the Schoolyard

James G. Gimpel and Shanna Pearson-Merkowitz

The 2004 presidential election taught us some valuable lessons about what could be accomplished by institutions outside schools when it came to political learning and engagement. Up until the fall of 2004, it had appeared that politicians, political parties, and the interest groups aligned with both had largely failed to stir up the political interest of Generation Y. For more than 30 years, the turnout of voters ages 18 to 24 had been steadily on the decline. The response to this decline was predictable. There were mounting calls for high schools to come up with innovative ways to inject political skill and activism into the student body. High schools, meanwhile, had been busy doing what they have always done: try to prepare students for college and the workforce, with some doing it better than others.

Into the early years of this decade, and particularly following the razor-thin margin of the 2000 presidential contest, academics looked at schools as critical venues for policy intervention to halt civic decline, spurred on in this direction by the financial support of philanthropic foundations (Zukin, Keeter, Andolina, Jenkins, and Delli Carpini, 2006; Macedo et al., 2005; Gimpel, Lay, and Schuknecht, 2003). When in anticipation of a close 2004 election, political parties, interest groups, and candidates steered millions of dollars toward youth mobilization efforts, and the response was a surge in the turnout of young people, it was a helpful demonstration to observers that the solution was not simply located on school grounds and that other political institutions could play a highly effective role in the political learning and socialization process. Statistics from that election suggest that the turnout of youth sharply increased by 9 to 12 points, depending on the survey. No school-based intervention has ever been shown to have this kind of impact. Reflecting on these remarkable results has led us to use the pages of this essay to challenge the school-oriented focus of much of the civic engagement research and to encourage a consideration of alternative institutions sometimes thought to be too challenging to alter through public policy. We are certainly refreshed that the editors of this volume have included essays that present a more rounded view of the civic engagement efforts currently under way.

Let the Schools Do It!

One cannot help but sympathize with public school administrators and teachers for the changing mandates and pressures they face from all directions. Politicians, interest groups, and citizens turn to schools not just for math, science, and history but also for social work, day care, police work, health care, drug counseling, morality and character, psychotherapy, family planning, and myriad other services and programs that vary by location. Schools are expected to be the locus of the solutions for so many of the nation's problems, the place where corrective policies are to be fashioned and implemented (Applebome, 1997; Ravitch, 2000; Dye, 2005, 125). One easily obtains the impression that no other institutions matter or that the 91 percent of the week that students spend outside of school is beyond the reach of policy makers (Chimerine, Panton, and Russo, 1993).

In recent months, we have watched with a peculiar mix of disquiet and amusement as various state legislatures have leveled their aim at the nation's obesity epidemic. Without question, childhood obesity is a grave and mounting public health threat. But fighting the obesity epidemic has become only the latest national crisis around which to remake the school curriculum and save children from imprudent parents and malevolent fast-food vendors. State legislatures around the country are presently considering bills to require more school time for physical education, not long after school districts at many locations reduced or eliminated gym class because it did not serve the academic needs of students.

Throughout the country, citizens should be thankful that their legislators are taking soda and candy machines out of schools and forcing school systems to reassess the quality of cafeteria food—much of which had no nutritional value. No one is for junk food in school, except perhaps for the corporations who have made millions vending the poisonous stuff. But one can only imagine how whipsawed the administrators and teachers must feel now that they must shoehorn in and expand a fitness program that they had cut just a few years ago. Regardless of their own viewpoints about the merit of these changes, they must make major readjustments. In the process, other aspects of the curriculum will be cut back, and some will be eliminated.

Nationally, we have become habituated to a familiar line of thinking, to wit: Where families fail, along various dimensions, schools are expected to pick up the slack. Where communities have failed, schools should be there to compensate. When any problem emerges, particularly one affecting large numbers of children, schools are expected to provide the fix.

In 1992, Maryland became the first state in the nation to require its students to perform community service as a condition for receiving their high school diplomas. The requirement was designed to make up for society's increased lack of bondedness and low levels of community participation and voluntarism.[1] More than 17 years later, there is no evidence that it has accomplished this goal, *or even that it could*, although evaluations of other service-learning programs have revealed mixed results, often because their goals have been scaled back. The best evaluations suggest that community service can build engagement among youth if it is highly structured and organized, rather than episodic and half-hearted (Youniss and Yates, 1997; Niemi, Hepburn, and Chapman, 2000).

Surely no one would argue that physical fitness, voting, community service, and political activism are unimportant elements of a robust, functioning citizenry. These virtues should be acquired somewhere. But there is no reason why we should expect schools to be the only place for remedial instruction or training when other institutions have failed to inculcate these values. The impression obtained from much of the civic education literature is that schools are an easy and appropriate target for policy experimentation because they are uncomplicated natural field laboratories.

Without question, some of the school-based interventions are worthwhile, and in related work we have proposed more than a few ourselves, directed specifically at classrooms (Gimpel, Lay, and Schuknecht, 2003). We are also realistic enough to note, however, that the mandates and expectations are already burdensome, and we are persuaded by those we have met who say that jamming more into the already crowded mission statement of the public school system has drawn attention away from essential and core foci of schools. Sadly, to date, there have been few rigorous evaluations of how existing programs have worked or any demonstration of what value they have added, particularly in areas of low political participation and engagement. The troublesome fact remains that high poverty schools are largely ineffective at raising student achievement, reducing dropout rates, and mitigating out-of-school inequalities (Pogrow, 2006). For being natural field laboratories, we have a surprising dearth of field experiments detailing how program interventions have worked, with one excellent exception: the youth voting experiment conducted by Elizabeth Addonizio from Yale University's political science department in which random assignment to a voting instruction program elevated turnout substantially over those not assigned such lessons (Addonizio, 2004).

To be sure, schools have a civic mission, and most Americans insist that they do (National Conference of State Legislatures, 2003). But how meaningful can it be when 90 percent of Americans say that schools have a civic mission, when Americans would say that schools have a mission to do nearly everything? Here is the complication. Asking survey questions about how time should be spent in schools is analogous to asking how money should be spent on the federal budget. It is easy for respondents to think of worthy ways to spend money, but more challenging for them to think of ways to cut when forced to make trade-offs. Similarly, people will say that the school curriculum should be filled with manifold content, as if the school day were of infinite length, not quite realizing that each additional item takes something away from a previous priority. No survey has yet surfaced that asks respondents to consider realistic exchanges between, say, obesity programs and math, or athletics and civics education, or science and day care, or music education and new computer labs.

There are a limited number of goals that any institution can achieve successfully. Rather than unimaginatively foisting all of our problems only upon teachers and administrators, we need to be setting some goals for other societal institutions. Perhaps schools should do what schools have always done best: teach the usual academic subject matter—doing it well, regulating conduct appropriately to accomplish that mission; preparing students for college or the workforce; and providing extracurricular activities in the form of athletics and related interscholastic activities (Kramer, 1991). Stop looking at schools as if they were the solitary place where policy can be implemented to salve society's ills, including low and declining citizenship. An education traditionalist might argue that schools are not laboratories for social activism and change. Schools are places for old-fashioned learning of basic subject matter. Further, the purist might add that school-based efforts in civics education did nothing to stall the decline in political engagement from the 1970s to the 1990s and that the uptick in youth participation in the 2004 election may demonstrate that other institutions, and not schools, are truly responsible for youth involvement because they can get results when they expend effort.

Troubling Outcomes of Institutional Failure

Attitudes toward Police and Law Enforcement

Suppose, for the sake of argument, that the school traditionalist was right and that there are other institutions of society that are responsible for important elements of developing good citizenship. What aspects of civic education might we expect these other institutions to promote among youth? Local governments through their police forces might be expected to improve and maintain a good relationship with local citizens, keeping crime and criminal behavior under control, responding to police calls promptly, treating citizens with a high level of professionalism and respect, maintaining honesty and integrity within their personnel ranks, and dealing promptly with instances of corruption when it does occur.

In recent fieldwork, our research confirmed for the Baltimore and Washington area neighborhoods what has been widely known about many other areas in the United States for several decades: that many students from ethnic minorities harbor hostile attitudes toward the police and related law enforcement authorities. To be sure, some of this is the result of a generally oppositional stage of development in which youth are seeking independence from parental and adult supervision as they move toward adulthood themselves. Much of it, however, results from the direct experience of inept police work and a mistrust of the police acquired over years of discriminatory policing and overly aggressive actions.

While it may seem beyond the capacity of any police administration to correct long entrenched habits of thought and perception about the corruption of local law enforcement, this does not mean that it is a school problem to repair this damage. Individual attitudes toward law enforcement generalize to other aspects of the political system, and therein lies their relevance for civic and political engagement later in life (Weissberg, 1972a, 1972b). If you distrust and despise the police, you will likely take a dim view of governmental authority in general. But defiant or hostile attitudes toward the police have never been a school problem but a local government, police, and parent problem. And having no evidence that schools have made much progress toward regulating or correcting this mind-set, there is certainly no reason to believe that the schools should have the primary responsibility for taming it now. To the extent that hostile attitudes toward law enforcement stem from police and court contact due to illegal behavior, that still has nothing to do with school. After all, many of the most ungovernable youth do not want to be in school and are chronic truants or dropouts. Given these difficult facts, it is beyond time to move the responsibility for this civic engagement problem elsewhere.

Political Cynicism among Ethnic Minority Youth

Latino and black youth in our research, and that of others, have shown significantly lower levels of internal and external political efficacy—or higher levels of cynicism about their voice in government and government's responsiveness—than white youth, regardless of their socioeconomic status or the socioeconomic status of their neighborhood (Gimpel, Lay, and Schuknecht, 2003) (see Figure 4.1). These findings are consistent with the work of others who have concluded that civics education is not acting as a corrective because it seems much less relevant to African Americans and other minorities than to other students (Niemi and Junn, 1998, 155). Without question, much of the distrust and scorn of the system we have seen expressed stems from attitudes developed toward law enforcement authorities. Some of it was also anchored in the experience of unequal treatment by local government authorities when it came to public policy. Even the students' observations of such seemingly mundane services such as

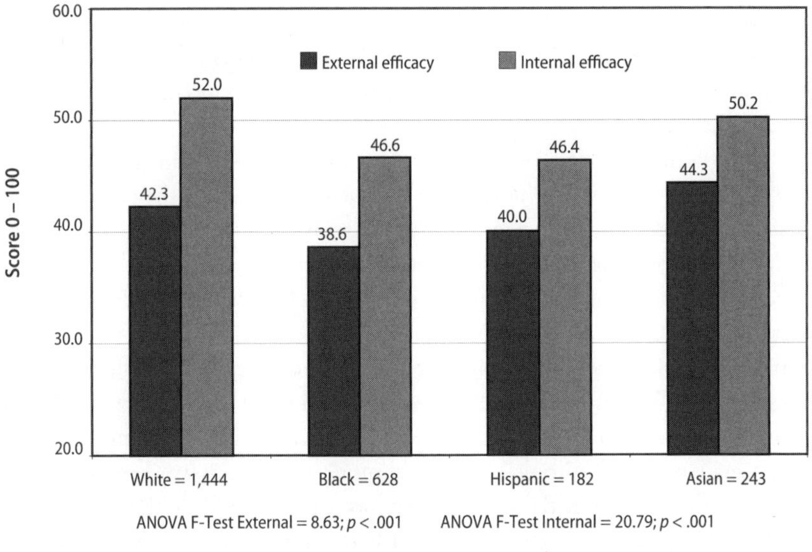

Figure 4.1: Differences in external and internal efficacy, by race, controlling for individual and neighborhood socioeconomic status

Source: Metro Civic Values Survey

street maintenance, trash collection, and snow removal mattered to the judgments they formed. For many low-income minorities, even welfare program experiences provide unpleasant points of reference from which to generalize about how government works (Soss, 1999, 376).

The suspicions and doubts raised among black and Latino youth were also the product of distance from the frequent experience of vigorous political campaigns that remind citizens of their importance in a community. Low levels of adult turnout in a locale were most directly detrimental to both the internal and external efficacy of white youth. Internal efficacy is one's sense that one's voice counts and that voting and other forms of political expression are worth the effort. External efficacy is the individual's impression that the political system works, that it is responsive to public demands, and that it is not hopelessly corrupt, wasteful, or insulated from expressions of public will.

Among Latinos and African Americans, low internal and external efficacy often has a number of sources, suggesting that the risk factors associated with low engagement often come in combinations—rarely is there only one institution at fault (Gimpel, Lay, and Schuknecht, 2003, 201). Furthermore, the absence of adult models of political activism in many places struck us as a basic institutional malfunction—but not one that finds its principal source in the local school system. These failures point to other institutions of local governmental performance and political arrangements that do not promote political challenges that encourage citizen input into civic life.

Residential Segregation and Minority Youth

Many students in our research also entered school displaying signs of racial prejudice or resentment. This resentment flowed in multiple directions: black toward white, white toward black, black toward Latino, Latino toward black, and so forth.

Racial and political intolerance is not only an education problem but also a housing problem, anchored in segregated and racially isolated living environments. Sometimes it is directly a product of racial discrimination, and sometimes it is the indirect result of housing prices, which determine the kinds of homes blacks, Latinos, and whites can afford. Racially discriminatory housing practices by realtors persist, such as "steering" blacks only toward certain kinds of neighborhoods (National Fair Housing Alliance, 2006; Ondrich, Stricker, and Yinger, 1998; Farley, Steeh, Krysan, Jackson, and Reeves, 1994). Discriminatory banking practices limiting black and Latino housing choices also remain in place, explaining why patterns of segregated housing have persisted over the past 30 years, in spite of steady socioeconomic upward mobility by

African Americans (Iceland, Weinberg, and Steinmetz, 2002). Schools are often used as a proxy for the racial and ethnic composition of neighborhoods by real estate agents who regularly make illegal comments about which schools are "good" and "bad," knowingly violating the law (National Fair Housing Alliance, 2006).

Public schools have a role to play in mitigating the negative impact of socioeconomic segregation on both racial attitudes and scholastic achievement, as they have in the past. But school integration would be less controversial, perhaps even a nonissue, if it were preceded by fair and open housing policy, including policies that permitted multifamily development alongside more exclusive, low-density residential areas. The consequences of integrated housing were striking in our own field investigations.

For example, we commonly found a far greater tendency for black youth to exhibit lower internal and external political efficacy and far more negativity toward police and law enforcement, as well as intense opposition to diversity, when they were living in racially segregated, predominantly black areas rather than in areas of greater racial integration (Figure 4.2). They also scored considerably lower on measures of political knowledge, corresponding to their performance on general achievement tests in areas of high residential segregation (Rumberger and Palardy, 2005). Higher incomes typically mitigate the negative impact of racial segregation only slightly. In our research in the metropolitan Washington area, when we compared middle-income segregated areas with integrated areas, test scores were still significantly lower for the segregated black students than for those from more residentially integrated areas (Gimpel, Lay, and Schuknecht, 2003).

Why is residentially integrated housing better for black or Latino youth than living in a segregated area? There are multiple reasons; for example, contact with whites signals some exposure to populations where political efficacy and knowledge levels are high, and at least some of these minority youth will receive the message that civic engagement is worthwhile. The activism of one population may rub off on the others, although it may take some time.

More than this, however, local governments serve integrated communities better than they serve segregated black or heavily Latino areas. In many of the segregated black locations we visited, even in lower-middle-class suburbs, blacks and Latinos could see bald-faced inequalities and came to view them as the product of a deeply flawed system in which opportunities for achievement were not distributed equally. The black and Latino youth we interviewed were all too aware that the police responded more quickly to those calling from white neighborhoods than from black neighborhoods. They were also acutely aware of inequalities across neighborhoods in other government services, from

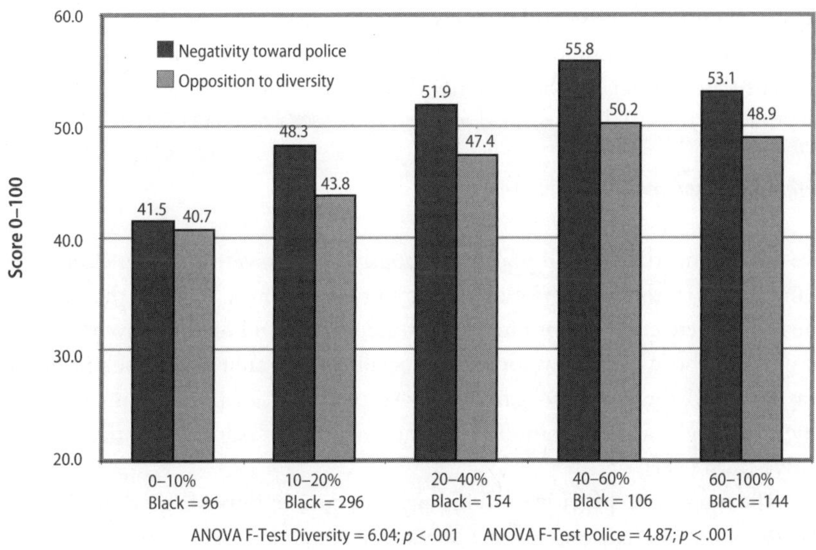

Figure 4.2: Attitudes of Latino and African American youth toward police and toward diversity by African American composition of neighborhoods, controlling for individual and neighborhood socioeconomic status

Source: Metro Civic Values Survey

street repair and garbage pickup to access to health care. The anger and despair in these remarks and observations were disconcerting even to the most experienced fieldworker among us.

Experiences with various state and local bureaucracies have taught black, Latino, and immigrant youth living in highly segregated locales that they are ill served by these governments—a completely sound conclusion based on ample observations. None of their contacts with government have indicated to them that civic engagement is worthwhile or that government can act responsibly to do good things for people. Racially integrated neighborhoods receive better service, on average, suggesting that government is responsive to citizen contact or can at least be counted on to fulfill its minimum functions.

We also have good reasons to suspect that the political behavior of council members and legislators from well-integrated districts will be more responsive to constituency demands than that of districts that are racially homogeneous and poor. This is because more diverse constituencies generally make reelection more challenging for legislative incumbents. An integrated district is likely to be more politically active and perhaps sponsor some modicum of political competition, at least within an occasional party primary. The political institutions operating in integrated urban neighborhoods may not be the picture of health, but they are not totally enfeebled either.

Latino and Immigrant Youth Civic Literacy

We also found that Latino youth did poorly on all civic literacy measures, in some locations the poorest of all ethnic minority groups. Usually this was because they were coming from immigrant households and did not have the benefit of native-born parental resources or socialization. Parental literacy in English was low, and there was no parental grasp of American political institutions. The offspring from these families were at a major disadvantage relative to their native-born peers.

The interaction of native and immigrant youth in impoverished urban areas where we conducted some of our previous research also raises questions about the values that immigrants pick up from the more numerous native-born peer groups among whom they find themselves embedded. Previous studies have indicated that Latinos and some Asian immigrant youth may learn to identify with native-born minority groups, acquiring the social and political values prevalent in existing Latino, black, and Asian communities (Fernandez-Kelly and Schauffler, 1996). If they are settling among native populations where the predominant posture toward the political system is one of estrangement, isolation, or hostility, the values they learn will contain the same component of cynicism borne by the natives.

Thrust upon the schools throughout the United States is the responsibility to compensate for the impoverished civic literacy, knowledge, and engagement of both the immigrant and native populations. In the case of immigrants, in particular, however, there are other institutions and organizations in the community able to assist, including faith-based institutions, which have often been instrumental to the immigrant assimilation process throughout American history. Adult English literacy (ESL), citizenship education, and pro bono assistance with naturalization paperwork are invaluable charitable services that are never in abundant supply in immigrant-receiving communities. These also have the indirect impact of building the confidence and knowledge of immigrant children growing up in these locations, reducing the achievement gap between themselves and the native-born. By enhancing parental literacy, presumably the improved parental resources then interact with the resources of the school to improve the child's chances of success.

The Accumulation of Risk Factors in Failed Institutions

The related findings from several years of research and reflection have led us to identify the young adults who are most at risk for a lifetime of low engagement as the ones who have been exposed to settings where politically relevant institutions—those that play a role in the political learning process—have persistently failed. Commonly at the intersection of these multiple institutional failures are legions of black, Latino, and poor white youth, as well as many children of immigrants (Gimpel, Lay, and Schuknecht, 2003).

Imagine that each institutional failure is a risk factor adding, say, a 10-pound weight to the inertia preventing an individual from realizing the goal of responsible citizenship (Plutzer, 2002). Viewed through this metaphor, school reform or even a raft of school reforms aimed at curriculum, facilities, and administration might remove only 7 pounds. This can enable those students afflicted only with mediocre schools. But for those who face multiple institutional malfunctions, some of which do not lie with the schools, it isn't even a beginning. Those most heavily burdened may never reach the point where they even register to vote, much less volunteer for a campaign.

The most burdened citizens possess such a high number of risk factors that poor socialization looks like an inevitable outcome. For the respondents who possess more than a few of these risk factors, the likelihood of nonparticipation as an adult is exceedingly high. For the respondents who possess only two or three of these traits, there is a possibility that the presence of countervalent forces in an adolescent's environment may neutralize or overcome the ones that diminish participatory impulses.

Police and Local Government Operations

The editors of this volume have set no limits on our policy ambition or constraints on political realism. Moreover, we have often been surprised at how proposals that appear politically out of reach one year may return to become feasible only a short time later. Where there is political will, there are political ways. In this unchained spirit, we recommend that state government should take a more active role in the lives of the citizens of its larger and lower-income jurisdictions because, as we have seen, these are the inhabitants whose civic lives are most at risk as a result of exposure to persistent inequality.

In our work, two types of local public service inequalities were demoralizing to youth in lower-income neighborhoods: those occurring within individual jurisdictions, and those which they observed across jurisdictions. Both served to undermine their confidence in the fairness and efficacious operation of government institutions as well as their confidence in their own voice.

Inequalities across jurisdictions, such as new school construction in a neighboring town, while the school nearby disintegrates from neglect, are difficult to change without politically controversial resource redistribution from one locality to another. Some jurisdictions are poor, others are rich, and this has been true for generations. Tax reforms and refinancing schemes have passed into law (for example, in Michigan) to assist poorer jurisdictions while holding harmless allocations to wealthier ones. Such policies close the wide gaps that can exist between the bottom and the top, providing a needed injection of relief for the poorer areas.

Inequalities occurring within jurisdictions, such as better garbage collection in one neighborhood than in another, are more alarming because they signal potential corruption within particular administrations or agencies of the same local government. Arguably, these inequalities are also subject to policy manipulation and political will more often than those that exist across local governments. Since municipalities and counties are considered creatures of states under constitutional law, local government administration is subject to state government oversight and even takeover. In many cases, state government takeover or close supervision of local government institutions may be required to root out corruption and bring an end to the kind of demoralizing inequities that local citizens find so corrosive to the meaning of their citizenship rights.

Perceptions of police behavior are particularly important. One of the surer means for obtaining higher levels of civic engagement among youth in big cities is to improve the quality, responsiveness, and fairness of local law enforcement. Through community policing, local residents now identify their priorities and express them to police department representatives in community and police forums. The cooperation of the community in targeting crimes and neighborhood problems has reportedly proven effective for many cities and neighborhoods (Stewart-Brown, 2001).

Apparently the community policing paradigm has virtually become the "normal" way to conduct police business in many parts of the United States, Canada, and Europe. If additional evaluation reveals that the community policing movement is taking hold nationwide, while remaining an effective crime fighting strategy, then we should begin to monitor citizen attitudes to see if there has been any improvement in response to this now well-entrenched police management change. Aside from more responsive locally based policing, strides can be made simply by reducing the number of unjustified stops and searches and by curbing instances of verbal abuse, excessive force, and other forms of treatment that strongly suggest racial profiling (Weitzer and Tuch, 1999).

Housing

Segregated neighborhoods produce segregated and unequal schools. Henceforth, housing policies should seek a balanced mix of multifamily and single-family development, rather than exclude low- and moderate-income families through construction of exclusive, high-end, low-density developments.

We require more aggressive monitoring and enforcement of compliance with federal, state, and local fair housing laws. This monitoring can be carried out both by government agencies and by locally based housing nonprofits that offer legal assistance to citizens in minority and low-income communities. Rather than offering only complaint-based services, more of these agencies should conduct regular (annual) nationwide paired tests of discriminatory housing and lending practices, the results of which are then reported to state and federal housing authorities with enforcement authority.[2]

The role of state law in housing policy and planning is worth further discussion because states have a greater role in the monitoring and performance of local government and services. There are states that have adopted state land use laws and regulations, ordinarily to preserve green space. Increasing the state role in housing is important, though, primarily because the federal role has contracted and shows no sign of expansion. Certainly a commitment to integrated housing on the national level would benefit individuals living in states lacking the political will to make efforts to diminish segregation. Given this uncertain federal commitment, however, state appropriations for affordable housing construction should increase and be targeted for locations where the construction is integrated with other types of residential land use. Most states have established housing trust funds that dedicate a source of public revenue to support the construction and rehabilitation of affordable housing. The source of these trust funds is ordinarily through the taxation of real estate transactions, although some states obtain this revenue from fees or from general funds. These trust funds should be considered in states that have not yet established them for the promotion of affordable housing.

Housing patterns determine racial and school patterns. Realizing that segregated schools exist chiefly as a result of segregated housing, we need to back up and treat the underlying cause and prevent it from taking hold in future neighborhoods, ultimately leading large segments of a population to conclude that they are lost and forgotten.

Religious Charities and Services

During the early months of the Bush presidency, much lip service was paid to the role of faith-based organizations as societal building blocks and community service providers. Churches are poised, perhaps better than any other societal institution, to help immigrants and their families find their way through the confusing maze of a new culture and community. Since 2001, the costs of waging a major war, opposition from deficit hawks, and fierce objections from civil libertarians concerned about church-state separation have drowned out much of this policy initiative. Modest support has been awarded to church-based programs that specialize in prisoner reentry, addiction treatment and counseling, and mentoring for at-risk youth.

Support for church-based provision of nonreligious services to immigrants is certainly worth further consideration. Churches have extensive infrastructure already in place in immigrant-receiving neighborhoods. Immigrants often turn to faith-based organizations as a place located within the community that they can trust. And these organizations often provide services in the native language of the immigrant, something few government agencies are readily equipped to do. The preexisting network and physical infrastructure provided by the nation's religious institutions, whether Roman Catholic, mainline Protestant, Evangelical, Jewish, Muslim, or of less common eastern origin, could not be replicated by government effort. There are good economic and administrative reasons, then, to support the secular components of the mission of religious institutions in the communities where they operate.

Religion is a national resource for addressing many of the major problems that have been directed toward schools. Churches, mosques, and synagogues are usually located in places where they stand out and are easily identifiable as a welcoming place for community support and development. "Far more numerous than the occasional Masonic temple, much more visible than the offices of a community's nonprofits, worship communities occupy a prominent place in America's civic landscape" (Foley and Hoge, 2007, 115).

Most American religious traditions are rooted in immigrant communities and have traditions of teaching their own members to engage in American civic life for reasons anchored in their own faith. Religious institutions are known to offer opportunities for acquiring the skills necessary for active participation in the public sphere. Whether through participation in the worship service itself, organizing or sponsoring activities not related to worship (such as organizing a Bible study or other "small group" activity), or participating in a governance role for the institutions, religious institutions help individuals overcome the costs associated with political and civic participation (Verba, Schlozman, and Brady, 1995; Foley and Hoge, 2007).

The Catholic Church, for example, has long been at the forefront of immigrant and refugee service provision, and a number of their models are known to be effective. Briefly, church-based language and legal service programs shore up the tenuous economic and legal status of immigrant families through exposure to English and gratis assistance with legalization and naturalization paperwork. Parenthetically, participation by volunteers also meets the civic engagement goals of youth seeking service-learning opportunities among needy populations.

Cynics complain that churches have a stake in providing these services, because they hope that parishes that were once nearly abandoned will be repopulated with new immigrants. There is undoubtedly some truth to this, but providing for immigrants is also a doctrine broadly consistent with charitable teaching and religious tradition. Certainly, the history of Judaism, Catholicism, and many Protestant denominations in the United States was built on the strength and determination of successive waves of immigrant families.

Contemporary religious institutions continue to assist immigrants in fostering skills that facilitate assimilation and civic engagement, even if they do not stand to benefit by building an enlarged membership base in doing so. For instance, Jewish support for immigrant citizenship education follows quite sensibly from well-known Jewish scriptures as well as from the historical struggles of the Jewish people. Through the hand of Moses, God reminds the Israelites to be kind to strangers, for they too were foreigners in the land of Egypt (Leviticus 19:33–34).

Moreover, it is difficult to credibly complain that the Council of Jewish Federations and the Hebrew Immigrant Aid Society are self-interested when providing services to resettle and assimilate immigrants, given that few of their benefactors are Jews. Although both groups have spent millions to resettle Ethiopian, Eastern European, and former Soviet Jews in Israel and the United States, recent activity has included large investments in improving the life prospects for Latin American and Asian refugees and immigrants, few of whom are ever likely to darken the door of a Jewish temple or synagogue.

Religious organizations have proven themselves to be valuable partners for reaching out to people who may not trust government officials or cannot count on those officials even if some may be trustworthy. Because they are usually located within the communities in which immigrants settle, faith-based organizations are best positioned to reach these newcomers because they understand them and have earned their trust. Arguably, no other local institution is better suited to assist in the socialization of immigrants than churches. Even if they can play only a partial role, it is surely an important one. Every labor economist agrees that there is a high wage premium in the United States associated with English language acquisition. For adolescents, bilingual students who become fluent in English do far better in school than those who are slower to pick up the language (Rumberger and Larson, 1998). Among the functions that these community organizations can perform, then, supplementary English language instruction is surely preeminent. Beyond this, immigrant families commonly need assistance with accessing childcare, employment, social services, legal services, and medical and educational resources.

Political Districts, Political Competition, and High Turnout

For the millions of citizens who are not going back to high school to experience someone's curriculum-based silver bullet, there is a need to keep looking to alternative institutions. Fortunately, much of what needs to be learned to exercise responsible citizenship can be picked up from sources outside school. Adults working full-time jobs and youth who are high school dropouts or who never take another social studies course can become politically active citizens if they obtain some exposure to models of good citizenship or experience political campaigns that remind them that their participation is worthwhile.

Writing in the middle of the last century, political scientist V. O. Key pointed to the value of partisan diversity and high turnout as vital forces behind democratic governance. The habit of not voting resulted in a shrunken electorate in one-party states. The limited electorate, in turn, influenced the nature of factional politics within a single party by practically eliminating from the voting population substantial blocs of citizens whose political interests and objectives, if activated, would furnish the motive for important political movements and demands (Key, 1949, 508). Key noted that a government founded on democratic principles became some other sort of regime when large proportions of its citizens failed to vote.

Political party competition and the associated mobilization efforts by parties and candidates were seen by Key to be the instrument of democratic restoration in the corrupt and morally decrepit Old South. Notably, no mention is made in his landmark work of improving formal education in schools, although he does attack the indefensible presence of suffrage restrictions in state law, which have since been ruled unconstitutional.

The fundamental insight of Key's work remains as sound today as it was then: maximizing one's sense of civic membership requires competitive party politics, at least a majority of the time an election is held. One means of ensuring this sense of membership is through proper institutional design. For example, the political district-drawing process should group people not on the basis of their similarity but on the basis of their dissimilarity. The guiding criteria for drawing political boundaries should be to maximize economic and political diversity within a district. True, given the concentration of certain economic and racial groups in certain areas of the country, there are limits to the extent to which any set of boundary adjustments will promote this diversity everywhere without a significant move toward housing integration. But stepping away from the bad idea of always blocking together the like-minded would be a move in the appropriate direction.

In the last several years, social scientists have rediscovered the problem of low turnout, alarmed by the fact that in spite of amazing improvements in the level of education over the course of the last century and the elimination of suffrage restrictions, participation rates have steadily declined. Gerber and Green (2000), echoing the argument made previously by Rosenstone and Hansen (1993), argued persuasively that turnout had dropped because people were no longer being mobilized by political parties. Party and candidate mobilization efforts had diminished with the extinction of politically competitive elections in many areas, along with a shift toward professionalized campaigns that relied more on glossy but impersonal technology than on door-to-door canvassing. The 2004 campaign, in particular, proved them right on the contacting front, as turnout surged coincident with a dramatic rise in grassroots outreach efforts. Not coincidentally, this election also saw impressive surges in youth participation.

Certainly we found impressive compensatory power in the institution of competitive elections and the sterling example of highly active adult populations. Adolescents' sense of political efficacy and level of political knowledge was greatly enhanced in politically active areas that exhibited partisan diversity and high turnout. There was some door-to-door campaigning going on in the highly participatory neighborhoods we visited, but more than this we found adults who were interested in discussing politics with young people and modeling good citizenship behavior by voting regularly. Even if participatory behavior is not being modeled by a teenager's parents directly, the adolescent could still see relatives, neighbors, and other adults in the community taking elections seriously.

Conclusions

If tackling the problems associated with low civic engagement from beyond schoolhouse walls sounds daunting, it may well be. But usually the facile solutions are the ones that don't work—and it doesn't make any sense to invest in paths that lead down blind alleys. We are not saying that everything matters—a most unhelpful conclusion. But we are also not satisfied with concluding that what matters is limited to what teachers and principals do. What we have tried to do is take an inventory of the institutions that make a difference outside of schools and initiate a preliminary policy discussion about what those institutions need to change.

Beyond the all-important institution of the family, it is religious institutions and local governments, and particularly the police, that have an important responsibility for the civic health and education of youth in a community. This education does not take the form of police officers teaching civics courses, but the conduct of police will send indisputably clear signals about obedience and respect for the law and equal, fair, and just treatment under the law. The role of state and federal government in controlling blatant corruption and mitigating the extent of inequality in local public service delivery is also important in communicating the hope that American society is not one of bleak castes and permanent underdogs. Public investments in local social capital formation are also eminently reasonable, including support for faith-based initiatives.

Perhaps civic engagement can be most usefully thought of as the product of a contextual matrix of overlapping institutions that together convey the message that participation is worthwhile. Even if participation does not pay off every time, and experience with government institutions is sometimes frustrating, at least there is no reason to abandon hope or to conclude that one's efforts are fruitless. In some of the places we have visited, the institutions that head off this kind of desperation are not present, either singly or in combination, and hence the sagging levels of engagement persist in spite of continual legislative tinkering and new mandates.

Nothing has been more encouraging for the goal of civic engagement than to see young voters surging to the voting booth in 2004 and returning again in 2006. In the wake of the measurable improvement in youth voter turnout, the necessity for rigorous evaluation of policy interventions both inside and outside of schools cannot be overstated. Our knowledge of what works to improve civic engagement, in the short term or the long term, given the number of programs that have been implemented, is inexcusably low. The field experimental model, with randomized treatment and control groups, is the most promising method for generating information useful for measuring the value added by new policy initiatives. In summary, we hope that our discussion contributes not only to additional studies of the effectiveness of school-based civic education programs but also to more aggressive efforts to evaluate the effects, both direct and indirect, of efforts moving forward outside of school as we travel into the new century.

Notes

1. Even when religion, combined with parenting, has failed, schools are sometimes called upon to teach things commonly covered by religious instruction: moral character, charity, humility, and other centeredness. With societal consensus declining on such matters, apparently children can no longer be expected to show up to school already knowing how to behave, but must be taught how to behave before they are ready to learn.
2. A "paired" test is when each test consists of visits by two teams of testers, typically a white tester and a black counterpart.

References

Addonizio, E. (2004). Reducing inequality in political participation: An experiment to measure the effects of voting instruction on youth voter turnout. Conference paper presented at the annual meeting of the American Political Science Association, Chicago Hilton and Palmer House Hilton, Chicago, September 2.

Applebome, P. (1997). Schools as America's cure-all. *New York Times*, Week in Review, January 12, p. 5.

Chimerine, C. B., Panton, K. L. M., and Russo, A. W. W. (1993). *The other 91 percent: Strategies to improve the quality of out-of-school experiences of Chapter 1 students.* Report prepared for the Office of Policy and Planning, U.S. Department of Education, by Policy Studies Associates, Inc. Washington, DC: U.S. Department of Education.

Dye, T. R. (2005). *Understanding public policy.* 11th ed. Upper Saddle River, NJ: Prentice Hall.

Farley, R., Steeh, C., Krysan, M., Jackson, T., and Reeves, K. (1994). Stereotypes and segregation: Neighborhoods in the Detroit area. *American Journal of Sociology, 100* (3), 750–80.

Fernandez-Kelly, M. P., and Schauffler, R. (1996). Divided fates: Immigrant children and the new assimilation. In A. Portes (Ed.), *The new second generation* (30–53). New York: Russell Sage Foundation.

Foley, M. W., and Hoge, D. R. (2007). *Religion and the new immigrants.* Oxford: Oxford University Press.

Gerber, A. S., and Green, D. P. (2000). The effects of personal canvassing, telephone calls, and direct mail on voter turnout: A field experiment. *American Political Science Review, 94* (3), 653–64.

Gimpel, J. G., Lay, J. C., and Schuknecht, J. E. (2003). *Cultivating democracy: Civic environments and political socialization in America.* Washington, DC: Brookings Institution Press.

Iceland, J., Weinberg, D. H., and Steinmetz, E. (2002). *Racial and ethnic residential segregation in the United States, 1980–2000.* Report CENSR-3. Washington, DC: Census Bureau.

Key, V. O., Jr. (1949). *Southern politics in state and nation.* New York: Alfred A. Knopf.

Kramer, R. (1991). *Ed school follies: The miseducation of America's teachers.* New York: Free Press.

Macedo, S. M., with Alex-Assensoh, Y., et al. (2005). *Democracy at risk: How political choices undermine citizen participation and what we can do about it.* Washington, DC: Brookings Institution Press.

National Conference of State Legislatures. (2003). *The civic mission of schools.* Report from Carnegie Corporation of New York and CIRCLE: Center for Information and Research on Civic Learning and Engagement. New York: Carnegie Corporation.

National Fair Housing Alliance. (2006). *Unequal opportunity—perpetuating housing segregation in America.* 2006 Fair Housing Trends Report. Washington, DC: National Fair Housing Alliance, April 5.

Niemi, R. G., Hepburn, M. A., and Chapman, C. (2000). Community service by high school students: A cure for civic ills? *Political Behavior, 22* (1), 45–69.

Niemi, R. G., and Junn, J. (1998). *Civic education: What makes students learn.* New Haven: Yale University Press.

Ondrich, J., Stricker, A., and Yinger, J. (1998). Do real estate brokers choose to discriminate? Evidence from the 1989 housing discrimination study. *Southern Economic Journal, 64* (4), 880–901.

Plutzer, E. (2002). Becoming a habitual voter: Inertia, resources, and growth in young adulthood. *American Political Science Review, 96* (1), 57–74.

Pogrow, S. (2006). Restructuring high poverty schools for success. *Phi Delta Kappan, 88* (3), 223.

Ravitch, D. (2000). *Left back: A century of failed school reforms.* New York: Simon and Schuster.

Rosenstone, S. P., and Hansen, J. M. (1993). *Mobilization, participation, and democracy in America.* New York: Macmillan.

Rumberger, R., and Larson, K. A. (1998). Toward explaining differences in educational achievement among Mexican American language-minority students. *Sociology of Education, 71* (1), 69–93.

Rumberger, R., and Palardy, G. J. (2005). Does segregation still matter? The impact of student composition on academic achievement in high school. *Teachers College Record, 107* (9), 1999–2045.

Soss, J. (1999). Lessons of welfare: Policy design, political learning, and political action. *American Political Science Review, 93* (2), 363–80.

Stewart-Brown, R. (2001). Community mobilization. *FBI Law Enforcement Bulletin, 70* (6), 9–17.

Verba, S., Schlozman, K., and Brady, H. E. (1995). *Voice and equality.* Cambridge: Harvard University Press.

Youniss, J., and Yates, M. (1997). *Community service and social responsibility in youth.* Chicago: University of Chicago Press.

Weissberg, R. (1972a). Adolescent experiences with political authorities. *Journal of Politics, 34* (3), 797–824.

Weissberg, R. (1972b). Adolescents' perceptions of political authorities: Another look at political virtue and power. *Midwest Journal of Political Science, 16* (1), 147–68.

Weitzer, R., and Tuch, S. A. (1999). Race, class, and perceptions of discrimination by the police. *Crime and Delinquency, 45* (4), 494–507.

Zukin, C., Keeter, S., Andolina, M., Jenkins, K., and Delli Carpini, M. X. (2006). *A new engagement? Political participation, civic life, and the changing American citizen.* New York: Oxford University Press.

5

Civic Participation and Development among Urban Adolescents

Daniel Hart and Ben Kirshner

Poor urban neighborhoods are often viewed as bad contexts for child and adolescent growth. Policy makers and researchers are deeply concerned with the high rates of crime in such neighborhoods (e.g., Sampson, Raudenbush, and Earls, 1997). Criminal activity endangers the youth who live in such neighborhoods and, through processes as yet not fully understood, facilitates their own entry into crime. Poor urban cities also seem unsuccessful in preparing youth academically; there are innumerable reports detailing the shortcomings of urban school systems and the resulting achievement deficits evident in America's biggest cities. No doubt urban environments—particularly those characterized by the high levels of disorder that are associated with poverty—can be obstacles to successful development.

Our goal in this chapter is to explore youth civic participation in poor urban neighborhoods. Civic participation is rarely discussed by those concerned with the effects of neighborhoods on development. In part, civic participation is eclipsed by the truly disastrous effects that crime and educational failure have on adolescent development: a low level of volunteering among urban adolescents can seem unimportant relative to the tragedy of high rates of incarceration and dropping out of school characteristic of high-poverty cities.

Yet the state of civic participation among minority and low-income adults and their children should alarm anyone who is concerned about the future of the United States. Jamison, Day, Shin, and the Census Bureau (2002) report that adults with family incomes less than $10,000 a year voted in the 2000 elections at about half the rate as those in families with incomes higher than

$75,000 (41 vs. 75 percent, respectively). Findings such as these led the American Political Science Association to conclude, "The privileged participate more than others and are increasingly well organized to press their demands on government. Public officials, in turn, are much more responsive to the privileged than to average citizens and the least affluent. Citizens with low or moderate incomes speak with a whisper that is lost on the ears of inattentive government, while the advantaged roar with the clarity and consistency that policy makers readily heed" (APSA Task Force on Inequality and American Democracy, 2002).

It is perhaps not surprising that the relative political disengagement characteristic of low-income adults is reflected among their children. The 2006 National Assessment of Educational Progress (NAEP) test for civics suggests that students from low-income households have much less of the knowledge necessary to participate effectively in a democratic, civil society than those from affluent households (Lutkus and Weiss, 2007). Indeed, the average 8th-grade student from a low-income family (eligible for free school lunches) has less civics knowledge than 75 percent of students from affluent families.

Yet in our view there is great potential for revitalized civic participation among adolescents living in urban America, for several reasons. The first of these stems from the preponderance of evidence showing that they are developmentally ready for meaningful participation under conditions of support. The second decade brings increased cognitive potential—youth interpret social issues and are capable of formulating complex solutions (Larson and Hansen, 2005). Questions of identity come to the fore, as teenagers grapple with questions of right and wrong and sociopolitical ideologies (Erikson, 1968).

Second, civic participation provides an opportunity for adolescents to develop skills that are underdeveloped by poor experiences in school and to bind to institutions that can buffer the deleterious effects of stress and crime so often found in high-poverty areas. In other words, civic participation can lead to healthy development.

Third, too often policies toward youth are built around their perceived deficits or the problems they pose to social order. Recognizing the developmental potential of young people may engage them rather than alienate them. There are usually serious economic and social issues, within neighborhoods and citywide, that can capture the energy and effort of adolescents who see a role for themselves as political actors. Indeed, there are innumerable examples of sophisticated, committed social and civic activism in urban neighborhoods across the country. Much of this civic activity is overlooked in assessments of civic participation that focus on indicators of conventional activity such as voting. The ubiquity of this kind of activity suggests considerable commitment to social issues; often, then, adolescents have the motivation for civic participation but lack the opportunities to develop the skills to act effectively in the civic sphere.

Finally, urban neighborhoods are often in desperate need of savvy, committed, active citizens. Preparing adolescents to become such citizens is a sensible strategy for achieving this end.

We begin our chapter by exploring the qualities of adolescence that lead to civic engagement in adulthood, then discuss the nature of poor urban neighborhoods and their relations to civic development. Next, we explore some successful strategies for engagement as well as the choices that must be made in implementing such strategies. We conclude with some recommendations for public policy.

What Adolescent Qualities Foster Civic Engagement?

The effective promotion of civic engagement requires facilitating its constituents. Many theorists have identified civic knowledge, civic attitudes, and civic action as crucial components for engaged citizenship.

Civic Knowledge

Adults knowledgeable in civics understand public policy. They judge politicians by their leadership rather than by their personal character, and they trust institutions, are more likely to vote, and can tolerate minority groups (Delli Carpini and Keeter, 1996). For all of these reasons, our society seeks to impart this knowledge to its youth. Much of this effort is focused on schools, which often require students to take courses on civics, American history, and so on. However, there is abundant evidence that schools are not terribly effective in inculcating civics knowledge in adolescents. For example, Hart, Donnelly, Youniss, and Atkins (2007) found that the number of history and civics courses taken by adolescents in high school had only a weak relationship to their civics knowledge. Niemi and Junn (1998) found that while political knowledge is higher among students who had extensive coursework in civics, the number of civics courses and the recentness of enrollment in them accounted for only 4 percent of the variation among students in civics knowledge scores. American adolescents' understanding of politics is surprisingly dependent on the knowledge possessed by their parents; those who have politically knowledgeable parents and who talk frequently with them about civic matters are far advanced in their knowledge relative to adolescents whose parents are ill informed about political matters (McIntosh, Hart, and Youniss, 2007).

Civic Attitudes

A number of authors have argued that civic attitudes of one sort or another are crucial for civic engagement. Putnam (2007) has been particularly persuasive in suggesting that social trust, which rests in part on the belief that others in one's community are fair-minded and trustworthy, is crucial in motivating civic participation. Trust is only one of many civic attitudes that appear to contribute to civic participation in democratic societies; tolerance appears to be another. In the absence of tolerance, majorities become tyrannical, and the polity fractures (see Sullivan and Transue, 1999). Indeed, it is difficult to imagine political philosophy in which civic attitudes are not central constituents, and political scientists have long studied civic attitudes. (See Beck and Jennings, 1982, for an early study of the relationship between adolescents' civic attitudes and their political participation as young adults.)

While civic attitudes are generally viewed as important for sustained, committed civic participation, surprisingly little is known about their roots. Stolle and Hooghe (2004) used longitudinal data to demonstrate that these attitudes can be discerned in childhood and that they reflect, in part, the influence of culture and parents.

Civic Action

Although lay psychological theories often posit that behavior is the outcome of knowledge and attitude, psychologists have shown convincingly that action may precede and create knowledge and attitudes. But this insight was reached more than 170 years ago by one of the most distinguished commentators on nineteenth-century American democracy, Alexis de Tocqueville:

> An American should never be led to speak of Europe, for he will then probably display much presumption and very foolish pride. He will take up with those crude and vague notions which are so useful to the ignorant all over the world. But if you question him respecting his own country, the cloud that dimmed his intelligence will immediately disperse; his language will become as clear and precise as his thoughts. He will inform you what his rights are and by what means he exercises them; he will be able to point out the customs which obtain in the

> political world. You will find that he is well acquainted with the rules of administration, and that he is familiar with the mechanisms of the laws. The citizen of the United States does not acquire his practical science and his positive notions from the books; the instruction he has acquired may have prepared him for receiving those ideas but did not furnish them. The American learns to know the laws by participating in the act of legislation; and he takes a lesson in the forms of government from governing. The great work of society is ever going on before his eyes and, as it were, under his hands.

Tocqueville's argument that democracy is learned through action is one of the principal tenets of educators like Dewey, who proposed to teach children civic-mindedness by encouraging them through action. The implication is that if we aim to promote civic knowledge and civic attitudes, then one route is to structure environments to elicit civic behavior.

Poor Urban Neighborhoods

What are poor urban neighborhoods like? And how do they influence the development of the three constituents of civic engagement just identified? In our view, three demographic characteristics of poor urban neighborhoods shape the course of civic development: poverty, child saturation, and racial/ethnic diversity.

Poverty

The percentage of families in a neighborhood with incomes at or below the poverty line is predictive of poor environments for adolescent development. Leventhal and Brooks-Gunn (2000) reviewed the literature on the effects of neighborhoods on children's development and reached several conclusions relevant to the goals of this chapter. First, they found that there is substantial evidence to indicate that neighborhoods influence child development in academic and behavioral domains. Second, they inferred that indicators of neighborhood economic vitality were generally the best predictors of development. Neighborhoods in which a large proportion of families have incomes below the poverty line and a small proportion of adults have professional occupations seem unfertile grounds for successful development.

How do poor neighborhoods deflect healthy development? Mayer and

Jencks (1989) proposed that the institutional resources of neighborhoods may explain the association of neighborhood deprivation to childhood outcome. For example, young children in poor neighborhoods may be less likely than their peers in affluent neighborhoods to attend preschool. The lack of preschool experience may hinder children in the development of academic and other abilities. Morenoff and Sampson (1997) proposed that neighborhood disadvantages lead to neighborhoods that have weak social control and little consensus on values. They were able to show that the association of neighborhood disadvantages with antisocial behavior in adolescence was substantially mediated by informal control measured at the neighborhood level. The backdrop to both of these possible explanations of the association of neighborhood economic disadvantage to developmental outcome is the fact that highly impoverished neighborhoods are stressful environments. Very poor neighborhoods have high levels of crime, noise, dilapidated housing, and other problems (Evans, 2004). It seems likely that the stress associated with life in economically depressed neighborhoods saps adolescents of the psychological resources necessary to benefit fully from developmental opportunities.

There is abundant evidence that children residing in high-poverty neighborhoods do not fully develop the skills and dispositions necessary to participate in civic life. For example, Hart, Atkins, Markey, and Youniss (2004) examined the association of neighborhood poverty levels with adolescents' tolerance for divergent perspectives. Tolerance is a cardinal virtue for democratic societies; in its absence, majorities become oppressive, and the polity splinters (see Sullivan and Transue, 1999). Hart et al. found that, controlling for a variety of background and demographic factors, adolescents living in poor neighborhoods were less likely to be tolerant of divergent perspectives than were adolescents residing in affluent neighborhoods, a pattern that is consonant with work with adults (e.g., Persell, Green, and Gurevich, 2001). Tolerance is likely to be an effortful extension of goodwill toward others who disagree with the self. The energy to extend goodwill may be diminished by the chronic stresses associated with life in poor urban neighborhoods.

While poor urban neighborhoods are stressful and likely to be poor contexts for civic development, they are not without opportunities. Adolescents living in such neighborhoods are able to perceive quite easily some of the needs of their families and neighbors—safe and clean streets, for example—and the clarity of the issues can be helpful for engaging adolescents. As we suggest in a later section, clear, present, and compelling issues are more likely to engage adolescents in civic and political activity than are complex concerns, and in this regard poor urban environments provide contexts for civic development.

Child Saturation

Child saturation refers to the ratio of children to adults. For example, child saturation can be used to array countries. According to the World Bank, in 2006 48 percent of the population of Mali was below the age of 15; in contrast, only 21 percent of the United States was younger than 15, and in Japan the percentage was 14 percent. Mali could be said to be high in child saturation, while Japan would be very low. Child saturation can also be used to explore differences within countries. For example, data assembled by Rupasingha, Goetz, and Freshwater (2006) suggest that counties in the United States in which the percentage of children is 30 percent or higher have lower levels of social capital—a composite index composed of voting rates and the number of community and political organizations—than do counties in which the percentage of children is less than 25 percent.

For our purposes in this chapter, child saturation is most useful in understanding poor urban communities. Poor communities are higher in child saturation than affluent communities. The correlation between a city or town's poverty rate in 2000 and the percentage of its population below the age of 18 is .23.[1] Neighborhoods are represented in U.S. Census data by census tracts; the correlation between a tract's poverty rate and its child saturation is .24. We conclude, then, that poor neighborhoods in 2000 tend to be young neighborhoods.

What are the implications of child saturation for adolescent civic development? Hart, Atkins, Markey, and Youniss (2004) suggested that in neighborhoods with high child saturation, the influence of children is likely to be greater than it is in neighborhoods characterized by low child saturation. One implication of this hypothesis is that characteristics more common among children than in adults will be acquired by youth more readily in child-saturated neighborhoods, and conversely, characteristics more typical of adults than of children will be transmitted more readily to youth living in neighborhoods with many adults (low child saturation). Adults generally know more about the political system than do children, and consequently, according to the hypothesis just outlined, adolescents living in neighborhoods low in child saturation ought to acquire more civic knowledge than adolescents living in neighborhoods high in child saturation. Hart et al. analyzed data from two national surveys of adolescents and found evidence consonant with this prediction.

Hart, Atkins, Markey, and Youniss (2004) also predicted that because volunteering is more common in children than in adults, neighborhoods with high child saturation ought to increase volunteering. Analyses of national data were generally consistent with this prediction, with one exception. Hart et al. reported that at very high levels of neighborhood poverty, a high level of child saturation was associated with a low level of adolescent volunteering. One possible interpretation is that high levels of child saturation and high levels of poverty together overtax a neighborhood's capacity to direct youthful enthusiasm into productive, pro-social civic activities.

Neighborhood child saturation and poverty have not always been correlated. In fact, as recently as 1970, there was no association between neighborhood poverty and child saturation; this means that the potentially deleterious interaction for adolescent civic engagement of poverty and child saturation is a new challenge.

Racial/Ethnic Diversity

Racial and ethnic diversity is increasing rapidly in the United States and most advanced countries around the world. As Putnam (2007) has noted, the consequences of increasing diversity are both positive and negative. Putnam suggests that research from various fields indicates that, once people become accustomed to it, diversity becomes a wellspring of innovation, creativity, and economic expansion. In the short term, however, racial and ethnic diversity may isolate people. Using data from national surveys, Putnam has shown that racial/ethnic diversity in the United States, measured at the level of neighborhoods, is associated with lower levels of civic engagement and social trust in adults.[2]

What are the implications specifically for poor urban neighborhoods? In the 2000 census, racial diversity was correlated with both neighborhood poverty ($r = .35$) and child saturation ($r = .18$). This means that poor urban neighborhoods are more likely to face the challenges of relatively few adults and racial diversity than are affluent neighborhoods. To the extent that poverty, high child saturation, and racial diversity pose challenges to civic development that are yet to be solved, adolescents in America's poor urban neighborhoods are more likely than adolescents elsewhere to fail to reach their potential as civic actors.

Facilitating Civic Development in Urban America

While there are both great needs and genuine obstacles to the promotion of civic development in urban America, real opportunity exists to facilitate civic engagement of urban teenagers. Like Tocqueville, we believe that the most effective of the available strategies promote development through civic action.

Community Service

Recruiting adolescents to community service—work in their neighborhoods that benefits others, such as working in soup kitchens, cleaning parks, tutoring children, and so on—is one effective strategy to promote civic development (for reviews, see Hart, Atkins, and Donnelly, 2006; Hart, Matsuba, and Atkins, 2008). In a recent analysis of national longitudinal data, Hart, Donnelly, Youniss, and Atkins (2007) found that adolescents involved in community service in high school were substantially more likely as young adults to vote and to volunteer. Moreover, they discovered that adolescents who reported being required to perform community service were nearly as likely to benefit as those who reported that their community service was voluntary; both groups were more likely to vote than those who reported no high school community service. A series of clever studies by Metz and Youniss (2003) demonstrate that these effects are likely to be a consequence of the community service and not of unmeasured, endogenous factors. Finally, Hart et al. found that community service was more efficient in promoting engagement in adulthood than was civic education in high school.

Both research and practical experience suggest that one key to engaging adolescents in community service is providing them with the opportunity to do so. Volunteering is more the result of being recruited by others than it is a reflection of personality traits or self-concept (Matsuba, Hart, Atkins, and Donnelly, 2007). In other words, those who are asked to participate often do so.

Our experience with the Camden STARR Program, a youth development program in one of America's poorest cities, suggests that adolescents who are members of an ongoing group are easily recruited for community service (Hart, Atkins, and Watson, 2005), and they readily appreciate the value of participation. The problem, in our view, is that there are too few opportunities for adolescents to engage in these activities. Because community service is associated with institutions, and because institutions and their associated social capital are less likely to be found in poor and highly child-saturated and racially diverse areas (Rupasingha, Goetz, and Freshwater, 2006)—all three characteristic of poor urban neighborhoods as just discussed—social structures that do exist in these areas need encouragement to provide opportunities for adolescents to become involved.

Youth Organizing

Youth organizing, in which young people work collectively to solve problems facing their neighborhoods or schools, is a second route to civic engagement. Whereas altruism is one of the principal virtues of community service, youth organizing focuses on recognizing interests and fighting for them in the public square (Kahne and Westheimer, 1996). In this sense, participants in organizing engage directly in the practices and skills of public work (Boyte, 2004). Ginwright (2003) pointed out that activism and organizing are particularly suited to areas where youth suffer from discrimination or lack of resources. For example, if one goes to a school with a high number of unlicensed teachers or where textbooks are out of date, then it makes sense to direct one's civic energies to improving one's own situation and that of one's peers.

Like many typologies, this one between service and organizing starts to break down when inspected closely. For example, Hart et al.'s 2007 data demonstrate that enrollment in high school community service predicts later voting, and therefore describing service as "apolitical" is not accurate. Also, the emphasis on "interests" in youth organizing does not preclude altruistic or pro-social goals. Studies of youth activist groups show that participants typically describe their work in terms of pro-social goals, such as helping the community or speaking for those who don't have a voice (Kirshner and Geil, 2007; Rogers, Morrell, and Enyedy, 2007). Lastly, some mandatory community service programs include volunteer placements in political or advocacy organizations, suggesting that service is not necessarily in opposition to political engagement or action (Metz and Youniss, 2004).

Nevertheless, we treat youth organizing here as a separate phenomenon because, for the most part, it embodies a distinct path to civic participation for youth, and it has proliferated in high-poverty urban areas, as witnessed by recent journal articles and books devoted to the subject (e.g., Delgado and Staples, 2007; Ginwright, Noguera, and Cammarota, 2005; Schutz, 2006). A recent publication concluded, "Indeed, youth organizing groups . . . are expanding so rapidly that it is difficult to assess the exact number of groups in existence. Research conducted in 2002 identified at least forty such groups in the San Francisco Bay Area alone, and suggested that many more are active throughout the country" (Shaw and Mediratta, 2008).

This emerging literature on contemporary youth activism is nascent compared with that about community service. With some exceptions (Gambone, Yu, Lewis-Charp, Sipe, and Lacoe, 2004), it comprises qualitative studies that describe single projects or organizations; these studies are just now making their way into peer-reviewed journals and edited books (e.g., Deschenes, McLaughlin, and Newman, 2008; Ginwright, Noguera, and Cammarota, 2005; Larson and Hansen, 2005). From this we identify three common features that help to illuminate youth organizing practices.

Focus on systems, particularly schools

Youth organizing groups seek policy change in the various systems that shape young lives, including schools, school districts, juvenile justice departments, and transportation boards. Although in rare cases groups target federal laws or policies, most focus on issues in the neighborhoods and cities where members live (Deschenes, McLaughlin, and Newman, 2008). For example, after identifying the need for safer, more productive places for youth to go, activism groups in Oakland led a successful ballot initiative to promote Measure K, which set aside 2.5 percent of the general city budget for youth programs (Ashley, Samaniego, and Cheun, 1997). Youth in Changemakers, a program of the San Francisco School District, persuaded the school board to revise its policy on sexual harassment after conducting research on its prevalence in middle schools (Sherman, 2002). Members of Youth Making a Change worked with public officials who oversee policies for the San Francisco juvenile justice system in an effort to reduce the disproportionate number of youth of color who were incarcerated for minor offenses.

Since the 1990s, youth organizing efforts have taken a distinct turn toward school reform in inner cities (Warren, Mira, and Nikundiwe, 2008). This is not so surprising, given that high schools are a gateway to opportunity and equality for youth in high-poverty areas while at the same time they so often fall short in delivering on that promise.

Youth-led efforts to reform schools abound: students in Philadelphia exposed corrupt test-giving practices and helped to create new policies for test preparation (Shaw and Mediratta, 2008). Students in Baltimore sustained a campaign over several years (still ongoing) that mobilized hundreds of their peers to call for the state to honor its obligations to provide adequate funds to Baltimore schools (Warren, Mira, and Nikundiwe, 2008). In Denver, students responded to a decision to close their school by engaging in protest politics (staging a walkout) and sustained engagement (carrying out a participatory research study to document the impact of the closure and generate recommendations for future school policies) (Kirshner and Pozzoboni, 2008).

Such efforts often take place outside officially sanctioned high school leadership bodies, sometimes in response to students' perceptions of the limited scope of participation they are offered through student councils. McFarland and Starmanns (2008) reviewed the student government practices in 362 high schools across the United States and found that schools with fewer financial resources, typically in the inner city, were less likely to have student councils and constitutions; when they did have them, they had fewer official powers. Similarly, Kahne and Middaugh (this volume) reported that students in high-poverty schools in California have fewer opportunities for civic deliberation and participation. These quantitative findings are consistent with the efforts of youth organizers in a high-poverty urban district who developed a campaign to make student leadership "more than just planning proms" (Kirshner, 2008).

Despite their outsider status, the work of youth organizing groups is much closer to Boyte's notion of "public work," in which ordinary citizens engage in the hard work of solving problems together, than it is to stereotypical perceptions of activism as illegal activity or a politics of complaint. Indeed, the examples above demonstrate how these groups work with school districts and school leaders to create lasting change—there is a pragmatic strain among such groups to see change happen. Often this means working strategically, in collaboration with systems, to enact changes, rather than treating political officials solely as adversaries (Boyte, 2004; Larson and Hansen, 2005). This pragmatic strain was articulated by one youth organizer when she was asked to describe what her group was "all about":

> I think that it gives youth opportunities to . . . actually help out in the community as in making the school a better place. Or, if something's not fair in the community, I feel that they actually go out and actually do something about it instead of just sitting there like other organizations. I'm not trying to talk about the other ones, but I heard that they just sit down and talk and complain about it. But I feel that with Youth Rising, they actually go out and solve the problem. Like you see a fly and say that fly is bugging me and that's all you do is complain. But I feel as Youth Rising, they'll go out and actually swat the fly. (Kirshner, 2005)

Sociopolitical development

Like many youth development agencies, such groups have shifted from a prevailing "deficit model," which designs programs to address certain problems of at-risk youth, to an "asset model," which designs programs to build on young people's strengths and hopes (Eccles and Gootman, 2002; Roth, Brooks-Gunn, Murray, and Foster, 1998). A central goal is that youth participants are encouraged to become partners in decision making and leadership. A recent multi-site evaluation of youth organizing groups reports that a higher percentage of members of such groups experience consistent opportunities to contribute to program decision making than youth in more traditional youth development organizations (Gambone, Yu, Lewis-Charp, Sipe, and Lacoe, 2004). Groups seek to position young people as democratic actors who have legitimate opinions about social policies and who deserve to have these opinions heard in the public square (Camino and Zeldin, 2002).

In addition to general leadership skills, many groups promote sociopolitical awareness (Watts and Flanagan, 2007). In groups that have a social justice ideology, this means an awareness of histories of racial oppression, analysis of economic systems, and analysis of the distribution of political power (Ginwright and James, 2002). Such an outlook challenges youth development programs to look beyond the needs of individual youth and address broader social conditions. As Ginwright and James write, such groups treat youth "as agents capable of transforming their toxic environments, not simply developing resiliency and resistance to them" (40).

Adult guides

The literature on youth activism emphasizes its youth-led character, but most studies describe essential roles played by more experienced adults as guides and mentors (Kirshner, 2008; Larson and Hansen, 2005; Nygreen, Kwon, and Sánchez, 2006). Typically, these leaders are in their twenties. A theme that emerges again and again (illustrated in the titles of many papers) is the balancing act that adults strive to achieve between supporting youth autonomy and providing guidance and scaffolding (Larson, Walker, and Pearce, 2005; Mitra, 2005; O'Donoghue and Strobel, 2007). Researchers have begun to uncover some variations—from "apprenticeship" approaches, where veterans coach novices, to "facilitative" approaches, where adults adopt neutral advisory roles. What is important is that, whatever the specific guidance strategy, these adults catalyze social capital in neighborhoods with high levels of child saturation. Ginwright's 2007 case study of Leadership Excellence in Oakland, California, provides evidence of the important ways that African American adults help youth develop social capital and civic competences.

Challenges facing the field of youth organizing

Groups work on dual fronts: they foster civic development while ministering to members' more immediate needs for caring relationships, academic mentoring, and skill development. These dual roles can place a strain on organizational staff and justify greater infrastructure support from foundations and government sources. Finding ways to sustain organizations in poor communities is a long-term challenge but one that is being met with increasing support from private foundations (Yee, 2008).

A second challenge pertains to achieving what we call *youth participation*

2.0. Youth have demonstrated their ability to carry out campaigns, mobilize their peers, and present their ideas to policy makers. Groups have gained access to the halls of power in cities, states, and Washington. But, with some exceptions (e.g., Kwon, 2006), the tangible impact of these efforts on policies or laws has been limited. The challenge facing advocates of youth participation is figuring out how to move from making impressive presentations to influencing meaningful policy.

A recent presentation by youth organizers on Capitol Hill (observed by Kirshner) epitomized this challenge. Students from across the country traveled to Washington to share findings from action research that called for greater attention to their rights to quality education and safe neighborhoods. The presentations were politely received; congressional staffers in the audience lauded the students' accomplishment and the persuasiveness of their case. But after its completion, there was a collective sigh. What next? Policy makers offered assurances that they had listened and would write memos based on the presentations, but it was unclear what steps would—or could—be taken. Suggestions that youth should write letters to their representatives fell flat. Surely there are more effective ways to follow up on a face-to-face meeting than sending a postcard?

This experience illustrates the challenge that youth face when trying to influence policy. The reasons are numerous. Youth under 18 do not vote, so representatives have little incentive to respond to their concerns. Policies affecting youth are made at so many levels (city, state, and federal) and by so many institutional sectors (school districts, juvenile justice, health and human services) that it can be difficult for groups to figure out which levels of power they need to push. Sometimes youth groups lack the political expertise to know how to be effective proposing or writing policy. And, of course, substantive improvements to inner cities have been slow in coming for adult residents, too, suggesting a deeply entrenched set of structural problems and a lack of political will among elected officials.

Policy Recommendations

We began this chapter with a discouraging overview of civic participation and civic knowledge among citizens living in poor urban areas, and we described how this state of affairs arises, in part, from broad demographic characteristics of poor urban neighborhoods. The demographics of urban neighborhoods—poverty, child saturation, racial heterogeneity—present broad, structural obstacles that ought to be incorporated into discussions of why neighborhoods vary in success in launching their adolescents into civic life. For this reason we believe it is neither fair nor helpful to imagine that poor urban neighborhoods could mimic affluent suburban neighborhoods on budgets, if the residents of poor urban neighborhoods simply chose to adopt different values and practices. The confluence of high poverty, high child saturation, and racial heterogeneity create an ecology that is substantially different from those found in the suburbs.

While the long-term civic vitality of urban neighborhoods probably requires an end to the economic, age, and racial segregation characteristic of the United States—a project so daunting that it seems out of reach without a significant social movement to address it—our review also suggests that there is much that *each of us can do now* to prepare urban adolescents to be civic participants and leaders in the twenty-first century.

First, we need to recognize that urban adolescents—like adolescents elsewhere—are interested in, and can contribute to, civic life. Poor urban adolescents typically know less about politics and have fewer experiences in civic participation than their suburban counterparts, but this is not because of a lack of interest or an absence of civic capacity.

Second, we believe that participation and opportunity are the keys to scaffolding civic development in urban neighborhoods. Community service and political activism are enormously powerful influences on civic development in adolescence. Those who serve and participate acquire civic habits, civic knowledge, and civic attitudes. The benefits of participation for civic development dwarf those from traditional civics and history instruction in schools; we know of no research suggesting that adolescents can be prepared for civic life through mere attitude change.

Participation requires opportunities; community service and political activism usually occur in the context of institutions—schools, churches, youth groups, and the like. As we noted earlier, these kinds of institutions and the opportunities they provide are less often found in poor urban neighborhoods than in affluent ones. This means that institutions that are in poor urban neighborhoods should be supported—both financially and through human capital—in order to broaden their missions to include providing opportunities for civic engagement to the adolescents they serve, and encouragement should be given to those seeking to form institutions of this sort.

Social institutions are typically effective in promoting civic development because they consist of knowledgeable, civically capable adults. It is these adults who bridge the gap between institution and adolescent. Adolescents are typically connected to institutions by invitation: teachers asking students to join student governments, church leaders asking adolescents to volunteer, coaches requiring team members to contribute to community efforts, youth leaders recruiting groups to political action. While few can end segregation across the nation, many Americans can support the institutions that serve urban adolescents, and many others can invite adolescents in these communities to participate.

Lastly, we invite policy makers to reach out to existing youth groups that seek to make a difference in their schools and neighborhoods. Policy makers can do more than listen when youth come to their doors—they can develop partnerships with such groups that capitalize on youths' ability to mobilize their peers and policy makers' knowledge about what it takes to see change implemented.

Both long-term efforts to eliminate segregation and immediate efforts to provide opportunities for civic engagement to urban adolescents ought to guide our social policy deliberations. There are millions of adolescents who can become our leading citizens—altruistic, effective, knowledgeable political actors—with the help of America's adults.

Notes

1. This number is generated using U.S. Census 2000 data from Geolytics.
2. Racial/ethnic diversity is often indexed by summing the squared proportions of each racial group in a population, and subtracting this sum from 1.

References

APSA Task Force on Inequality and American Democracy. (2002). American democracy in an age of rising inequality. *Perspectives on Politics, 2,* 651–89.

Ashley, J., Samaniego, D., and Cheun, L. (1997). How Oakland turns its back on teens: A youth perspective. *Social Justice, 24,* 170–77.

Beck, P. A., and Jennings, M. K. (1982). Pathways to participation. *American Political Science Review, 76* (1), 94–108.

Boyte, H. (2004). *Everyday politics: Reconnecting citizens and public life.* Philadelphia: University of Pennsylvania Press.

Camino, L., and Zeldin, S. (2002). From periphery to center: Pathways for youth civic engagement in the day-to-day life of communities. *Applied Developmental Science, 6,* 213–20.

Delli Carpini, M. X., and Keeter, S. (1996). *What Americans know about politics and why it matters* New Haven: Yale University Press.

Dewey, J. (1916). *Democracy and education.* New York: Macmillan.

Delgado, M., and Staples, L. (2007). *Youth-led community organizing: Theory and action.* New York: Oxford University Press.

Deschenes, S., McLaughlin, M., and Newman, A. (2008). Organizations advocating for youth: The local advantage. *New Directions for Youth Development, 117,* 11–25.

Eccles J., and Gootman, J. A. (Eds.). (2002). *Community programs to promote youth development.* Washington DC: National Academy Press.

Erikson, E. (1994/1968). *Identity: Youth and crisis.* New York: Norton.

Evans, G. W. (2004). The environment of childhood poverty. *American Psychologist, 59* (2), 77–92.

Gambone, M., Yu, H., Lewis-Charp, H., Sipe, C., and Lacoe, J. (2004). *A comparative analysis of community youth development strategies.* Paper presented at the biennial meeting of the Society for Research on Adolescence, Baltimore.

Ginwright, S. (2003). *Youth organizing: Expanding possibilities for youth development.* New York: Funders Collaborative on Youth Organizing.

Ginwright, S. A. (2007). Black youth activism and the role of critical social capital in black community organizations. *American Behavioral Scientist, 51,* 403–18.

Ginwright, S., and James, T. (2002). From assets to agents of change: Social justice, organizing, and youth development. *New Directions for Youth Development, 96* (winter), 27–46.

Ginwright, S., Noguera, P., and Cammarota, J. (Eds.). (2006). *Beyond resistance! Youth activism and community change: New democratic possibilities for policy and practice for America's youth* Oxford: Routledge.

Hart, D., Atkins, R., and Donnelly, T. M. (2006). Community service and moral development. In M. Killen and J. Smetana (Eds.), *Handbook of moral development* (633–56). Hillsdale, NJ: Lawrence Erlbaum Associates.

Hart, D., Atkins, R., Markey, P., and Youniss, J. (2004). Youth bulges in communities: The effects of age structure on adolescent civic knowledge and civic participation. *Psychological Science, 15,* 591–97.

Hart, D., Atkins, R., and Watson, N. C. (2005). How to start your own youth development micro-program. *SRA Newsletter* (spring), 1.

Hart, D., Donnelly, T. M., Youniss, J., and Atkins, R. (2007). High school predictors of adult civic engagement: The roles of volunteering, civic knowledge, extracurricular activities, and attitudes. *American Educational Research Journal, 44,* 197–219.

Hart, D., Matsuba, K., and Atkins, R. (2008). Service-learning and character development. In L. Nucci and D. Narvaez (Eds.), *Handbook of Moral and Character Education.* New York: Routledge.

Jamison, A., Day, J. C., Shin, H. B., and U.S. Census Bureau. (2002). *Voting and registration in the election of November 2000.* Washington, DC: Dept. of Commerce, Bureau of the Census.

Kahne, J., and Westheimer, J. (1996). In the service of what? The politics of service learning. *Phi Delta Kappan, 77,* 593–99.

Kirshner, B. (2005). *Democracy now: Activism and learning in urban youth organizations.* Unpublished doctoral dissertation, Stanford University.

Kirshner, B. (2008). Guided participation in three youth activism organizations: Facilitation, apprenticeship, and joint work. *Journal of the Learning Sciences, 17* (1), 60–101.

Kirshner, B., and Geil, K. (2007). "I'm about to really bring it": Access points between youth activists and adult policymakers. Manuscript under review.

Kirshner, B., and Pozzoboni, P. (2008, March). *Youth responses to high school closure.* Paper presented at the annual conference of the American Educational Research Association, New York.

Kwon, S. A. (2006). Youth of color organizing for juvenile justice. In S. Ginwright, P. Noguera, and J. Cammarota (Eds.), *Beyond resistance!* (215–28). Oxford: Routledge.

Larson, R. W., and Hansen, D. (2005). The development of strategic thinking: Learning to impact human systems in a youth activism program. *Human Development, 48* (6), 327–49.

Larson, R., Walker, K., and Pearce, N. (2005). A comparison of high quality youth-led and adult-led youth programs: Balancing inputs from youth and adults. *Journal of Community Psychology, 33,* 57–74.

Leventhal, T., and Brooks-Gunn, J. (2000). The neighborhoods they live in: The effects of neighborhood residence on child and adolescent outcomes. *Psychological Bulletin, 126* (2), 309–37.

Lutkus, A. D., and Weiss, A. R. (2007). *The nation's report card: Civics 2006* (NCES 2007-476). U.S. Department of Education, National Center for Education Statistics. Washington, DC: Government Printing Office.

Matsuba, K., Hart, D., Atkins, R., and Donnelly, T. (2007). Psychological and social-structural influences on involvement in volunteering. *Journal of Research on Personality, 41,* 889–907.

Mayer, S. E., and Jencks, C. (1989). Growing up in poor neighborhoods: How much does it matter? *Science, 243,* 1441–45.

McFarland, D., and Starmanns, C. E. (2008). Inside student government: The variable organization of high school student councils. *Teachers College Record, 111* (1), 27–54.

McIntosh, H., Hart, D., and Youniss, J. (2007). The influence of family political discussion on youth civic development: Which parent qualities matter? *PS: Political Science and Politics, 40,* 495–99.

Metz, E., and Youniss, J. (2003). A demonstration that school-based required service does not deter—but heightens—volunteerism. *PS: Political Science and Politics, 36* (2), 281–86.

Metz, J., and Youniss, J. (2004, March). *Community service as a means to promote civic participation.* Paper presented at biennial meeting of the Society for Research on Adolescence, Baltimore.

Mitra, D. L. (2005). Adults advising youth: Leading while getting out of the way. *Educational Administration Quarterly, 41* (3), 520–53.

Morenoff, J. D., and Sampson, R. J. (1997). Violent crime and the spatial dynamics of neighborhood transition: Chicago, 1970–1990. *Social Forces, 76,* 31–54.

Niemi, R., and Junn, J. (1998). *Civic education: What makes students learn.* New Haven: Yale University Press.

Nygreen, K., Kwon, S., and Sánchez, P. (2006). Urban youth building community: Social change and participatory research in schools, homes, and community-based organizations. *Journal of Community Practice, 14,* 107–23.

O'Donoghue, J. L., and Strobel, K. R. (2007). Directivity and freedom: Adult support of activism among urban youth. *American Behavioral Scientist, 51,* 465–85.

Persell, C. H., Green, A., and Gurevich, L. (2001). Civil society, economic distress, and social tolerance. *Sociological Forum, 16* (2), 203–30.

Putnam, R. D. (2007). E pluribus unum: Diversity and community in the twenty-first century. The 2006 Johan Skytte Prize Lecture. *Scandinavian Political Studies, 30* (2), 137–74.

Rogers, J., Morrell, E., and Enyedy, N. (2007). Studying the struggle: Contexts for learning and identity development for urban youth. *American Behavioral Scientist, 51,* 419–43.

Roth, J., Brooks-Gunn, J., Murray, L., and Foster, W. (1998). Promoting healthy adolescents: Synthesis of youth development program evaluations. *Journal of Research on Adolescence 8* (4), 423–59.

Rupasingha, A., Goetz, S. J., and Freshwater, D. (2006). The production of social capital in U.S. counties. *Journal of Socio-Economics, 35* (1), 83–101.

Sampson, R. J., Raudenbush, S. W., and Earls, F. (1997, August 15). Neighborhoods and violent crime: A multilevel study of collective efficacy. *Science, 277,* 918–24.

Schutz, A. (2006). Home is a prison in the global city: The tragic failure of school-based community engagement strategies. *Review of Educational Research, 76,* 691–744.

Shaw, S., and Mediratta, K. (2008). Negotiating reform: Young people's leadership in the educational arena. *New Directions for Youth Development, 117,* 43–59.

Sherman, R. (2002). Building young people's lives: One foundation's strategy. *New Direction for Youth Development, 96* (winter), 65–82.

Stolle, D., and Hooghe, M. (2004). The roots of social capital: Attitudinal and network mechanisms in the relation between youth and adult indicators of social capital. *Acta Politica, 39* (4), 422–41.

Sullivan, J. L., and Transue, J. E. (1999). The psychological underpinnings of democracy: A selective review of research on political tolerance, interpersonal trust, and social capital. *Annual Review of Psychology, 50,* 625–50.

Tocqueville, A. (2000). *Democracy in America.* Trans. H. Mansfield and D. Winthrop. Chicago: University of Chicago Press.

Warren, M. R., Mira, M., and Nikundiwe, T. (2008). Youth organizing: From youth development to school reform. *New Directions for Youth Development, 117,* 27–42.

Watts, R., and Flanagan, C. (2007). Pushing the envelope on civic engagement: A developmental and liberation psychology perspective. *Journal of Community Psychology, 35,* 779–92.

Yee, S. M. (2008). Developing the field of youth organizing and advocacy: What foundations can do. *New Directions for Youth Development, 117,* 109–24.

6

City Government as Enabler of Youth Civic Engagement

Policy Designs and Implications

Carmen Sirianni and Diana Marginean Schor

In this essay, we examine the role that city governments can play in promoting youth civic engagement in a systematic and strategic fashion, especially through such innovations as youth commissions as well as related efforts to make youth empowerment part of the culture of city agencies and nonprofits that contract with the city. We analyze in detail two cities that have demonstrated notable success since their initial innovations in the mid-1990s: Hampton, Virginia, and San Francisco, California. These cities are widely recognized as two of the leaders in the field, and yet they have proceeded from very different starting points in terms of key initiators and action frames, as well as demographics and political culture. Each represents a different "model" of sorts, though each shares some common elements, and the two have begun to converge in emphasizing culture change of bureaucratic and service delivery systems. Following this comparison, we broaden the analysis to the networks critical to the diffusion of similar models in other cities. That cities have been able to initiate reform from a variety of leverage points holds much promise for enabling youth civic engagement through city governments around the country. In the concluding section, we explore how federal policy might support cities in such endeavors.

Of course, the ecology of organizations supporting youth engagement in any given city is generally complex and can range from YMCAs and 4-H clubs to youth organizing around issues of social justice, identity, and policy advocacy (Ginwright, Noguera, and Cammarota, 2006; Checkoway and Gutierrez, 2006; Delgado and Staples, 2007). There is often much overlap, especially in larger cities, as well as multiple forms of membership, strategic complementarities, and leadership pathways. Thus a middle-school student involved in a YMCA leadership program might become a militant youth organizer in high school, and a youth organizer might later focus on collaborative forms of neighborhood development. We know from our interviews with youth leaders over the past seven years that such pathways are diverse (see also Irby, Ferber, and Pittman, 2001), but there exists little quantitative data revealing typical and less typical patterns. Needless to say, among organizations promoting youth engagement, there is also competition, with some types of organizations claiming that they engage young people in ways that are more effective and consequential than others, that they employ action frames that better address the root causes of problems, and that they develop leadership in ways that are more transformative. This kind of competition is familiar and virtually inevitable within the larger ecology of organizations in any given field of action (Baum, 1996), including adult-led community organizations (Sirianni and Friedland, 2001, chap. 2; Orr, 2007).

City Government as Civic Enabler

Our focus on city government's role in enabling youth civic engagement is thus selective but nonetheless potentially broad. It rightly excludes some kinds of activities, such as promoting partisan political activity or organizing *against* city government itself. As important as these activities often are, they are not part of city government's rightful role, but best promoted by independent organizations with nongovernmental funding. But city government clearly can claim a legitimate interest in, and normative responsibility for, promoting other forms of youth civic engagement: community service, civic education and service-learning, policy review and development, and collaborative problem solving that promises to add value to the city's role as producer of public goods, such as safe streets and schools, restored urban streams, open space, community-supported agriculture, public art, and neighborhood revitalization. The city can provide robust roles for young people on youth commissions, on advisory boards, and in city and neighborhood planning. These are the kinds of activities that can bridge some of the divide between political and civic engagement, which has widened for youth over the past two generations and poses a serious long-term challenge to our democracy (Zukin, Keeter, Andolina, Jenkins, and Delli Carpini, 2006).

The broader literature on city government's role in enabling certain forms of civic engagement among adults leads us to believe that there are some genuine advantages to be had from well-designed models of city support. The now classic quantitative and comparative study by Jeffrey Berry, Kent Portney, and Ken Thomson, *The Rebirth of Urban Democracy* (1993), shows robust effects of citywide systems of neighborhood associations, such as those in Portland, Oregon, and St. Paul, Minnesota, compared with non-citywide systems and independent organizing. Chicago's citywide system of community policing, with its infrastructure of beat meetings in which citizens and beat officers engage in collaborative problem solving, provides extensive evidence of effectiveness in reducing crime, as well as reduction of some of the racial and class biases that accompany many forms of neighborhood participation (Skogan, 2006; Fung, 2004). Sirianni's 2007 study of Seattle's neighborhood planning system demonstrates the potential of city-supported neighborhood planning groups to produce good technical plans that are well integrated with the comprehensive plan and that generate enhanced legitimacy, decreased NIMBYism, increased inclusiveness of traditionally excluded groups, new forms of collaboration among city departments and neighborhoods, and continued mobilization of community assets by civic associations. Other city models have had notable successes as well (Fagotto and Fung, 2006; Kathi and Cooper, 2005; Ozawa, 2004; Leighninger, 2006).

City governments can become enablers of robust civic engagement, community asset mobilization (Kretzmann and McKnight, 1996), and coproduction (Boyte, 2005) because they are able to provide, promote, and/or require the following, in some fairly rich combination and on a citywide basis, should they so choose: (1) *resources*, such as staff support, training, technical and data analysis, and funding for projects, consultants, and facilitators; (2) *templates for problem solving*, such as neighborhood beat plans, asset mapping models, and citizen toolkits of various sorts; (3) *formal mandates*, such as for diverse representation, inclusive visioning, or service-learning; (4) *reciprocal accountability* among citizens, civic groups, other organized stakeholders, city departments, city council, and the mayor, through both formal review and intensive relationship and trust building by city staff (Behn, 2001; Fung, 2004; Sirianni, 2007); and (5) *high-level leadership and vision* by elected leaders, city managers, and department heads.

The research for this study is based on a variety of sources. We conducted three cycles of interviews (2001–2002, 2005, 2007) with key municipal innovators, youth leaders, and local nonprofits in five cities, as well as directors and staff in national and regional youth development intermediaries that have focused on urban youth engagement. In all, we interviewed 87 individuals, some multiple times. Second, we conducted field observations of meetings of the youth commission, superintendents' and principals' advisory groups, youth planning and neighborhood groups, and various other youth advisory and activist groups in Hampton in 2002 and 2007. Third, we examined an array of documents (policy reports, evaluations, surveys, annual reports, meeting minutes, websites, toolkits, and curricula) from Hampton and San Francisco. We analyze these two cases in terms of the logic of equifinality (George and Bennett, 2005) or identifying different causal paths that lead to a (roughly) similar outcome in different cases. City agency culture change, enabling more robust engagement and collaborative problem solving among youth and adults, emerged through two distinct pathways in Hampton and San Francisco—reinventing government and social movement, respectively—reflecting the different political cultures of the two cities. Fourth, one of our four three-day national strategy conferences on youth civic engagement, attended by key local innovators, national intermediaries, and academic scholars in 2001–2002 and funded by the Pew Charitable Trusts, focused on youth development, including citywide models. In addition, we participated in a four-day national conference in Hampton in April 2007, designed to help learn from Hampton's model, as well as share lessons across the 10 other cities that sent teams of public officials, nonprofit staff, and youth leaders to participate. This conference was convened by the City of Hampton and Alternatives, Inc., with funding from the city's Innovations in Government Award (2005), sponsored by the Ash Institute for Democratic Governance and Innovation at Harvard's Kennedy School of Government. Unless otherwise indicated, all direct quotations are from our interviews and field observations.

Hampton and San Francisco

In this section, we compare the models of youth civic engagement institutionalized by the city governments of Hampton and San Francisco along a number of dimensions: policy initiators, mission and frame, institutional and network capacity, and agency culture change.

Policy Initiators

Policy innovation in youth civic engagement emerged from distinctly different sources in Hampton and San Francisco. In Hampton, reform began as an extension of reinventing government within city hall, whereas in San Francisco a youth advocacy organization successfully waged a referendum campaign against city hall to amend the city charter to establish a youth commission with a mandate to review all youth-related city policy initiatives.

Hampton is a medium-sized city of 146,000 on the coast of Virginia, roughly half white and half black, with a modest economic base and few income extremes. It has a nonpartisan council/manager form of government, with the mayor chosen as the one with the most votes among city council members. It had little tradition of grassroots community or youth organizing before the 1990s, with the exception of neighborhood associations. In the mid-1980s, facing serious problems of economic development and local revenues (Stone and Worgs, 2004), Mayor James Eason and City Manager Bob O'Neill embarked on a series of initiatives to reinvent local government by flattening bureaucratic hierarchies and devolving initiative downwards, and then by extending power outwards to citizens through collaborative neighborhood planning (Osborn and Plastrik, 1997, chap. 8; Bayer and Potapchuk, 2004). As various innovators at the time recall, the city manager would continually tell them, "Don't bring me more programs. Change systems." When the city turned to the problems of youth in 1990, it was thus predisposed to a collaborative planning process oriented to systems change, which received funding through a three-year $320,000 Community Partnership Grant from the Center for Substance Abuse Prevention (CSAP) at the U.S. Department of Health and Human Services. A key organizational player in the collaborative planning process was Alternatives, Inc., a local youth service organization with a national reputation for its substance abuse work. Cindy Carlson, the Alternatives staff person who wrote the CSAP grant proposal, became the key facilitator of the collaborative, subsequently named the Hampton Coalition for Youth.

The collaborative planning process generated a number of surprises. First, the group of 20 who had been recruited by Alternatives to provide their own perspective told the youth service workers that they did not want to be viewed as broken and in constant need of fixing. They wanted to be challenged and given opportunities to make real contributions to the community. They viewed as most successful those programs of Alternatives that had involved them in problem solving, such as youth-to-youth programs. In response, Alternatives decided to reinvent itself as a learning organization (Senge, 1990; Light, 1998) to focus on youth leadership development, and it was helped in reframing its work by a national youth development network that had begun to stress "positive youth development" and "community youth development," in which young people were viewed as assets to communities rather than bundles of deficits (Lofquist, 1989; Hughes and Curnan, 2000). The second big surprise was that the process produced a consensus vision built on youth empowerment. Each stakeholder group—youth, parents, community groups, businesses, and youth workers and advocates—met separately for months, with extensive outreach and skilled facilitation to develop their own ideas for youth and family programs. But when they came together in a two-day retreat in the summer of 1992, they embedded their specific proposals in a broad statement of principles:

> *Our Mission:* Hampton will create an environment in which youth contribute to the community in a manner that positively impacts the quality of life. We will empower our youth to meet their full potential. . . . To empower someone means to give them both authority and responsibility.
>
> *Partnership in the Community:* All young people in Hampton are entitled to be seen, heard, and respected as citizens of the community. They deserve to be prepared, active participants—based on their level of maturity—in community service, government, public policy, or other decision making which affects their lives and their well-being. (Hampton Coalition for Youth, 1993, 2, 6)

Other cornerstones of the vision included the importance of families, a commitment to the whole child, an emphasis on strengths and assets brought by families and neighborhoods, respect for diversity of every kind, and lifelong learning in and out of school. Collaboration was highlighted as essential in an era when "no longer can we look to single programs and fragmented approaches to solve problems." The report insisted, however, that "strong public policy" could lead the way by outlining the kind of community to which all children are entitled. But over and over, the document returned to empowering youth as the most fundamental mission and called for "a comprehensive system of opportunities for youth to be involved in the life of the community" (Hampton Coalition for Youth, 1993, iii). To catalyze such efforts, the city transformed the Hampton Coalition for Youth into a small office of city government, albeit one with extensive networks into public, nonprofit, and business institutions. The creation of a youth commission several years later would become a linchpin in this system.

In San Francisco, the policy initiators were different than in Hampton. A much larger and more ethnically and economically diverse city of 776,000 on the West Coast, San Francisco has a strong progressive political culture, with an extensive array of community, ethnic, and youth organizing groups—many favoring protest and direct action—and a strong mayor/council system organized on a partisan basis (DeLeon, 1992; DeLeon and Naff, 2004). Among youth advocacy groups, one stood out. Coleman Advocates, founded in 1975 around issues of children in juvenile justice and foster care systems, stepped to the forefront to lead a "children's movement" or "youth movement," especially with its successful ballot campaign for a Children's Amendment to the city charter in 1991 (McLaughlin, 2005; Coleman Advocates for Children and Youth, 1994; Briggs, 2008, chap. 5). The amendment dedicated 2.5 cents of every $100 of the assessed value of local property taxes to children's services. Although a small staff-based organization, Coleman mobilized a broad coalition and sponsored Youth Making a Change (Y-MAC) to bring youth leadership to the field of children's advocacy. Several years later, it also sponsored the Community Coalition of Youth and Adults, which campaigned to get a youth commission written into the city charter. When the board of supervisors rejected this, the coalition successfully waged a referendum campaign and the supervisors approved it on a second vote. As its former executive director, Colleen Montoya, told us, the youth commission was a result of a "grassroots fight," a "bottom-up movement," and elected leaders were "reactive rather than proactive."

Mission and Frame

These diverse origins of officially sponsored youth civic engagement in Hampton and San Francisco have shaped their respective missions and action frames (Schön and Rein, 1994; Benford and Snow, 2000). Because of its origins in a strong advocacy and referendum campaign in a city with a contentious, "hyperpluralist" progressive political culture (DeLeon, 1992; DeLeon and Naff, 2004), San Francisco's youth commission has predominately employed a "youth rights" and "youth movement" frame. This is reflected in its various policy reports, public meetings, training sessions, and summer retreats, which draw from the history of youth movements as well as from Alinsky-style community organizing principles as interpreted by national intermediaries such as the Alliance for Justice and the Midwest Academy. The mission of the youth commission is to advise the mayor and the board of alderman on children's and youth issues, with a charter mandate to review all laws, policies, and regulations affecting youth, as well as any proposed changes in these. All proposed bills affecting youth must be sent to the commission for review. The youth commission also proposes policy changes and reviews budgetary priorities of departments that may impact the type and quality of services, such as protecting community-based services for juvenile probation. One task force focused on the rights of lesbian, gay, bisexual, and transgendered youth in 1998–2000 by getting city departments to sign memoranda of understanding (MOUs) on its treatment of such youth, as well as requiring all city employees and certain city contractors who work with them to undergo sensitivity training to create safe spaces. In addition, the commission has been active in state policy, such as its (unsuccessful) coalition campaign in 1999–2000 against Proposition 21, which, among other things, permitted juvenile offenders as young as 14 to be tried as adults.

The predominant frame in Hampton, by contrast, is one of "relationship building as democratic community building," the phrase repeatedly employed by Hampton's leaders at the Innovations in Government Award ceremony during the network learning conference of 2007. This frame places emphasis on trust, collaboration, partnerships, dialogue, and social capital for the purpose of empowering youth and citizens generally. This civic "master frame" (Sirianni and Friedland, 2005, 132–48; see also Benford and Snow, 2000) is richly interwoven with several others: (a) *youth as assets*, which derives from the positive youth development frame that emerged as a critique of much research and practice focused on youth as problems and deficits; (b) *developmental assets*, which has been articulated and diffused by the Search Institute (Benson et al., 1998) and stresses 40 assets that young people need to become healthy and responsible; and (c) *creativity*, which views the capacity for serious play and artistic creation as closely tied to leadership competency and problem solving. Adult leaders in the youth civic engagement system, as well as a good number of the youth leaders, employ this common language in their work, though with distinct emphases in different settings. It anchors their persistent efforts to transform organizational cultures.

The Hampton Youth Commission does not have a charter mandate to review all policies affecting youth, but it has a great deal of moral authority to choose to work on policy issues it sees as relevant, as we shall see further below. After the Coalition for Youth was transformed into a city office in 1994, the first institutional reform was to employ two teenagers in the planning department on a part-time basis (Carlson, 2005). The youth commission has utilized the city's comprehensive plan as a framework for much of its policy work, especially since the comprehensive plan and strategic plan were merged into an overall community plan.

The contrasting frames in Hampton and San Francisco should not be overstated. Hampton's original vision did include the idea that youth were "entitled" to be empowered and respected as citizens, and the Hampton youth commission held a lively public forum at city hall with 240 participants in September 2002 on "the rights of youth," with five lawyers volunteering to help clarify legal issues. In turn, as the San Francisco youth commission has come to recognize that more of its work needs to be focused on long-term transformations of institutional cultures of various city agencies and contracting nonprofits, and not just on policy making and budgets, it has begun to place more emphasis on the language of relationship building and collaboration. Training to map community assets (Kretzmann and McKnight, 1996) reinforces this tendency.

Institutional and Network Capacity

Hampton and San Francisco both have youth commissions with adult staff to support youth leadership and policy development. Each is also embedded in a set of broader institutional and network relationships that shape the overall configuration and relative capacity of their youth civic engagement systems. Because the Hampton system emerged as part of a multi-stakeholder reinventing government initiative, its infrastructure has been progressively reinforced by a collaborative network of civil servants committed to the youth engagement mission through the youth commission and within their own agencies, as well as by a youth services nonprofit that contracts with the city to provide extensive leadership development. Having emerged from grassroots advocacy and a charter revision campaign, San Francisco's system, by contrast, has relatively fewer institutional resources directly supporting the youth commission. But it has network linkages to a greater array of independent youth advocacy and youth organizing groups. With increasing recognition of the need to change institutional cultures, and not just policies and budgets, the San Francisco system shows some convergence with Hampton. The biggest opportunity for this emerged when Margaret Brodkin, the executive director of Coleman Advocates from 1978 to 2004 and the spearhead of many successful advocacy campaigns, was appointed by the mayor to head the Department of Children, Youth, and Their Families in 2004. She has thus been faced with the challenge of making youth empowerment a key component of how a city bureaucracy and its network of grantees operate. In Hampton, there has also been some convergence from the other direction, as Alternatives found it necessary to help develop a youth-led advocacy organization independent of the city in order to fight proposed city budget cuts for leadership training for the youth commissions and various advisory groups.

Hampton's Civic Engagement System

Hampton's system has a number of institutional components that are designed to be complementary and to provide structured pathways for service and leadership development, ranging from the simple and episodic (e.g. service day, stream cleanup) to the more complex and sustained (e.g., youth commission, youth planner). Youth are broadly recruited across the city to enter the most democratic portals of community service and service-learning projects, which are open to virtually everyone, and then are more selectively identified, recruited, trained, and mentored to assume more ambitious leadership roles. At this point, the system stretches from middle school through high school, although young people on the neighborhood youth advisory board or the parks and recreation advisory board might go beyond high-school age. Not everyone who becomes engaged, of course, enters from the lower rungs of the ladder; some are directly recruited to the youth commission as 9th-graders because they have quickly demonstrated leadership potential. But many youth are motivated by the structured pathways that are presented to them visually as a pyramid of opportunities for developing their civic capacities and enabling them to make ever more substantial contributions to the community (Carlson, 2006). Thus when we questioned 14-year-old Michael Bock, a member of the youth commission in 2007 and, before that, of his middle school principal's youth advisory group, on how it happened that he became involved in these various activities, he could point to specific individuals who nurtured his leadership capacity, but finally blurted out, "It's just in the water here!"

The major institutional components of the Hampton system are the following: youth commission, youth planners, principals' advisory groups, superintendent's advisory group, and neighborhood youth advisory group.

Youth commission

The Hampton Youth Commission, established in 1997, is composed of 24 students from four public and three private high schools serving the city. Commissioners serve two-year staggered terms and are recruited through broad outreach to schools, community centers, youth and faith-based organizations, and public meetings. In the spring of 2007, for instance, there were 47 applications for 12 available slots. Students apply and are selected by existing commissioners and adult training partners who may have mentored them in various other leadership capacities, such as the principals' or superintendent's advisory groups, or other neighborhood and faith-based groups, with increasing avenues from middle-school leadership programs as well. This ensures structured pathways of leadership development based on experience, trust, and performance, though all applicants must go through a rigorous set of interviews and group exercises before being chosen. The commission is broadly representative of the youth demographics (race, gender, income) in the city and is intentionally not designed for just an elite group of high GPA students.

During the school year, the commission meets twice a month, once in a work session of the entire commission, with the last 30–45 minutes of the two-hour meeting given over to subcommittee business, and the other as an extended subcommittee session in which almost all the time is devoted to the specific subcommittee projects on which the commission has chosen to work that year. There are three standing subcommittees, each with responsibility for working on two of the six general goals contained in the youth component of the city's official community plan. Each committee organizes a large annual public forum on one issue within its purview, and the commission as a whole organizes one large public forum.

Commissioners thus attend general and committee meetings three to six times a month, sometimes more frequently, depending on the issue, the deliberative public process selected, and their level of commitment. Most of the larger forums are convened in city council chambers, where commissioners sit in the councilors' seats to conduct business. Twice annually, the youth commission presents formally to the city council, which is televised, and to the planning commission. Commissioners commit to active outreach to involve a broad range of young people in commission deliberations, and efforts extend to school groups, teachers, and friendship networks. An outreach video, DVD, and website help in recruitment and publicity. The youth commission published a detailed manual in 2001, recently updated (Carlson and Sykes, 2007), on how to start and improve youth commissions and advisory groups to empower young people.

Youth commissioners develop a progressively more expansive civic skill set through formal training, as well as through various kinds of formal and informal mentoring by a coordinated network of adults and youth within and outside of city government. Newly selected commissioners receive training by Alternatives and more experienced youth leaders during the summer prior to assuming their positions. They typically refer to this as "boot camp," because it signals the discipline and seriousness of their work, although these and other youth events are almost always intermixed with a good dose of creative fun. In addition, the Coalition for Youth, the city office under whose jurisdiction the youth commission falls, provides continual mentoring as well as help with coordination, logistics, and transportation. But the network of mentors in April 2007—all with highly developed civic skills and mind-sets for working with youth and citizens generally—extended to the director of planning, plus a senior and junior planner, the superintendent of parks and recreation, the director of In-SYNC Partnerships between schools and neighborhoods, the director of secondary education, two youth planners, and two individuals who have been vital to building the network of mentors: Cindy Carlson, director of the Coalition for Youth, and Allyson Graul, director of the Youth Civic Engagement Center at Alternatives. Many, if not most, of this network attend the youth commission staff meeting every Tuesday afternoon, when they assist commission and subcommittee chairs in developing agendas and debriefing their various meetings, workgroups, and public events.

Graul, who oversees youth commission and high school leadership training, notes that Hampton utilizes a philosophy of relationship building and close mentoring and coaching of youth commissioners, with continual feedback to enable them to refine their leadership skills. As she notes, "We help them through a process of personal-level learning. But we don't directly worry about their personal development. We tell them, 'You have a job to do, a public role.' And they generally step up to the task." Tamara Whitaker, a youth commissioner in 2000–2002 and member of the school superintendent's youth advisory board, concurred, adding: "Relationship building is essential. People keep coming back because of the relationships." Though without any direct line of influence, this model of relational leadership development is closest to that utilized by the IAF and PICO community organizing networks (Warren, 2001; Wood, 2002).

When the commission meets in open session on an important issue (e.g., diversity in Hampton, youth rights, candidates' forums), the city council chambers are often packed to capacity. In March 2004, the commission hosted a candidates' forum for the city council and mayoral election, using a Wheel-of-Fortune game-show format that other civic groups, such as the League of Women Voters, then borrowed for their own election forums. Youth commission forums typically combine general discussion with lively breakout sessions. The breakouts engage in serious, nuanced deliberation that is facilitated by commissioners in a highly professional manner. Indeed, in observing these and other meetings with the school superintendent, high school principals, and other community partners, one is struck immediately by the poise and skill that youth display as they lead large and small group discussions, brainstorm ideas on flip charts, develop strategies, consult with authorities, plan outreach to parents, teachers, and other youth, and hold each other accountable for the work commitments they make to see a project through to completion.

The mayor and other city officials also bring ideas to the youth commission to consider before making formal policy proposals. In January 2007, for instance, the mayor brought his idea of building a second trade school in the city. He made a half-hour presentation, and youth commissioners questioned him for another 15 minutes or so. In follow-up discussions, the youth commission determined that this was not a very compelling idea, at least in its present form. The existing trade school was currently under enrolled, and the proposal did not address the main reasons behind high school dropout rates. Furthermore, the cost was substantial, and existing high school buildings could use the funding for much needed repairs. As a commission, they felt that they had responsibility to take into account the limited resources available to the city. But how do you turn down the mayor? As 16-year-old commissioner Jaron Scott put it, "We didn't want to stand him down, so we wrote him a letter and said that the dialogue was still open." The letter, signed by commission chair Gregory Harrison, was phrased diplomatically and noted that the commission would consider this or another proposal if it addressed a list of specific concerns. The mayor wrote back thanking the commission, and the proposal was put on hold. As both the planning director and the superintendent of schools told us later, the youth commissioners had zeroed in exactly on the core problems with the trade school idea.

The youth commission, while primarily focused on policy, supports the work of other youth groups in the city through its youth grants, which amount to $40,000 per year, allocated to the commission from general funds. This practice has become commonly known as "youth philanthropy" (Garza and Stevens, 2002). There are two basic grant categories: service and initiatives. Service grants are small, generally several hundred dollars, designed to help a group, such as a youth ministry at a church, with a short service project. Initiatives grants are larger, ranging sometimes as high as $15,000, and are generally tied to the core policy goals of the subcommittees and the community plan. Those groups receiving grants are held accountable for their work by the youth commission—a form of what Archon Fung (2004) calls "accountable autonomy." Commissioners often negotiate with groups over proposals before giving their final approval, and they are encouraged to make site visits. Contracts for the larger initiatives grants, which can run one or two years, require two site visits. Commissioners examine the product, such as the quality and distribution of a youth action magazine they have funded, and even give feedback on the quality of the leadership of the group, in one recent case holding back on further funding until the leadership was reorganized. In 2006–2007, the commission gave out 23 grants, the largest being an initiative grant of $7,500. In years when commissioners feel they don't have enough high-quality proposals, they return money to the city, the first commission ever to do this, which earned it enormous credibility.

Youth planners

The planning department hired two youth planners beginning in 1996 after Terry O'Neill, the director of planning, had an eye-opening experience facilitating a local planning meeting in the Aberdeen neighborhood of the city. "A light bulb came on for me. The room was filled with thirty-somethings and retirees. Where were the young people?" So he decided to convene another dialogue with youth. "Quite frankly, they participated at a better level than the adults."

Youth were then invited to join with adults in neighborhood planning. In fact, O'Neill noted, the youth came up with a much better plan for the proposed recreation area that saved the city tens of thousands of dollars. "I realized that it was in my self-interest to involve youth. . . . I don't like making bad planning decisions and spending money I don't need to."

Youth planners work, on average, 15 hours per week all year round and serve two-year staggered terms, so that a senior youth planner is available to help break in a junior one, typically a rising junior in high school. The senior planner received $8.65 per hour in 2007 and the junior one $8.09 per hour. In any given year, there might be 6–12 applicants for the one open slot, and those chosen have already proven themselves in a range of other leadership roles, such as the youth commission or various youth advisory groups. Thus they start with a good set of skills for running meetings and focus groups, making public presentations, and conducting one-on-ones with other relevant staff and stakeholders. The adult staff members of the planning department are available to help them learn a range of other skills and to mentor them through phases of any given project that they might undertake at the behest of the youth commission. In addition, youth planners conduct research and projects for other youth advisory groups and city departments. Because they have the full cooperation of the school system, they can administer surveys through the schools and move relatively quickly from data collection to writing reports (e.g., on neighborhood youth safety and youth spending power), then to deliberation in the youth commission, and finally to action. Youth planners learn how to conduct and analyze statistically valid surveys, do field observation, analyze census data, use basic GIS and plot mapping tools, conduct design charrettes, and present findings in Excel spreadsheets and Power Point. Though not generally involved in land use and rezoning activities, youth planners have accompanied professional staff to study transportation layout in other cities to help youth determine options for their own bikeways and for bus routes that serve the needs of young people. They provide reports to the city's planning commission for 10 minutes at the beginning of its monthly meetings.

Like other staff members in the planning department, youth planners work as a self-managing team, generally seeking assistance from a half-dozen or so other planners, although they have access to all planning staff, should they need it, and meet with the network of adult mentors for a half hour every week before the Tuesday youth commission executive meeting. Youth planners are treated as full members, not interns, and they attend all staff retreats and similar events. Their office is next to the director's, and they have their own keys to the city hall building and planning department should they wish to come in on weekends or evenings. While their pay is capped for any two-week period, they often put in more than 30 hours because they find the work so interesting and at times urgent.

The youth of Hampton are about to see one of their bigger planning ideas come to fruition: a teen center designed by young people working with professionals. The idea for the center emerged from focus groups and "speak outs," as well as a formal survey of 1,099 teens conducted by the youth planners. Youth who participated in the original planning process in 1998–1999 expressed a strong desire for youth-driven programming and a mixture of activities, including sports, dance, computers, clinics, media center, arts, arcade, meeting rooms, and a recording studio. The center should also provide a "strong sense of membership/ownership" by teens and should have youth participation in governance of the space itself. Youth recognize the need for a safe space with supervision by adults, such as security personnel, but in a way that is not intrusive and does not entail adult dictation (City of Hampton, 1999, 4–14).

When a private health and fitness center became available for purchase, the youth commission had to compromise on some of its original goals, such as location. Then, when the existing center was delayed in moving to a new space, the project lost some of its momentum. But the youth planners returned to the project once a date was announced by the city. Seventeen-year-old senior youth planner Will Bane coordinated a design charrette in the fall of 2006 with the four architects hired by the city. Some 85 young people attended, and youth commissioners facilitated eight groups in brainstorming and priority setting. They drew floor plans and placed ideas on Post-it Notes. They discussed with the architects the safety features of alternative designs. They also designated those elements of the design that were not negotiable, in case the budget would not support everything they wanted. Four groups then carried the work forward: (a) a youth board to determine the details of programming; (b) a multi-stakeholder steering committee that included youth planners and commissioners, but also representatives from business, police, schools, and the neighboring golf course; (c) a project team to oversee the construction phase, with representatives from the Hampton Coalition for Youth, as well as planning, engineering, and parks and recreation; and (d) the Move subcommittee of the youth commission to help plan transportation to and from the center. The teen center was scheduled to open at the end of 2008.

Youth planners in Hampton have also helped develop a *Youth-Friendly Guidebook* and certification program to rate businesses and service organizations and to enable them to learn what it means to become "youth-friendly," if they are not already so. The planners held focus groups throughout the city to determine the criteria that young people felt constituted a welcoming environment. As Alicia Tundidor, one of the youth planners involved at this earlier stage, explained, the focus groups came up with some 75 characteristics, and the planners grouped them into three categories with 21 questions for the initial survey of 240 businesses (to be followed later by nonprofits, community centers, and libraries). The questions concerned such things as cleanliness, respect for youth, safety, youth hiring, and whether youth were followed while on the premises. Youth evaluators, paid through a youth commission grant, conducted the site visits. Those businesses that passed got a youth-friendly window sticker to display in their establishment and a letter of certification, and they were honored at an awards breakfast in council chambers attended by the mayor.

Needless to say, those not making the grade were often upset. But the planners and youth commissioners have offered assistance, via the guidebook and personal consultation, on how to improve in order to attract more young people and win certification. Another round of site surveys is planned. Bradford Knight, a youth commissioner, explained the evaluation process as "realizing the power of youth as consumers," in a vein similar to what political scientist Cliff Zukin and his colleagues (2006) see as the increasingly common practice of youth to be engaged through boycotting and "buycotting." But youth planners and commissioners view the site visits and consultations as an opportunity to build relationships with business owners and supervisors—a relational, community-building variant of the larger phenomenon. As Tundidor noted, "The youth commission and planners were trying to help them pass." In this, as with the other activities she was involved in, "The most important thing in the whole process was the relationship building."

Since the creation of the youth commission, youth have had a formal role in the development of the city's comprehensive plan, which has now been combined with its strategic plan into an overall community plan. The teen center proposal, discussed above, was the key recommendation on youth space emerging from the research, focus groups, and public meetings conducted by the youth commissioners and planners for the 1999 *Youth Component of the Comprehensive Plan.* But youth also focused on issues of transportation, employment, and community interaction. Youth planners in Hampton received a Virginia Planning Award from the American Planning Association's Virginia chapter and honorable mention for the youth component in the 2010 plan, where it competed against adult professional planners as well. After this initial document was developed, the youth commission's comprehensive plan committee continued to conduct surveys and public forums on the plan, worked successfully to get several of its recommendations implemented, and reported regularly to the planning commission and city council. When the new community planning process was set in motion, youth claimed a role as one of the eight main "vision and goals" groups and also provided feedback to the seven other groups, such as healthy business climate, healthy neighborhoods, and diverse community (City of Hampton, 2006). As senior planner Donald Whipple noted, they provided a "youth filter" for the work of all the groups.

To refine their own goals, youth planners and commissioners conducted a new round of surveys and focus groups. As Tundidor recalls, they did at least 50 focus groups in high schools and neighborhoods across the city. "We did ice breakers, . . . had stations around the room, posters, to keep them moving, and divided them into teams to compete for good suggestions." Youth commissioners and planners then organized the results of this public process into six categories of goals: (1) caring relationships, (2) youth share leadership, (3) essential life skills, (4) career preparation for all youth, (5) places to go and things to do, and (6) getting around. Under each goal, they listed specific objectives, backed up by their reasoning and research. This new *Youth Component of the Community Plan* (City of Hampton, 2006), 47 single-spaced pages in all, was officially adopted by the city council, along with the general plan. In order to maintain momentum on implementation, the youth commission then established three subcommittees, each to take continuous responsibility for two of these sets of goals and objectives. At the youth commission's summer retreats, commissioners and planners now decide on the key focus of each subcommittee for the school year, so that momentum is established early in the fall when the new commission formally convenes.

Principals' advisory groups

Each public high school in Hampton has a principal's advisory group. Members meet with the principal on a regular basis and typically run the meetings themselves, though with training by Alternatives staff. Like the youth commission meetings, they plan and brainstorm in a deliberative fashion and have rigorous standards of accountability for follow-through on commitments. Some schools have more ambitious projects and more extensive participation than others, of course, but most deal with a range of issues such as peer mediation training, youth-to-youth mentoring, school safety, and inclusion of students who feel left out due to teasing and bullying. Most now have projects aimed at transforming attitudes and behavior on sexual harassment and dating violence. The advisory groups plan events such as student-teacher breakfasts. Some tackle academic improvement issues as well as staff hiring, including in at least one case the search for a principal.

At Kecoughtan High School, with some 1,900 students, the Principal's Advisory and Consulting Team (PACT) meets monthly with the principal in an evening session, and various committees meet during the week. Participation has varied over the years, from a core group of 20 active students to as many as 60–100 working on various projects. Principal Arnold Baker has become a believer in "youth as resources." He began with a dialogue group when he was a 6th-grade teacher, and then developed an advisory group when he became a middle-school principal. As principal of Kecoughtan, he initially utilized this dialogue and gripe session model. But when the city received some grant money to train youth, he says, "We shifted to partnerships and became project oriented in order to improve the school." As a result, the number of students involved increased substantially. He also set strict rules that the PACT meetings were not a venue for complaints against specific teachers—"no names," he tells them. Most teachers have come along. "Teachers often don't want to give up power to kids. But we are not equals. We are partners."

With a core group of teachers and administrators in support of its civic problem-solving work in the school, the Improving Student Achievement committee and others on PACT at Kecoughtan High initiated a project in 2001 on how to make classrooms more stimulating. Keisha Ashe, vice chair of the committee, noted that "teachers felt very restricted by the SOLs [Virginia's standards of learning], so we decided to get more creative ideas . . . and to create stronger bonds with teachers." Students interviewed other students, as well as teachers they especially respected, and then classified effective teacher practices and attitudes into categories, such as teacher ability to build relationships, manage the classroom, create high expectations, manage time, and engage students as resources in learning. PACT then published the *Kecoughtan High School Idea Book* filled with innovative learning techniques, pictures of teachers and students working together, quotations from famous educators and leaders, and small tips to help all teachers create a caring and learning environment. They distributed it to all teachers. Much impressed with the product, Baker agreed to use the booklet in new teacher orientation at the beginning of the next school year and to have PACT leaders serve as co-facilitators of training. Several years later, the students decided to develop a second, more substantial edition of the *Idea Book*, using the developmental assets framework more systematically, but weaving their own heartfelt experience and field research around the eight assets they chose as relevant for school, such as commitment to learning, boundaries and expectations, social competencies, and constructive use of time. They convened youth/adult forums to get more ideas and examples, and then held a roundtable editing session paying much more careful attention to the language that adults would find convincing. Instead of waiting for fall orientation of new teachers, they presented the revised product at faculty meetings on May 7–8, 2007, and engaged the teachers in a "scavenger hunt" as a reflective learning exercise. While there are certainly skeptics among the faculty—one teacher was overheard saying, "I feel welcome. Can I go now?"—the school deeply respects the practical knowledge of students as a democratic resource and utilizes it to inform the professional practice of teachers in their school community.

The principals' advisory groups in the public high schools have systematically taken on issues of sexual harassment and violence, as well as verbal and physical bullying. With funding from the Center for Injury and Violence Prevention at the state department of health, Alternatives, along with youth leaders from the advisory groups, developed a peer trainers' manual based on national research and participatory pedagogy. It then began to provide rigorous two-day training sessions for classroom peer education in 9th-grade health classes. The RELATE project (Relationship Education Leading Adolescents Toward Empowerment) aims to enhance students' understanding of sexual and peer violence and to engage them in developing competencies for recognizing and resisting it, while building healthy relations based on respect. Working in pairs in classes that range in size from 12 to 30 and utilizing creative skits and role-playing, peer trainers lead a weeklong module, generally with the health teacher or some other staff member present but not playing any direct role in the instruction. Shauna and Imani Adams, twins who served as RELATE trainers at Phoebus High School through their 10th, 11th, and 12th grades, became trainers as an extension of their other work on the principal's advisory group because, as Imani noted, "we see harassment every day." Lydia Huey, a trainer at Bethel High School, added, "I really wanted my younger brother and his friends to get what was happening, to change the way they act."

The RELATE project at Phoebus, with 12 peer trainers in 2006–2007, encompassed the entire 9th-grade class, more than 400 students in all. As part of the 100-member school band, Shauna and Imani Adams were able to recruit other trainers through its networks and to leverage its prestige in getting students to take their work seriously—including a prominent football player who laughed off the training in his freshman year but later came around as a big supporter. Their approach is not just to teach a discrete set of classes and hope for behavioral changes, but also to help establish and nurture lasting networks of support among students, as well as between students and teachers, throughout the school year. While the pre- and post-test survey of attitudes that accompanies each RELATE module shows a positive impact, the student trainers stress how much they see a change in actual behavior—less visible harassment, greater use of assertive language and boundary setting. To the extent that sexual and other forms of harassment and peer violence limit youth—and especially girls—from becoming full citizens in the public square (Sapiro, 1993; Fullwood, 2001), Hampton's young leaders have been hard at work trying to ensure that no one feels excluded from the school polity as a result of being physically, sexually, or emotionally intimidated.

Superintendent's youth advisory group

The superintendent's advisory group involves student representatives from all the city's public high schools. Some two dozen student members generally attend the two evening meetings every month, which are facilitated by Alternatives. One of the monthly meetings is devoted to planning and work groups for various policy issues on the advisory group's agenda, which they set during a one-day retreat at the beginning of the school year, then revise as needed during the year. At these meetings, the Alternatives staff also works to build the civic skill set of the commissioners: making public presentations, doing one-on-ones with public officials and other adult stakeholders, facilitating workshops and focus groups, and doing research to help refine issues and develop policy agendas over a multiyear period. Dinner with the superintendent and the director of secondary schools starts off the other monthly meeting, followed by a lively community building exercise, such as circular rhythm-sticks, where all (including school officials) tap complex rhythms with those around them. Discussion then turns to serious matters of district policy. School officials display no sign of "professional knows best," but listen carefully and work collaboratively toward mutually acceptable solutions in an atmosphere that is at once thoughtfully deliberative and playfully energizing.

During the 2005–2006 school year, the superintendent's youth advisory group took up the issue of guidance counseling in the high schools, about which students citywide had voiced serious discontent. To get a better sense of what students felt the problems were, youth advisors began with one-on-ones with their peers, including members of the principals' youth advisories, with whom they often consult. They continued their one-on-ones with guidance counselors and other key stakeholders. The conclusion they came to from the one-on-ones was that guidance counselors often just did not have enough time to do adequate and timely counseling because they had become loaded down with responsibilities related to testing and Virginia's standards of learning. The youth advisory board then worked up a proposal for the superintendent that included two options: (1) hire a testing coordinator in each high school to unburden the guidance counselors, or (2) reassign staff to try to achieve the same result, so that guidance counselors could focus primarily on high-quality and timely guidance. In response, the superintendent created a new testing coordinator position in each school, largely by redesigning the registrar's role, thus enabling the school system to meet the students' policy proposals without spending nearly as much money as creating four new positions would require.

The superintendent's advisory group addressed the issue of service and service-learning policy in high schools during the 2006–2007 school year, although it had begun planning even earlier. Service-learning has developed at a slower pace in Hampton than in many other cities and certainly more slowly than anticipated in the original 1993 report and vision statement to the city council. Alternatives began by offering a yearlong leadership development course enrolling students from all four public high schools. With funding from a State Farm grant, as well as from Alternative's Youth Innovation Fund grant from the Kellogg Foundation, Hampton then piloted an 8th-grade course based on Project Citizen, a curriculum developed by the national Center for Civic Education with earmarked dollars from Congress. A public policy–based form of service-learning, Project Citizen requires students to collectively select a policy issue in their school, neighborhood, or city, determine what the problem is, and then develop a proposal for policy change and implementation.

The superintendent's youth advisory group made community service and service-learning an agenda priority for high schools when the superintendent asked the group to take up the specific question of mandatory service hours as a requirement for graduation. The youth advisors' initial deliberations revealed strong resistance to any mandates, so they decided to do a survey that might yield deeper insight into the patterns and preferences for volunteering among high school students. The survey showed a strong desire for greater opportunities to volunteer, as well as a strong preference to become engaged through school and with their friends. After further deliberation, the advisory group endorsed the idea of service-learning, as well as a graduation seal noting the number of hours of community service performed. Since this did not match up with the initial agenda of Superintendent Patrick Russo, he decided to bring the issue to a top administrative staff meeting at the end of the 2005–2006 school year. To his surprise, he got only two questions from his staff: "Have you asked students in the International Baccalaureate Program?" and "Have you considered service-learning for elementary schools?" After no further questions were forthcoming, he responded, "So can I take your silence as a yes for service-learning?" And the entire staff nodded in clear approval.

However, this was only the beginning of a yearlong process in which the policy design was researched, refined, and then finally approved by the school board in May 2007. The youth advisors did some preliminary research over the summer of 2006 and then brought the issue to the school board in October, which requested that a full policy proposal be presented by the end of the school year. Director of Secondary Education Donna Woods asked the youth advisors a fundamental question: "Do you want to own this policy, or do you want to turn it over to the school system?" And the advisors were clear in their response: "No, we want to own it." So they began much more systematic research on service-learning around the country. They looked at models in Philadelphia and Chicago, as well as in Michigan, New Hampshire, and Vermont.

They examined studies on mandated requirements and impacts on student achievement. According to Woods, who attended the advisory group meetings, the work groups did meticulous research on different aspects of service-learning and the general meetings engaged in "a very deep discourse." They also met with principals, teachers, and students in Hampton to better understand the opportunities and constraints. Youth advisors Eliott Clark, Yana Kupke, and Carmen Hills, along with school and Alternatives staff, visited with experts in Washington, DC, including Nelda Brown, director of the National Service-Learning Partnership, and Kenny Holdsman, deputy director of the Campaign for the Civic Mission of Schools. This traveling team of three youth and two adults also made a side trip to Stafford County, which had the best known service-learning model in Virginia, though one different than that which the Hampton advisory group eventually developed.

The group's design called for a multiyear rollout, beginning in the second year with the 12th-grade government classes, which did not have state standards of learning, followed by world geography (9th grade) and world history (10th grade), and finally by U.S. history (11th grade). By the end of the five-year rollout period, students in every grade in high school would have at least one service-learning opportunity each year, and teachers in these subjects would be required to offer at least one opportunity in one of their courses every year. Teams of teachers would work across these and other disciplines to develop their service-learning curricula. During the first year of the rollout (2007–2008), a planning coalition of students, parents, teachers, administrators, and community groups would work on the details of implementation.

In addition to doing Internet-based and field research, building relationships through research one-on-ones with teachers and principals, deliberating among themselves and with top school officials in the advisory group's monthly meetings, and developing an actual policy proposal, the youth advisors had hoped to do one-on-ones with school board members before the board's upcoming meeting. But, as Eliott Clark, a 17-year-old senior from Kecoughtan High School and member of the traveling research team, told us, "The timelines were a roadblock," especially given the advisors' other commitments to school, work, and still other activist projects in which they were involved. Nonetheless, at the school board meeting of May 1, 2007, nearly the entire advisory group attended, and several presented the results of their research and their proposed plan. What most impressed the school board, according to Ann Bane, director of community and legislative relations for the Hampton City Schools, was not just the thoroughness of the students' research and their polished presentation but also the fact that "they just came back so passionate" from their trip to

Washington and that when questioned by the school board on topics for which they had not prepared, "to the school board's amazement, they were so good at thinking on their feet." The board passed the proposal unanimously.

Facing relentless fiscal and demographic pressure, with an aging white population becoming increasingly disconnected from the majority school-age black population, Russo and his administrative team also decided to launch an annual Community Priorities Workshop that builds upon the city's early designs for collaborative planning for youth, as well as his own experiences with the youth advisory group. On February 25, 2005, 140 people participated in the first three-hour workshop and developed a set of six broad goals. Participants represented a broad range of stakeholder groups, including students, parents, administrators, teachers, elected officials (city council, school board, constitutional officers), city personnel, higher education, neighborhoods, civic organizations, realtors, military, business, and faith communities. Each stakeholder group was chosen so as to include broad representation based on age, race, gender, and geography. Stakeholder groups met separately and then in mixed groups to refine the goals, which the school board then adopted as divisionwide community priority goals. The superintendent tasked each central administrative department and individual school with developing three to five simple and quantifiable written objectives, resulting in some 200 tools to implement the six goals. As a result of continued collaboration among stakeholders during the following year, teachers were given a substantial raise, the board agreed to finance significant new school construction, seven new school/church partnerships were created, the first preschool for children ages 3 and 4 was started, and student's AYP (Adequate Yearly Progress) scores rose more than 20 percent. Critical for democratic legitimacy in this demographically asymmetrical community, 95.9 percent of the community reported in a survey that they now understood the school division's mission and vision. After its second year, the school system's community priorities workshop won a prestigious award from Virginia Tech University's School of Education.

San Francisco's Youth Commission and Engagement System

San Francisco's system of youth engagement has fewer formally authorized components than Hampton, but a richer set of network linkages to independent youth advocacy and youth organizing groups. With the Department of Children, Youth, and Their Families (DCYF) playing a more energetic and strategic role in changing the culture of its own agency over the past few years, as well as providing grant incentives and youth-led evaluation of its contracting nonprofits to make youth leadership and youth-initiated projects more central to their work, San Francisco's system is now building capacity in a more integrative manner.

The San Francisco Youth Commission is composed of 17 youth between 12 and 23 years of age. While a smaller number than in Hampton, especially relative to the size of its population, the commission can draw upon college-age youth from local universities, which are far more numerous than in Hampton. This enhances its policy-analytic potential, especially given some institutional partners (e.g., San Francisco State University, University of California–San Francisco, University of California–Berkeley) that place a high value on service-learning and civic engagement among its students. Commissioners are recruited and selected through an application process, in which the adult staff play a major role. The pathways of recruitment are diverse, and as in Hampton, staff seek those who have generally proven their leadership capacity in a variety of settings, as the bios posted on its website as well as our interviews clearly show. Final approval of staff recommendations, however, rests with the supervisors and mayor. Each of 11 supervisors gets to pick one youth commissioner; the mayor gets one regular choice, plus five additional ones to ensure diversity on the commission.

Commissioners receive training during a two-and-a-half-day retreat over the summer that covers the basics of the commission's role within San Francisco's city government, team building among commissioners themselves, and advocacy skills. Some mini-trainings are conducted periodically on public speaking, legislation, budgets, and related skills, and a midyear retreat helps commissioners assess and refocus, if necessary. The commission has three adult staff, who are skilled and highly committed to the mission of youth empowerment. Compared to Hampton, however, they tend to be considerably younger, receive less pay, and have higher turnover. When Hampton's network of other senior civil servants who serve as mentors to the youth commissioners and youth planners is factored in, along with long-term mentors from Alternatives, it seems clear that there are considerably fewer city resources devoted to training and mentoring in San Francisco's youth commission. The adult staff in San Francisco are conscious of the impact of such limited resources. With more to work with, they could provide greater training to the commissioners themselves and build capacity for a far-reaching peer-to-peer training network across the city, utilizing both commissioners and youth leaders from other organizations (e.g., Center for Young Women's Development, Chinatown Community Development Center, Youth United for Community Action, Homies Organizing the Mission [District] to Empower Youth, Oasis for Girls). Since many youth organizations, as well as youth engagement projects within larger community development and advocacy organizations, operate in silos that are often ethnically and racially based, the youth commission staff and leadership aspire to provide much greater connectivity and coordination.

While relatively smaller and understaffed compared with Hampton, the youth commission in San Francisco is active on a wide range of fronts: legislative and budget reviews, advice and advocacy, convening public forms, funding youth-initiated projects, and conducting periodic citywide "youth votes" to register the views of young people, especially before city elections.

Legislative and budget review

The primary mission of the youth commission, as established in the city charter revisions of November 7, 1995, is to collect information, identify concerns and needs, develop and propose plans, and review and comment on all proposed legislation and budgets impacting on youth. The scope of the latter task is broad, and because the commission is required to respond within 12 days, much of its agenda is driven by the array of policy and budget proposals or regulatory revisions that are continually sent its way by the board of supervisors or city departments. Thus the commission can, at any given meeting, consider a resolution urging the department of public works to engage in more vigorous efforts to reduce graffiti citywide or one urging the mayor's office on homelessness to implement and modify existing homeless service benchmarks. It can consider a resolution urging the police department to de-prioritize criminalizing sex workers and prioritize instead convicting those who attack sex workers. In times of fiscal crunch, the commissioners can review proposed budget cuts to youth programs and suggest alternative savings from efficiencies in other departments, such as fire and police. Or it can recommend budgetary or zoning action for a specific community center or street intersection.

With staff support from the commission's adult policy coordinator, as well as regular consultation with Coleman Advocates, the city supervisor's staff, and other individuals and groups that might make their case at commission meetings, the youth commissioners seem to do a reasonably good job of deliberating and making recommendations on this broad range of policy issues. Their dependence on staff and professional advocates for help in refining their positions is not all that different than that of the city supervisors themselves. At the committee level, however, youth commissioners get greater opportunity to gather information more systematically and to develop more robust and long-term strategies.

Public forums

A good example of committee work that led to collaborative policy proposals and strategies is sexual assault and harassment in schools. An early task force of the youth commission worked with the Commission on the Status of Women—now a full city department—to improve services and leadership skills among girls and young women, and also developed educational workshops with San Francisco Women Against Rape. Some momentum on these issues was maintained by the Department on the Status of Women (DOSW), as well as by peer training in some high schools. After a highly publicized incident of sexual assault at Wallenberg High School, however, the youth commission's ad hoc Sexual Assault and Harassment Prevention Committee teamed up with the Student Advisory Council (SAC) of the San Francisco Unified School District (SFUSD), composed of two representatives from each public high school, to hold a public hearing on April 1, 2004. Youth commissioners Constance Mourning and Peter Lauterborn opened the hearing by making clear that its purpose was not "to point fingers" at anyone but to figure out the scope of the problem, best practices already in use for reporting and prevention, and how various city and county departments and SFUSD could further support students and school communities. Testimony and research were presented by a broad range of actors: Student Leaders Against Sexual Harassment, SAC, DOSW, Equal Rights Advocates, Peer Resources, Office of Adolescent Health of the city/county health department, SFUSD board members and staff, and the police department's School Resource Officer (SRO) program. After the hearing, Lauterborn was invited to write an op-ed for the *San Francisco Chronicle* (Lauterborn, 2004), in which he reiterated that the youth commission's approach was not to point fingers but to engage "all stakeholders," institutional and organizational ones, as well as students, parents, and teachers. The issue, he wrote movingly, "comes from our own relationships with people who have been victimized. . . . This has affected far too many of our closest friends and loved ones. This is a community issue that deserves a community response. This is why the Youth Commission is making the elimination of this threat from our schools a top priority."

Commissioners on the task force, led by Lauterborn, then proceeded to research the issue further, guided by suggestions from various participants at the hearing, as well as by further input from students. The following year they issued a detailed report (San Francisco Youth Commission, 2005) that reviewed relevant federal and state laws, national statistics, and their own survey findings from 6,000 local students. They examined efforts already in place, identified gaps, and outlined components of a strategy across various institutions. The report urged DSOW to conduct a public service announcement campaign in schools similar to the "Respect Is What's Sexy" campaign they had done for adult men, as well as build upon the video that Galileo High School students produced with Peer Resources. The report also urged that DSOW assign a liaison to the school system and that the mayor's school liaison take up this issue as well. It urged private and charter schools to follow the teacher training for handling student-to-student sexual harassment that SFUSD had put into effect after the initial public hearing that the youth commission convened, and for all schools to enrich their health curricula and collaborate with relevant community-based organizations. Although some advocates had discouraged using police in the schools, and the youth commission had a history of such stances (Checkoway, Allison, and Montoya, 2005), the report urged a genuine partnership of students and SROs in facilitating sexual assault and harassment workshops, another indication of a shift toward collaboration that we discuss further below.

Transforming Agency Culture

Because of its roots in a broad reinventing government strategy, Hampton's innovators have held from the beginning that youth civic engagement can realize its potential only if there is corresponding culture change in institutions, including administrative agencies of city government. Youth volunteering and having a voice are not enough; adults must change their own behavior at a deeper level. Administrators and professionals must encourage productive public work by young people. They must share expert knowledge, recognize youth as resources for problem solving, value their special insights, and offer public challenges of consequence to the life of the city. By contrast, given its roots in contentious grassroots advocacy, San Francisco's youth commission did not begin with such a strong focus on institutional culture change, but has moved increasingly in this direction over time.

Hampton's culture change strategy

The Hampton Coalition for Youth plays the key role in a coordinated, citywide strategy of institutional culture change. As former assistant city manager Mike Montieth explained, the coalition's role is to "catalyze best practices" and "establish a learning community throughout city government, not to run programs." The Coalition serves as a clearinghouse for youth development and capacity-building practices for agencies and other organizations. It coordinates the city's "youth as resources" and "developmental assets" strategies. Its budget (approximately $400,000) funds a small staff, as well as contracts for training and facilitation services by Alternatives (beyond the nonprofit's contract with the school system). The Coalition also helps raise money from national foundations to help the city continue to innovate. Cindy Carlson, its director from the beginning, serves as the key relational organizer within city government, including its top departmental and elected leadership. She reports directly to the city manager and mayor.

The planning department and school system, as we have seen, have made youth engagement a core component of how they conduct their business. The Neighborhood Office has also helped engage young people in neighborhood projects and planning. A product of the same collaborative planning that led to the creation of the Coalition for Youth as a city agency, the Neighborhood Office (along with local volunteers) set about helping neighborhood associations in the 56 neighborhoods consolidate around 10 planning districts. It also lent assistance to strengthen and build associations in neighborhoods where they were underdeveloped (Bayer and Potapchuk, 2004). The office operates on principles of assets-based community development (Kretzmann and McKnight, 1996) and provides small matching grants and larger neighborhood improvement funds for local projects. Working with the school system, the Neighborhood Office's InSYNC (Innovations for Schools, Youth, Neighborhoods, and Communities) partnerships operate through a network of some 40 organizations and their youth and adult volunteers—Girls, Inc., Boys and Girls Club, Foster Grandparents, United Way, Hampton University Leadership Program, and various city agencies—to provide after-school and community-based education programs. InSYNC has been recognized with a National Civic Star Award by the American Association of School Administrators. Neighborhood College, also sponsored by the office, provides courses in local government as well as neighborhood leadership development. While the courses began with an emphasis on how government works, the college has shifted much more in recent years to building partnerships with government, including youth/adult partnerships. The Neighborhood Commission, with representatives from all 10 districts, along with faith and school communities, other institutions, and city government, has two youth members. Youth also serve on a citywide Neighborhood Youth Advisory Board (NYAB).

To be sure, not all neighborhood associations or planning districts are as inclusive of youth as they might be. Neighborhood associations tend to be dominated by older homeowners, many of whom see young people as threats to neighborhood safety, appearance, and quietude. This has been changing as younger families move into many neighborhoods and as the Neighborhood Office has focused more attention on engaging youth. To become a "registered neighborhood," associations are now required to do a self-assessment every two years, which includes how they have been involving young people as assets.

Associations receive assistance from the capacity committee of the Neighborhood Office to help them figure out how to engage youth more effectively. Shellae Blackwell, a senior neighborhood development specialist and a member of the original youth coalition in the early 1990s, reflected in 2007 on the long learning process involved: "Fourteen years ago, when we started this, youth were viewed as problems. But with the help of the capacity committee [in the registering and assessment process], more neighborhoods are identifying youth engagement as important, especially in the last six years or so. It's become more a part of the culture."

The parks and recreation department has two youth on its nine-person advisory board. Superintendent Art Thatcher, who has a deep appreciation of the range of pathways for engaging youth, noted that in a resource-poor city, it is even more important to find ways to get young people to contribute: "We have little money, so we involve as many people as possible." Former superintendent Laurine Press, deeply committed to youth participation for many years, believes that the more voice young people have, the more they will utilize the facilities and programs. "They are my customers, just as if they were adult customers," she noted in a 2002 interview. But they are not just customers, she cautioned; they are also "citizens" who have the responsibility to engage directly in constructive dialogue and problem solving with local residents who may fear a skateboard park in their neighborhood or who are upset at late night basketball or profanity on the court in the presence of young children. To develop the ethos and skill at the street level for youth participation and co-ownership, Press and Thatcher have provided staff with three-day training sessions through Alternatives. They have also been energetic in getting their staff to participate in the BEST (Building Exemplary Systems of Training for Youth Workers) Initiative, which is a national training program to upgrade the professional skills of young workers, including their capacity to facilitate youth participation (Academy for Educational Development, 2002). Alternatives serves as a core partner both locally and nationally in this initiative. Youth on the Parks and Recreation advisory board have provided input to ensure that more recreation suits the needs of young people. But they are instructed that they are on the board to represent the needs of the entire community, not just youth. And they are challenged to imagine the kinds of recreation they would like to see for their own children. They do not approve of programs just because they are directed at youth, and they can be rigorous in evaluating, and sometimes rejecting, proposals for youth recreation.

The police department has also included youth as part of its larger community policing strategy in what is known as Y-COPE (Youth Community-Oriented Policing). A school resource officer program places officers in schools, where they perform traditional policing duties, but also build relationships and trust, provide mentoring, and teach law modules in classes. The department has sponsored a Citizens Police Academy as well as a Youth Citizens Police Academy. Youth and police have also written a curriculum for the police academy that embodies the principles and practices of "youth as resources" and "police as servants of youth," which aims to move beyond programs to deeper culture change. Officers meet to develop strategies with neighborhood associations, local youth groups, and NYAB representatives. Several neighborhoods initially targeted for Y-COPE reduced juvenile crime by half and received the Governor's Excellence in Safety Award. As detective Tony Perkins noted of the collaborative Y-COPE work at a 2002 community meeting, "In our group [in Newtown], we vote. My vote counts only as one. If I am outvoted by youth, that's OK." Youth leaders are trained to educate the community about domestic violence and to organize "speak outs" among previously incarcerated residents. Officers are recognized and rewarded for their work with youth and communities. In 2002, for example, Perkins and William Davis were named among six "exemplary assets builders" in the city, and Davis was named "detective of the year" and promoted to captain, with special recognition for his youth work.

San Francisco's culture change strategy

The primary mission of the youth commission, as established in the city charter revisions of November 7, 1995, was to collect information, identify concerns and needs, develop and propose plans, and review and comment on proposed legislation and budgets. Changing the culture of agencies and nonprofit contractors was not an explicit charge. However, the charter did recognize that the youth commission should conduct its work by developing "personal contact" with a broad range of youth, civic, church, service, and business organizations, as well as with school officials and citywide neighborhood planning collaborative efforts for children, youth, and families. In the early years, this mission was relatively submerged by the enormous press of work to review legislation and budgets, especially on the tight 12-day schedule required by the board of supervisors, as well as by the primacy of the youth rights frame and efforts at citywide mobilization through youth summits. But the issue of agency culture change, enabled by the chartered mission of relationship building and collaboration, increasingly came to the fore as youth commissioners recognized that they would have to work with specific agencies over a period of years to effect lasting change.

By the time of our 2001–2002 interviews, this trend was already evident. The recreation and parks department had brought in members of the youth commission to assess all recreation centers in the city. The public health department had set up a youth advisory board to help it develop strategies for teaching high school students about the intersection of environmental health and social justice. The Committee on the Status of Women collaborated with the youth commission's task force on sexual assault of girls and young women to develop educational workshops across the city. DCYF had just established a citizens' advisory council composed of eight adults and four youth, and its community liaison had previously been a staffer of the youth commission. DCYF had also facilitated a coordinated citywide planning process for children and youth services, which included a youth-led evaluation component known as Youth IMPACT. In 2001, youth conducted evaluations of 40 DCYF-funded community-based organizations (CBOs). They were trained to develop performance measures of CBOs based on their own experiences. Youth in Focus, a nonprofit consulting and training organization (associated with the Tides Center), which supports youth-led research, evaluation, and planning, helped in this process. The stated goal was for Youth IMPACT to help make youth-led evaluation part of "the way the City does business."

The big opportunity came, as noted earlier, when Margaret Brodkin of Coleman Advocates was appointed to head DCYF in 2004 under Mayor Gavin Newsom. With the growth of revenues in the Children's Fund that Brodkin had pioneered, the previous mayor, Willie Brown, had been persuaded to establish DCYF as a full city department, and a referendum in 2000 reauthorized the fund with an increase to 3 cents per $100 of assessed property taxes ($33 million in 2007). Brodkin had long-standing commitments to youth empowerment and also had enormous experience in working with a variety of city systems and nonprofit institutions. Her fingerprints are all over the long-term strategy to transform the city to support youth civic engagement, as are those of her successor as Coleman's executive director, N'Tanya Lee, who had been youth empowerment coordinator and trainer for the youth commission and project director of Coleman's Youth Making a Change.

Culture change at DCYF and its network of nonprofit grantees proceeds on a number of fronts. First, youth are represented on important committees that set policy and guide evaluation, namely, the Children's Fund Citizens Advisory Committee and a recently established "youth team" within the agency, which is being trained and supervised by the Youth Leadership Institute, a major youth development and leadership training nonprofit in the Bay Area. Second, the Youth Empowerment Fund (YEF), a categorical set aside of 3 percent of the children's fund (roughly $1 million in 2007), goes exclusively to youth-initiated projects, and several youth commissioners sit on its advisory board. Third, and perhaps most important over the long run, is that a broader category of "youth leadership/youth-initiated projects" has been included in all funding applications from local nonprofits serving children, youth, and families. In the most recent funding cycle (as of mid-2007), we count 126 grants that included this category, out of a total of 290 given by the agency. Some clearly do not represent robust models of youth civic engagement and may just be add-ons to improve funding chances, but a good number of others represent clear attempts to make youth leadership an important part of how a program or an entire nonprofit agency operates. With continued leadership from the top of DCYF, energetic work by the youth team in consulting and evaluation, and a network learning strategy (Agranoff, 2007; Light, 1998) across the array of youth-serving nonprofits in the city, DCYF's grants have the potential to play a powerfully transformative role in the nonprofit sector.

In addition, Brodkin chairs the mayor's policy council on children, youth, and families, and several others with strong youth empowerment frames sit on it as well, such as N'Tanya Lee and Iqra Anjum, the 20-year-old chair of the youth commission in 2007. Anjum has also served on the advisory council of the juvenile probation department, which under director William Siffermann has developed peer leadership among youth exiting and entering the system to enable more successful transition. Perhaps most important for the long-term prospects of agency culture change is that the mayor has asked all department heads to develop a "youth inclusion" strategy. Brodkin coordinates this interagency effort, and Rachel Antrobus, staff director of the youth commission (as of 2007), has worked closely with her in aligning the various committees of the commission with a culture change strategy for each relevant city department. Through a different path than in Hampton, we now can begin to see a San Francisco network of innovators working strategically across multiple agencies to change organizational cultures to support youth civic engagement. The more this occurs, the more likely will the collaborative charge of the youth commission become more prominent, though not without greater investments in training commissioners to be effective relational organizers, in addition to policy advocates.

Networks for Learning and Diffusion

Hampton and San Francisco, while clearly leaders in city-sponsored innovations that engage youth in community problem solving and policy development, are hardly alone. As we noted in the introduction, other cities have been implementing a range of similar innovations. While there are no hard figures on how many have done so or with what staying power, the pace seems to have picked up in recent years. In this section, we provide a brief overview of these networks, and in the following section we consider a federal "policy design for democracy" (Ingram and Smith, 1993; Schneider and Ingram, 1997; Sirianni, 2009a) that could further strengthen them and promote diffusion both more broadly and with deeper culture change impacts within city agencies and non-profit youth organizations contracting with them.

There have been two main nodes of network learning (Agranoff, 2007; Goldsmith and Eggers, 2004; Wenger, McDermott, and Snyder, 2002) and diffusion (Rogers, 1995) over the past decade, each intersecting with the other and with several other youth development intermediaries. These are the National League of Cities (NLC) and Hampton's various champions active on the national stage.

The NLC, founded in 1924 as the American Municipal Association, advocates in Washington, DC, for cities and towns and provides various forms of training, education, and best-practice toolkits for its members, of which there are now some 1,600 of all sizes, as well as state municipal leagues that represent some 18,000 communities in all. In 1998, responding to local innovators as well as to the rising national focus on youth empowerment and civic engagement, NLC began encouraging elected officials to bring youth (ages 15–18) to its national conferences, especially its annual Congress of Cities, where there is a three-hour youth forum as well as other sessions to which youth are invited to contribute. Of the 5,000 city representatives typically in attendance, several hundred are youth, and they and many adult leaders attend the sessions designed to profile best city practices in youth commissions, youth philanthropy, and service and service-learning. In 2000, under the leadership of Mayor Thomas Menino of Boston, which developed its own mayor's youth council in 1994, NLC established the Institute for Youth, Education, and Families (IYEF), one of whose focus areas has been youth participation and youth development. Originally under the direction of John Kyle and now under Leon Andrews, the participation group has been active in promoting youth commissions and councils, among other models, at its national meetings, through dedicated trainings with a select number of cities, and through its widely used toolkit, *Promoting Youth Participation*. NLC now has a website called YouthScape (*www.nlc.org/IYEF/networks_assistance/youth_network/youthscape.aspx*), which provides a list of (and many links to) over 200 youth councils across the country, as well as periodic profiles and news updates. Several state leagues of cities—most notably California, Michigan, Indiana, and Florida—have also provided active support for the youth commission model, with diffusion in California also getting significant support from the Youth Leadership Institute and the San Francisco model.

Hampton's innovators provide the second major network for learning and diffusion. Several partners in Hampton have been especially important in national work: the Coalition for Youth, Alternatives, and Onsite Insights, a small consulting group headed by Richard Goll, the founding director of Alternatives. In various configurations, these Hampton innovators have engaged in network leadership and learning activities on a broad scale. First, they have presented the Hampton model at national conferences and training workshops, such as those sponsored by NLC, YMCA of the USA, Search Institute, National 4-H Council, Coalition of Community Foundations for Youth, National Youth Advocacy Coalition, Pew-sponsored Youth Civic Engagement Project, Habitat for Humanity, and others. Second, as noted above, they have been core partners in the BEST Initiative, especially in developing the youth participation components of its Advancing Youth Development curriculum, which includes the basic course modules and various toolkits for supervisors of youth workers and facilitators of training. BEST is housed at the National Training Institute for Community Youth Work (NTI) at the Academy for Educational Development (AED), and it has 18 city and regional training partners across the country participating in the project (National BEST Network), as well as a still broader network of local institutional partners, such as YMCAs, 4-H clubs, parks and recreation departments, after-school programs, Boys and Girls Clubs, Girls Scouts, neighborhood associations, youth ministries, and community colleges. Approximately 10,000 youth workers and supervisors have received training through BEST since 1996. Third, Hampton was a grantee and learning partner in the Kellogg Foundation's Youth Innovation Fund for several years, an important though much smaller network. Fourth, Hampton innovators have provided intensive consulting—often with Hampton's most accomplished youth leaders on the consulting team—to cities and counties interested in youth commissions, culture change strategies, and youth master planning (e.g., City of Brighton, 2007). Fifth, in addition to a variety of other training materials crafted for specific venues, Hampton's manual on youth commissions (Carlson and Sykes, 2007, updated from 2001) remains the best in the field, with distribution not only through Hampton itself but also through its listing in many resource guides in the youth development and youth civic engagement fields.

Finally, as winner of a 2005 Innovations in Government Award, Hampton has been able to convene leadership teams from 10 cities. These 10 cities have utilized various leverage points to advance youth engagement. Sacramento, for instance, established a rather narrow youth commission through the parks and recreation department, then shifted the pivot to the mayor's commission on youth development, whose agenda was approved by city council. Sacramento has now established an office of youth development in the city manager's office, with the goal of building upon more robust models such as Hampton and other cities in California. In Portland, Oregon, the mayor sponsored a public process that led to a Constitutional Convention on the Rights of Children and Youth, with a Bill of Rights for Children approved by the city council in 2006 and by Multnomah County in 2007. The mayor's office, which has also sponsored a broad community visioning process (visionPDX), then worked with the county to develop a joint city/county youth commission and hired two youth planners to work in the city's planning bureau. With a key staff member coming from the San Francisco youth commission, Portland has also built in components from that model, including an age range up to 21, which should permit greater coordination with the robust youth leadership and service-learning programs at Portland State University, Portland Community College, and Reed College, among others.

As should be clear, these two key network nodes are part of extensive networks of youth civic engagement innovators and intermediaries, many of whom focus their work on formal institutions of local government. Each of the two, of course, has particular strengths and limits. NLC has a broad reach into local governments, but also must remain ecumenical in terms of how it promotes various models, whereas Hampton, with more selective networks, is freer to concentrate on what it sees as high-end relational and culture-change practices. Both are underresourced relative to the demand and potential of diffusing city-based models of youth civic engagement.

Federal Policy to Support City Innovation

Today there exists a number of relatively robust and sustainable models of city-supported youth engagement, including ones we have not discussed in any detail. There is also increasing interest in such models among city officials, as well as a solid base of receptivity among youth for engagement in community problem-solving activities (Zukin et al., 2006; Levine, 2007). Municipal governments have been able to utilize a variety of levers to launch innovations, proceed through diverse pathways to institutionalize them, and find ways to collaborate with a range of nonprofit youth organizations and other partners to promote systems change. Various youth development and civic engagement intermediaries and national associations have reached a point where they can provide direct training and network learning opportunities to help build capacity on a broader scale, though they clearly have a long way to go before they can match the civic-capacity-building intermediaries in fields such as watersheds (Sirianni, 2009b) or service-learning and civic engagement in higher education

(Sirianni and Friedland, 2004). There is substantial opportunity for complementarity among city-supported youth commissions, youth planning, youth advisory groups in school systems and other city agencies, and other policy initiatives discussed in other chapters of this book, such as service-learning and civic education.

Nonetheless, many cities that have created youth commissions and similar bodies remain stuck at a relatively low level of development: youth councils that do not break out of a parks and recreation silo or move beyond simple service or youth philanthropy projects or policy deliberation that has little impact on city affairs or follow-up work by youth themselves. Cases of sustained culture change in city government departments and nonprofit agencies contracting with them are relatively rare, and for good reason. Such work requires long-term investments of staff time and funding, sustained and sophisticated relational and political work among youth and adults, and a willingness to confront the kinds of bureaucratic reflexes that hinder many other kinds of innovation, civic or otherwise (Light, 1998; Schorr, 1998). Even in the more robust cases, backsliding can occur as the head of a city agency retires or is replaced, mid-level teams are broken up (e.g., Hampton's Y-COPE police teams for National Guard Service in Iraq), or budgets are cut.

These challenges, of course, have to be confronted by local political leadership, above all. At this point, state agencies and youth commissions, where the latter exist, are not well positioned to support robust youth engagement in city government. But federal support can play an important role, especially if there is visible and sustained leadership by the president, key leaders of Congress, senior agency officials, and mid-level teams and networks, including interagency ones. Federal programs have been important in building civic capacity in a variety of fields in recent years (community service, service-learning, watershed planning and restoration, environmental justice, community health). If properly designed and supported, federal programs can avoid some of the pitfalls of the past and become civic enablers on a relatively ambitious scale. We are well beyond some of the design flaws and political dilemmas of the 1960s "maximum feasible participation." There is no need or predisposition to go around city government to set up independent community action agencies or some youth equivalent. Collaborative practice, including that of city governments themselves, has progressed enormously since that time, demonstrating substantial capacity for organizational and policy learning (Sirianni and Friedland, 2001; Sabatier et al., 2005).

Given the deeply rooted social, cultural, and economic factors that have been eroding the nation's social capital (Putnam, 2000, 2007; Rahn and Transue, 1998) and classic multitiered associations (Skocpol, 2002), it is more important than ever that government invest systematically and strategically in building civic capacities. With the increasing complexity of public problems, growing diversity of publics, and rising expectations for voice and inclusion, the costs of doing civic democracy well rise commensurately in terms of requisite organizational capacities of associations and skill sets of citizens, as well as agency capacities for partnering with them. As Holmes and Sunstein (1999) argue in parallel fashion on the issue of rights, liberty requires major investments by government at all levels—from court systems and legal training to consumer product safety and labor relations boards, and "the amount a [political] community chooses to expend decisively affects the extent to which the fundamental rights of Americans are protected and enforced" (31). It is the same with civic democracy: we get—and deserve—that for which we are willing to pay. The federal government can become a strategic investor in the civic capacity of youth and thereby help enable cities (and regions) to become the vibrant democratic polities needed for public problem solving in the twenty-first century (Innes and Booher, 2003; Healey, 2006; Sirianni, 2007).

While it is beyond the scope of this essay to offer a detailed proposal for a federal program to help catalyze and support citywide innovation in youth civic engagement, a promising policy design, which I shall call Youth Leadership for Cities (YLC), would include the following components:

- *Grants and cooperative agreements*: Two- to three-year grants, awarded on a competitive basis through the U.S. Department of Housing and Urban Development (HUD), offered for two levels of partnerships, namely, those with substantial proven capacity already and those demonstrating the emergence of a promising community vision, coalition, and design. A model for this might be the U.S. EPA's Community Action for a Renewed Environment program's level 1 and level 2 grantees (Sirianni, 2009a). The cooperative agreement would require the participation of the mayor, city council, and/or city manager's office, as well as at least one major city department (planning, parks and recreation, environment, school district, neighborhoods, children/youth/families), and one or more local nonprofit youth development agencies (YMCA, Girls Scouts, 4-H) or other relevant nonprofits (sustainable city coalition, young women's leadership development group, citywide council of neighborhood associations, university-based service-learning center, community foundation). Grants might range from $100,000 to $300,000 per year, depending on the size of the city, and could be renewed for one further two- or three-year cycle. (Recall the three-year $320,000

CSAP community partnership grant that made Hampton's youth civic engagement vision and strategy possible.) The explicit focus of the grant should be multi-stakeholder visioning and planning for and with youth, with a central component of institutionalizing youth's active participation and changing the culture of city and nonprofit agencies to support this. Perhaps add a matching formula to the grant. Where possible, seek business partners as well.

- *Begin small, grow strategically*: The first annual round of grantees could be as few as 10–12 and then be expanded in similar increments, depending on the range of worthy applicants, emerging capacity for training and technical assistance, and, of course, performance evaluation based on authentic community-developed metrics. Once critical mass has been achieved and appropriate state capacity has been built (e.g., with state leagues of cities and relevant state agencies that understand the mission of youth engagement and institutional culture change, proven through some funded state projects), Youth Leadership for Cities could possibly become a state block grant.

- *Competitive set aside funding for training and technical assistance*: Funds would be set aside for national, regional, and state intermediaries, on a competitive basis, to help assist local partnerships. One can thus imagine organizations such as the National League of Cities, Alternatives, Onsite Insights, Youth Leadership Institute, International City/County Management Association (ICMA), and state leagues of cities applying for funding to enable them to work with local grantees, with a broader range being chosen as the number of overall grantees expands. A relevant model might be EPA's capacity-building grants for the Targeted Watershed Initiative, which have gone to organizations such as the River Network, Center for Watershed Protection, Southeast Watershed Forum, and ICMA, among others (Sirianni, 2009b). What is to be avoided is a single national youth development intermediary, especially one with little on-the-ground experience in youth and adult partnership training and organizational transformation.

- *HUD team and interagency network*: A cross-program HUD team with experience in community development, university-community partnerships (Vidal, Nye, and Walker, 2002), and participatory planning should oversee the program and recruit several experienced youth engagement practitioners to help staff it. The HUD team should convene an annual conference or training and work with similar networks in other federal agencies (Corporation for National and Community Service, Department of Education, Health and Human Services, EPA) to ensure the greatest degree of complementarity of training and resources for grantees and among intermediaries.

This proposal is ambitious, yet it could be quite workable in terms of building capacity at various levels in an incremental fashion, including local government and nonprofits, training intermediaries, federal agency teams and networks, and eventually state agencies. Sustainable systems and culture change requires proceeding in a manner that builds local civic and political relationships (Stone et al., 2001; Sirianni, 2007) and is not confined to programmatic and bureaucratic silos (Light, 1998; Boyte, 2005). This is long, hard, embedded work, and no cookie-cutter model or superficial training regimen can ensure that city governments become transformative agents for youth civic engagement, or that youth learn to engage in ways that add real public value to their communities. This is what the initial Hampton group of 20 youth clearly stated as their overriding purpose—not being fixed, but doing real work as democratic partners contributing to their communities.

Note

Research and travel support was provided by the Pew Charitable Trusts, Innovations in Government Award at Harvard University, and the Norman Research Fund at Brandeis University.

References

Academy for Educational Development. (2002). *BEST strengthens youth worker practice: An evaluation of building exemplary systems for training youth workers.* Washington, DC: AED, Center for School and Community Services.

Agranoff, R. (2007). *Managing within networks: Adding value to public organizations.* Washington, DC: Georgetown University Press.

Baum, J. (1996). Organizational ecology. In S. Clegg, C. Hardy, and W. Nord (Eds.), *Handbook of organization studies* (77–114). London: Sage.

Bayer, M., and Potapchuk, W. (2004). *Learning from neighborhoods: The story of the Hampton Neighborhood Initiative, 1993–2003.* Hampton, VA: Neighborhood Office.

Behn, R. D. (2001). Rethinking Democratic accountability. Washington, DC: Brookings Institution Press.

Benford, R. D., and Snow, D. A. (2000). Framing processes and social movements: An overview and assessment. *Annual Review of Sociology, 26,* 611–39.

Benson, P. L., Leffert, N., Scales, P. C., and Blyth, D. A. (1998). Beyond the "village" rhetoric: Healthy communities for children and adolescents. *Applied Developmental Science, 2* (3), 139–59.

Berry, J., Portney, K., and Thomson, K. (1993). *The rebirth of urban democracy.* Washington, DC: Brookings Institution Press.

Boyte, H. C. (2005). Reframing democracy: Governance, civic agency, and politics. *Public Administration Review, 65* (5), 536–46.

Briggs, X. D. S. (2008). *Democracy as problem solving: Civic capacity in communities across the globe.* Cambridge: MIT Press.

Carlson, C. (2005). Youth with influence: The youth planner initiative in Hampton, Virginia. *Children, Youth, and Environments, 15* (2), 213–26.

Carlson, C. (2006). The Hampton experience: Creating a model and a context for youth civic engagement. In B. N. Checkoway and L. M. Gutierrez (Eds.), *Youth participation and community change* (89–106). New York: Haworth Press.

Carlson, C., and Sykes, E. (2007). *Shaping the future: Working together, changing communities. A manual on how to start or improve your own youth commission.* Hampton, VA: Hampton Coalition for Youth.

Center for Civic Education. (n.d.) *We the People . . . Project Citizen.* Calabasas, CA: Center for Civic Education.

Checkoway, B., Allison, T., and Montoya, C. (2005). Youth participation in public policy at the municipal level. *Children and Youth Services Review, 27,* 1149–62.

Checkoway, B. N., and Gutierrez, L. M. (Eds.). (2006). *Youth participation and community change.* New York: Haworth Press.

City of Brighton. (2007). *Brighton's 2007 children, youth, and family master plan.* Brighton, CO: City Council and School Board, and Hampton, VA: Onsite Insights.

City of Hampton. (1999, May 13 draft). Youth component of the 2010 comprehensive plan. Hampton, VA: Planning Department.

City of Hampton. (2006, February 8). *Youth component of the community plan.* Hampton, VA: Planning Department.

Coleman Advocates for Children and Youth. (1994). *From sandboxes to ballot boxes: San Francisco's landmark campaign to fund children's services.* San Francisco: Author.

DeLeon, R. E. (1992). *Left coast city: Progressive politics in San Francisco, 1975–1991.* Lawrence: University Press of Kansas.

DeLeon, R. E., and Naff, K. C. (2004). Identity politics and local political culture: Some comparative results from the social benchmark survey. *Urban Affairs Review, 39* (6), 689–719.

Delgado, M., and Staples, L. (2007). Youth-led organizing: Theory and action. New York: Oxford University Press.

Fagotto, E., and Fung, A. (2006). Empowered participation in urban governance: The Minneapolis neighborhood revitalization program. *International Journal of Urban and Regional Research, 30* (3), 638–55.

Fullwood, P. C. (2001). *The new girls' movement: Implications for youth programs.* New York: Ms Foundation for Women.

Fung, A. (2004). *Empowered participation: Reinventing urban democracy.* Princeton: Princeton University Press.

Garza, P., and Stevens, P. (2002). *Best practices in youth philanthropy.* Austin, TX: Coalition of Community Foundations for Youth.

George, A. L., and Bennett, A. (2005). *Case studies and theory development in the social sciences.* Cambridge: MIT Press.

Ginwright, S., Noguera, P., and Cammarota, J. (Eds.). (2006). *Beyond resistance: Youth activism and community change.* New York: Routledge.

Goldsmith, S., and Eggers, W. D. (2004). *Governing by network: The new shape of the public sector.* Washington, DC: Brookings Institution Press.

Hampton Coalition for Youth. (1993). *2 commit 2 the future/4 youth: Proposed plan of action.* Hampton, VA: Author.

Healey, P. (2006). *Collaborative planning: Shaping places in fragmented societies.* New York: Palgrave Macmillan.

Holmes, S., and Sunstein, C. R. (1999). *The cost of rights: Why liberty depends on taxes.* New York: Norton.

Hughes, D. M., and Curnan, S. P. (2000). Community youth development: A framework for action. *CYD Journal, 1* (1), 7–13.

Ingram, H., and Smith, S. R. (Eds.). (1993). *Public policy for democracy.* Washington, DC: Brookings Institution Press.

Innes, J. E., and Booher, D. E. (2003). Collaborative policymaking: Governance through dialogue. In M. A. Hajer and H. Wagenaar (Eds.), *Deliberative policy analysis: Understanding governance in a network society* (33–59). New York: Cambridge University Press.

Irby, M., Ferber, T., and Pittman, K. (2001). *Youth action: Youth contributing to communities, communities supporting youth.* Community and Youth Development series, vol. 6. Takoma Park, MD: Forum for Youth Investment.

Kathi, P. C., and Cooper, T. L. (2005). Democratizing the administrative state: Neighborhood councils and city agencies. *Public Administration Review, 65* (5), 559–67.

Kretzmann, J. P., and McKnight, J. L. (1996). *Building communities from the inside out.* Chicago: ACTA Publications.

Landy, M. (1993). Public policy and citizenship. In H. Ingram and S. R. Smith (Eds.), *Public policy for democracy* (19–44). Washington, DC: Brookings Institution Press.

Lauterborn, P. (2004, April 14). Rational discussion of irrational behavior. *San Francisco Chronicle.*

Leighninger, M. (2006). *The next form of democracy.* Nashville: Vanderbilt University Press.

Levine, P. (2007). *The future of democracy: Developing the next generation of American citizens.* Medford, MA: Tufts University Press.

Light, P. C. (1998). *Sustaining innovation: Creating nonprofit and government organizations that innovate naturally.* San Francisco: Jossey-Bass.

Lofquist, W. (1989). *The technology of prevention workbook.* Tucson: AYD Publications.

Martin, S., Pittman, K., Ferber, T., and McMahon, A. (2007). *Building effective youth councils: A practical guide to engaging in youth policy making.* Washington, DC: Forum for Youth Investment.

McLaughlin, M. (2005, April). *Coleman advocates for children and youth: Advocating to institutionalize children's rights.* Stanford, CA: John Gardner Center for Youth and Their Communities.

Orr, M. (2007). *Transforming the city: Community organizing and the challenge of political change.* Lawrence: University of Kansas Press.

Osborn, D., and Plastrik, P. (1997). *Beyond bureaucracy: Five strategies for reinventing government.* Reading, MA: Addison-Wesley.

Ozawa, C. P. (Ed.). (2004). *The Portland edge: Challenges and successes in growing communities.* Washington, DC: Island Press.

Potapchuk, W. R., Carlson, C., and Kennedy, J. (2005). Growing governance deliberatively: Lessons and inspiration from Hampton. In J. Gastil and P. Levine (Eds.), *The deliberative democracy handbook: Strategies for effective civic engagement in the twenty-first century* (254–67). San Francisco: Jossey-Bass.

Putnam, R. (2000). *Bowling alone: The collapse and revival of American community.* New York: Simon and Schuster.

Putnam, R. (2007). E pluribus unum: Diversity and community in the twenty-first century. *Scandinavian Political Studies 30,* 2, 137–74.

Rahn, W. M., and Transue, J. (1998). Social trust and value change: The decline of social capital in American youth, 1976–1995. *Political Psychology, 19,* 545–65.

Rogers, E. M. (1995). *Diffusion of innovations* (4th ed.). New York: Free Press.

Sabatier, P. A., Focht, W., Lubell, M., et al. (2005). *Swimming upstream: Collaborative approaches to watershed management.* Cambridge: MIT Press.

San Francisco Youth Commission. (2005, April). *Report on sexual assault and harassment in San Francisco schools.* San Francisco: Sexual Assault and Harassment Prevention Committee.

San Francisco Youth Commission. (2007). *Annual report, 2006–2007.* San Francisco: Author.

Sapiro, V. (1993). "Private" coercion and democratic theory: The case of gender-based violence. In G. E. Marcus, and R. L Hanson (Eds.), *Reconsidering the democratic public* (427–49). University Park: Pennsylvania State University Press.

Schneider, A. L., and Ingram, H. (1997). *Policy design for democracy.* Lawrence: University Press of Kansas.

Schön, D. A., and Rein, M. (1994). *Frame reflection: Toward the resolution of intractable policy controversies.* New York: Basic Books.

Schorr, L. (1998). *Common purpose: Strengthening families and neighborhoods to rebuild America.* New York: Anchor.

Senge, P. M. (1990). *The fifth discipline: The art and practice of the learning organization.* New York: Doubleday.

Sirianni, C. (2007, December). Neighborhood planning as collaborative democratic design: The case of Seattle. *Journal of the American Planning Association, 73* (4), 373–87.

Sirianni, C. (2009a). Investing in democracy: Engaging citizens in collaborative governance. Washington, DC: Brookings Institution Press.

Sirianni, C. (2009b). The civic mission of a federal agency in an age of networked governance: The U.S. Environmental Protection Agency. *American Behavioral Scientist, 54* (winter).

Sirianni, C., and Friedland, L. A. (2001). *Civic innovation in America.* Berkeley: University of California Press.

Sirianni, C., and Friedland, L. A. (2004). The new student politics: Sustainable action for democracy. *Journal of Public Affairs, 7* (1), 101–23.

Sirianni, C., and Friedland, L. A. (2005). *The civic renewal movement: Community building and democracy in the United States.* Dayton, OH: Kettering Foundation Press.

Skocpol, T. (2002). *Diminished democracy: From membership to management in American civic life.* Norman: University of Oklahoma Press.

Skogan, W. G. (2006). *Police and community in Chicago: A tale of three cities.* New York: Oxford University Press.

Stone, C. N., Henig, J. R., Jones, B. D., and Pierannunzi, C. (2001). *Building civic capacity: The politics of reforming urban schools.* Lawrence: University of Kansas Press.

Stone, C., and Worgs, D. (2004, July 30 draft). Community-building and a human capital agenda in Hampton, Virginia: A case analysis of the policy process in a medium-sized city.

Vidal, A., Nye, N., Walker, C., et al. (2002). *Lessons from the Community Outreach Partnership Center Program.* Washington, DC: Urban Institute.

Warren, M. R. (2001). *Dry bones rattling: Community building to revitalize American democracy.* Princeton: Princeton University Press.

Wenger, E., McDermott, R., and Snyder, W. M. (2002). *Cultivating communities of practice.* Boston: Harvard Business School Press.

Wood, R. L. (2002). *Faith in action: Religion, race, and democratic organizing in America.* Chicago: University of Chicago Press.

Young, I. M. (2000). *Inclusion and democracy.* New York: Oxford University Press.

Zukin, C., Keeter, S., Andolina, M., Jenkins, K., and Delli Carpini, M. X. (2006). *A new civic engagement: Political participation, civic life, and the changing American citizen.* New York: Oxford University Press.

7

Local Political Parties and Young Voters

Context, Resources, and Policy Innovation

Daniel M. Shea

During two very cold days in January 2007, youth mobilization activists and academics from across the nation convened at the Johnson Foundation Wingspread Conference Center at Racine, Wisconsin. The goal of the gathering was to discuss mobilization efforts in the previous midterm election. Funded by the Pew Charitable Trusts and organized by Young Voter Strategies and the Graduate School of Political Management at George Washington University, the event boasted many of the best and brightest in the youth engagement field.

There was considerable excitement, perhaps even jubilation, over the apparent rise in youth voting in the 2004 and 2006 elections. We had turned the corner, many proclaimed, and there was reason to celebrate. But not long into the event two nagging issues emerged. First, Peter Levine of CIRCLE reminded the gathering that while youth turnout seemed to be on the rise, a scant 22 percent of those under 30 went to the polls in 2006. In what many have suggested was a historic midterm election, less than one-quarter of young Americans had bothered to vote. It was a splash of cold water. While things *might* be improving, the challenge of truly engaging America's youth in the political process is daunting.

Second, and equally significant, a concern quickly termed the "low-hanging fruit" was raised by a few of the participants. In the drive to register and mobilize as many young Americans as possible, and to do so at the lowest possible costs, many youth engagement organizations focused on populations predisposed to becoming engaged. The quickest, most cost-efficient way to produce massive numbers of new registrations, for instance, is to head to a four-year college campus. While this is a valuable activity, college students are much more likely to register on their own than other populations of young citizens. And if they do not become involved in their college years, chances are quite high that they will become engaged after graduation—once again, especially compared with other populations.

Many of the philanthropic organizations that sponsor voter registration initiatives set ambitious goals and cost per registrant guidelines. This pushes engagement activists to find groups already predisposed to vote. A common technique is to prompt students to change their voting address from back home (where their parents live) to their school address. The student who moves is often considered a "new" registrant when it comes to the program's tally sheet.

A related problem of "more-is-always-better" registration initiatives is the premium put on quick contacts. If one technique registers 20 new voters per hour, and the other just 10, the former must surely be "better." This would even be something to extol: "Pay attention, young voter activist, for we have found a cheaper, more efficient way of registering new voters!" The logic of cost-efficient voter work is explicit in Green and Gerber's important book, *Get Out the Vote: How to Increase Voter Turnout* (2004). It is, they write, "a guide for campaigns and organizations that seek to formulate cost-efficient strategies for mobilizing voters" (2). The authors admit that the book is focused on "short term" considerations and *not* on "how voter turnout relates to broader features of society" (6).

For most of us working in the youth engagement field, the goal is to help create better citizens, not simply new voters. We view registration and voter mobilization as important (indeed, the organization that I direct participated in a large, goal-oriented registration program in 2006), but as an *initial* step toward broader engagement and expanded civic enlightenment. Voting is not an end but, rather, a beginning. Grabbing the shoulder of our college student outside the cafeteria to convince her to reregister at her campus address, and quickly moving to the next student in order to click off another "new" registrant, may boost registration figures, and it may even kick up turnout, but how it helps create a generation of better citizens is less clear. Does it really help this person better appreciate their potential in a democratic society? Does it promote a more in-depth understanding of the issues or candidates, and does it encourage other modes of participation such as helping a candidate with grassroots activities?

What is more, the reliance on registration and voting as the indicators of political engagement neglects other modes of involvement. Some assume that voting is the foundation of greater engagement, but others have suggested this is not necessarily the case. Would we consider a youth disengaged if he does not vote, even though he pays close attention to the news, writes to his congressman, discusses politics with friends and family, and is a member of several political interest groups? Once again, are we striving for more voters or for a more engaged, more active citizenry?

After a rather sobering conversation about the limitations of "efficient" registration techniques, our conversation at Wingspread turned to institutions that might promote long-term engagement in public life. The focus, noted one of the participants, should be on existing institutions that can draw youth into politics for the long term and in meaningful ways. But are there any such institutions?

Indeed there are. Two of the most important institutions for linking new generations to the political process are schools and political parties. This chapter will focus on the latter. Local political parties have been drawing new citizens into the political process for nearly two centuries. Rather than lumping all local parties together, however, the focus of this chapter will be on the internal and external forces that shape the likelihood of a party committee focusing on youth projects and the probability of its success. After the empirical analysis, five state-level policy recommendations are outlined. In the end it is argued that local political parties can make a difference in engaging America's youth but that policy changes must be considered.

Local Parties and Electoral Mobilization

A nagging issue for voter activists and scholars is establishing standards to gauge recent trends. We might all agree that an overall turnout of 50 percent for presidential elections and 30 percent for a midterm congressional election is low, but what would constitute robust electoral participation? One approach is to compare our turnout with participation in other nations. In his oft-cited book *Bowling Alone*, Robert Putnam writes, "Our turnout rate ranks us just above the cellar—narrowly besting Switzerland, but below all twenty-two other established democracies" (2000, 31). With regard to young voters, a cross-national comparison seems bleak. In 2006, the United States tied for last (with Japan) in a list of 18 advanced industrialized democracies for those under 30 who voted (Wattenberg, 2007, 107). This is a stark statistic. There are limitations to a comparative approach, however. First, many other nations impose requirements that compel voting. That has never been done here. While Americans may vote less often than citizens in other countries, we tend to be more active outside the ballot box. Membership in politically active groups, for instance, is much more common in the United States than in many other democracies.

Another common approach is to assess current voting rates through a historical lens, and in doing so our attention is quickly drawn to the second half of the nineteenth century. Although the voting age was 21 instead of today's 18, and many citizens were excluded from voting, turnout for several decades was remarkably high. In only three elections during this period did the presidential turnout dip below 70 percent, and on three occasions it breached the 80 percent mark (Shea and Green, 2007, 24). Politics during this "golden age of parties" was integral to the everyday lives of most Americans.

For a number of reasons, most notably women's suffrage and progressive reforms designed to reduce corruption in electoral politics, turnout began to decline. By 1920 it was down to just 50 percent. After World War II, there was a modest resurgence, and until 1968 roughly 60 percent of Americans came to the polls for presidential contests. Since 1972 the trend has been more or less downward, with several recent elections seeing turnout at or just below the 50 percent mark. "The period from 1960 to 2000," writes Thomas Patterson in *The Vanishing Voter*, "marks the lowest ebb in turnout in the nation's history" (2002, 4). In 2004, 54 percent of the eligible population cast a ballot.

There are less hard data on youth voting rates in the twentieth century, but a downward trend is also apparent in recent decades. We know that when 18-year-olds were first guaranteed the right to vote in 1972, 50 percent of those under 25 came to the polls. That figure dropped quickly, and by the 2000 election it measured a scant 35 percent. Martin Wattenberg argues in *Is Voting for Young People?* that "over the last three decades, politics and voting have indeed become more and more the province of the elderly" (2007, 1). In 2004, he writes, there was a jump upwards of those under 30 at the polls, to about 46 percent, but even here the ratio between younger and older voters is much larger than it was in the 1960s and 1970s (99).

Assessing levels of participation through a historical lens pushes us to consider why it was high at certain times. What were the forces that drove voter engagement? There are a number of possibilities, but one cannot look very deep into the nature of politics in the second half of the nineteenth century without noticing the preeminence of local party organizations. By the 1840s, parties had grown into a system of mass-based organizations, and through their efforts voter participation skyrocketed. Writing of the "golden age of parties," Cornell historian Joel Silby finds a powerful link between party activities and voter mobilization: "After 1838, parties were, and were accepted as, the key integrating mechanisms of all aspects of American politics." As a result, "the American electorate now contained few apathetic, poorly informed, or marginally involved voters" (1991, 11). In a very real sense, local parties manufactured mass electoral mobilization in America, and they also served as a key socializing agent for new citizens. Parties afforded a rationale for civic involvement, and clear avenues for involvement in a broad range of democratic activities.

A parties/voter mobilization nexus became a common theme in both normative and empirical political science. E. E. Schattschneider argued that "parties have extended the area of popular participation in public affairs enormously," and that "once party organizations become active in the electorate, a vast field of extension and intensification of effort is opened, the extension of the franchise to new social classes, for example" (1942, 208, 47). Several recent empirical works find local parties play a critical role in registering new voters and in getting out the vote (Frendreis, Gibson, and Vertz, 1990; Frendreis and Gitelson, 1999; Shea and Green, 2007; Brooks, Farmer, and Pagonis, 2001).

Nevertheless, local parties have not faired well in the twentieth century. Progressive Era reforms, innovations in communications, and loopholes in campaign finance laws have enhanced the role of national and state organizations, often at the expense of local structures. Local parties have found it increasingly difficult to perform their historic function of mobilizing voters. It is not just a coincidence that these difficulties occurred during the period when voter turnout declined, especially among the youth. As I have suggested elsewhere, the party system of the late twentieth century could be characterized as "baseless" due to its weak local structures and lack of direct connection to voters (Shea, 1999).

Party Variation and Youth Engagement Efforts

This is not to say all local parties have withered. To better understand local party dynamics and the extent to which they conduct youth initiatives, John Green and I, with assistance from CIRCLE, conducted a telephone survey of 805 local party leaders from across the nation in the fall of 2003. (For additional information on the sample and mode of administration, see the Appendix.) The results have been reported elsewhere (Shea and Green, 2007, chapters 2 and 3). In brief, we found that while most party leaders see youth engagement as a serious issue, only about half of the county party organizations across the nation conduct youth engagement programs. Many of these efforts were quite modest, rather "thin" initiatives, to be sure. When asked if party organizations can make a difference in drawing new generations into the political process, an overwhelming majority of the party leaders believed they could. We concluded our study with a call to local parties to shift resources to this important area of work. A "best practices" summary is provided.

Rather than simply suggest "innovative" parties will have greater success, this analysis will center on perceptual and contextual forces that shape the willingness of party committees to undertake youth-centered projects and the likely success of these efforts. The history of party politics in America is one of variation and distinctiveness. Local parties are composed of diverse social, ideological, and geographic subcoalitions, and they are found in a dizzying array of electoral contexts. In brief, we might expect that certain types of party committees—in certain electoral contexts—will be more successful at youth engagement than other organizations. This chapter will confront three key variables: overall party goals, party resources, and electoral competition.

Party Goals

What, exactly, are local parties designed to accomplish? What would distinguish a "successful" party from a "failed" party? This seemingly simple question has been the source of much debate, over time leading to two broad perspectives. Pragmatic, or "rational-efficient," parties are composed of a small group of elite, divorced from a mass base. They hold a singular goal of becoming more technically advanced. Although winning elections is an important outcome of party activity, "good" parties are believed to be those most capable of aiding candidates. The goal of party work is to help candidates win. On the other pole would be the ideological or "responsible" party model. Here party success is measured by a change in public policy. Winning elections is important, but only as it allows newly elected officials to express the party's policy concerns. An overview of several additional characteristics of these party models is found in Table 7.1.

Where do American parties fit into these theoretical perspectives? Most scholars would place the Democrats and Republicans leaning toward the rational-efficient end of the spectrum, but one must be cautious with blanket assessments. Numerous reforms during the early 1970s opened party organizations to greater involvement, and many local party organizations perform activities in nonelection periods—including those not directly related to winning office. At the very least there is significant variation.

It seems logical that organizational goals would shape a party's willingness to undertake youth engagement activities. Drawing new voters into the process can be a difficult, time-consuming chore, especially when attracting existing nonpartisan voters to a candidate. Writing in the *Atlantic*, Don Peck notes, "In recent decades parties have moved away from grassroots mobilization efforts, which reach out to nonvoters, to focus on 'switching' independents that have a strong history of voting" (2002, 48). We might hypothesize, then, that respon-

Table 7.1: Contrasting attributes of rational and responsible parties

Attribute	Rational-Efficient	Responsible
Functions	Election activities	Linkage Aggregation Articulation Participation Community service
Objectives	Win elections / control office efficiency	Policy Ideological unity
Structure	Professional	Mass membership Amateur
View of intraparty democracy	Hinders efficiency	Essential
Incentives for participation	Material	Mix of purposive, social, and material

Source: Adapted from Shea, 1995, 61.

sible parties—organizations interested in long-term movements around ideological concerns—would be more interested in making the investment necessary to draw new voters into the party fold than would purely election-centered organizations. What is more, we might speculate that responsible parties would be more willing to invest in the cultivation of more engaged *citizens*, compared with simply finding new voters for next election.

Party Strength

As we all know, some local parties have more resources than do other party organizations. This might be a function of the affluence of the community, the fund-raising prowess of party leaders, electoral competition, party history, and much else. There are also several ways to measure party "strength," such as financial resources, the number of active committee members, whether or not there is an ongoing headquarters, and even whether the committee has a website.

As noted above, mobilizing nonvoters can be a costly undertaking. We can assume, then, that stronger party committees would be more likely to shift resources to youth engagement initiatives. What is more, we might expect that viable responsible parties are more likely to work to engage young voters than are weak responsible parties.

Electoral Competition

In some communities voters are accustomed to highly competitive elections, but in other communities one party dominates. Many recent studies have suggested that youth voter levels are related to electoral competition (Franklin, 2004), but it is unclear whether this is a function of party organizations taking greater steps to engage potential voters or whether uncertainty pushes new voters to the polls. In fact, it may be the case that greater electoral competitiveness will push local party committees away from youth engagement initiatives. Perhaps when parties confront high-risk elections, resources will be shifted to persuading existing voters, rather than mobilizing new voters. This would be consistent with Peck's assessment.

The Data

To test these suppositions, several data sets were merged. The survey data from the 805 county party leaders, discussed above, provides a host of information regarding party functions, organizational viability, the electoral context, the extent to which the committee is concerned about youth participation, and whether the party engages in youth-oriented activities. This survey was merged with a large aggregate data set from the U.S. Census, which contains scores of county-specific variables. A third layer of information added to the data set is county-by-county results from the 2000 and 2004 elections. Finally, voter turnout data was purchased for 27 states.[1] This information allows us to assess overall turnout figures in the 2000 and 2004 elections, as well as youth turnout figures for 450 counties that match our survey data.

Several dependent variables were used, including whether the party committee boasts youth engagement programs, the willingness of the party membership to work to attract young voters, party committees' overall effort on youth engagement initiatives, whether they have registration programs, whether they boast "get out the vote" (GOTV) programs for young voters, the scope of particular programs, and the perceived success of various programs. Actual turnout figures for young voters in the respondents' county will also be used as a dependent variable, but some caution should be used here, given that numerous factors unrelated to party dynamics are likely to shape youth turnout rates.

Party Functions and Youth Engagement

Party leaders were asked questions designed to assess their outlook toward general party functions. Do they consider the goals of their organization to be more ideological or pragmatic? Table 7.2 provides the results of these questions. It seems that the split on most of the questions is about even.

There is solid evidence to suggest that overall party goals shape attitudes toward youth engagement initiatives and the success of these initiatives. Party leaders were asked how interested their committee was in developing programs designed to engage young citizens. Some 44 percent of respondents who suggested that "consistent issue positions" were important for their candidates said they were also "very committed" to youth initiatives. On the other hand, just 32 percent of those who viewed "electability" as important were committed to youth initiatives. A similar result was found when using a slightly different independent variable: whether it is the role of parties to help candidates win elections or to bring voters into the fold. The Chi-square statistic was significant for both of these cross-tabulations at the 95 percent confidence interval. Amateur-centered organizations were also more likely to have youth-centered programs than those that rely more on campaign consultants. When the dependent variable is switched to whether or not the county committee boasts voter

Table 7.2: Outlook toward party goals: Responsible vs. rational functions

	Rational position	Responsible position
Parties should . . .	Promote broad appeals (320)	Take consistent issue positions (450)
Parties should . . .	Help candidates win (489)	Help voters forge long-term attachments to party (297)
Who should manage party affairs?	Leaders/experts (346)	Rank-and-file members (425)
Campaign consultants are . . .	Important (301)	Not important (495)
Your organization relies on . . .	Campaign consultants (188)	Volunteers (595)

registration programs or whether they undertake youth-centered GOTV initiatives, findings are more or less the same.

To further analyze the importance of this dimension, an index was created using five rational/responsible questions: a 0 is assigned to the chairs who noted all of the responses dubbed more "rational," and a 5 was given to respondents who noted all of the "responsible" options. (This scale proved to be normally distributed, with 4 percent at the rational pole, 7 percent at the responsible pole.) Table 7.3 provides the results of a series of cross-tabulations between youth initiatives and the rational/responsible scale. Consistently, rational parties are less likely to engage in youth programs than are more responsible parties. For example, some 34 percent of the more responsible party committees (those noted as a 4 or 5) boast young voter registration programs, while only 13 percent of the rational committees (those noted 1 and 2) have these programs. About 35 percent of the responsible committees have youth GOTV programs, but just 12 percent of the rational parties have them.

Party Vitality and Youth Engagement

We can imagine that a party's willingness to conduct youth voter initiatives and the success of these programs would be a function of resources. Stronger parties—parties with more staff, more volunteers, a permanent headquarters, larger budgets, websites—would more likely turn their attention to difficult, time-consuming projects (such as youth engagement) than would organizations starved for assets. Prior studies, noted above, suggest such a positive relationship between party activities, more generally, and party resources.

Table 7.4 presents the results of a series of cross-tabulations between party resource measures and three youth outreach measures. Table 7.5 presents the same information based on budget. The budgetary information was collected as interval data and was recoded into "low," "moderate," and "high" levels. What is more, there is an overall budget variable and a per capita budget measure.

The table supports the notion that stronger parties are more likely to engage in youth-centered projects than are weaker organizations. For instance, while 67 percent of committees that maintain a year-round headquarters boast youth registration programs, just 58 percent without a permanent headquarters do the same. Some 66 percent of committees with a website work with college clubs and organizations, while just 44 percent without a website do the same. Every variable of party vitality suggests stronger parties are more likely to work with young voters than are less robust committees. The budgetary information is especially revealing, as it clearly indicates operating funds have a bearing

Table 7.3 Party leaders' commitment to youth initiatives

	Rational/responsible scale						
	Most rational 0	1	2	3	4	Most responsible 5	Total (*N*)
% with youth division	3.9	9.2	23.9	33.0	22.5	7.5	306
% work with college clubs	4.1	8.9	22.8	34.1	23.5	6.7	417
% with youth registration programs	3.2	10.1	23.4	29.5	25.5	8.2	376
% with youth GOTV program	3.0	9.4	22.5	30.0	25.8	9.4	267
% overall committee "very interested" in young voters	7.2	8.3	24.3	30.8	24.6	9.8	276

Table 7.4: Percentage of participation in youth initiatives according to party resources available

Party resource measures	Youth registration programs	Youth GOTV programs	Work with college clubs	*N*
Maintain year-round HQ	67%	47%	60%	414
Do not maintain year-round HQ	58%	41%	51%	248
Maintain a website	68%	48%	66%	399
Do not maintain a website	56%	40%	44%	264
Have any full-time staff	74%	52%	71%	50
Do not have full-time staff	62%	44%	56%	614
Have >75% committee spots filled	64%	50%	59%	345
Have <75% committee spots filled	64%	40%	51%	311

on whether or not a party committee will engage in youth-centered activities. Well-funded committees, for instance, were almost 50 percent more likely to boast youth registration programs than were poorly funded units.

The relationship between party vitality and the perception of success on youth engagement efforts is also robust. Using the perceptional measure—whether or not the chair believes his/her committee was successful with youth-centered projects—we find that stronger parties are less likely to have "failed" than weak parties. For example, of the respondents who suggested they were "not at all successful" with their youth initiatives, 43 percent were the lowest per-capita budget grouping, compared with just 5 percent in the high per-capita budget grouping. Those parties without a permanent headquarters were twice as likely as those with a headquarters to suggest their efforts were unsuccessful. Switching it around to measure of success, those committees with at least one paid staff position were nearly twice as likely to have suggested that their committees had been "very successful" in their youth efforts, than those without paid staff positions.

When we assess the relationship between various party resource measures with actual turnout figures, the relationship is difficult to discern. Independently, all of the resource measures are positively related to youth mobilization, but only one of these figures (whether the committee boasted a website) was statistically significant. And when the variables are combined in a multivariate analysis, the coefficients are once again in the expected direction, but the goodness-of-fit measure was modest. This result suggests that party activities play a role, but that many other forces also shape young voter turnout.

Table 7.5: Percentage of participation in youth initiatives according to party budget level

Budget level	Youth registration programs	Youth GOTV programs	Work with college clubs	*N*
Overall				
Low	57%	38%	44%	356
Medium	64%	47%	63%	205
High	78%	56%	73%	127
Per capita				
Low	58%	40%	57%	270
Medium	64%	47%	59%	337
High	74%	47%	58%	80

Electoral Competition

On the one hand, it would seem logical to assume that political parties would be more interested in attracting young voters where electoral competition is high. In areas where elections can swing in either direction, parties would be interested in mobilizing any latent group of nonvoters. On the other hand, when parties are facing stiff competition, they may choose to allocate resources to projects that yield an immediate electoral payoff, such as activities that persuade existing voters. Again, youth mobilizations are difficult, time-consuming, and require a great deal of resources. How, then, does electoral competition shape youth mobilization efforts? To answer this question, we created an electoral competition measure, using the 2004 presidential election.[2]

Table 7.6 supports the first supposition—that electoral competition pushes party committees toward youth engagement projects. In noncompetitive areas, 57 percent of the county committees developed youth registration programs, but in highly competitive areas this number jumps to 70 percent. Only 41 percent of the parties in noncompetitive areas had youth-centered GOTV programs, but 51 percent in highly competitive areas boasted such initiatives. For each of the cross-tabulations, the Chi-square statistic is significant at the .95 percent level. What is interesting about this data is that there is little difference between low and modestly competitive areas; the real change occurs in highly competitive areas.

Electoral competition does not seem to matter when it comes to perceived success with youth initiatives. That is, chairs in highly competitive areas re-

Table 7.6: Percentage of participation in youth initiatives according to electoral competition

Level of competition	Youth registration programs	Youth GOTV programs	Work with college clubs	*N*
Noncompetitive	57%	41%	54%	147
Modestly competitive	59%	40%	51%	292
Highly competitive	70%	51%	64%	324
Chi-square significance	.012	.049	.007	

port almost the exact same level of success with these programs, as do chairs in low and moderately competitive areas. A correlation between electoral competition and actual youth voting numbers, on the other hand, suggests young voters do, in fact, turn out more in competitive areas than in noncompetitive communities.

Policy Recommendations

Local party organizations *can* play a vital role in engaging young Americans in the political process. More than simply signing up new registrants or pushing voters to the polls, parties have the potential to help young Americans appreciate the broad responsibilities of citizenship in a democracy. Rather than dismiss party organizations as passé, we might consider public policies that enhance the likelihood that they would be engaged in youth-centered projects. Below are five state-level policy suggestions.

Eliminate Open Primary Systems

Nineteen states allow primary voters to cast ballots for candidates of a party to which they do not belong. Open and blanket primary systems are most common in the upper Midwest and the South and were originally designed to promote greater participation in nomination contests. There is little evidence, however, of higher turnout rates in these states. As noted by one scholar, "While we might suspect higher turnout in open primaries, as voters are free to participate in the party's contest which most excites them, aggregate research has found higher turnout in closed primaries" (Norrander, 1991, 641). Additionally, a byproduct of open primary systems is a willingness of candidates to break with their party's platform to attract independents—and even voters from the opposing party. In other words, open primaries push candidates in a pragmatic direction and reduce the chance that local parties will command "responsible" behavior. The Supreme Court noted as much in *California Democratic Party v. Jones* (2001, 530 U.S. 567), where it rejected mandatory blanket primaries. Scholar David Ryden notes that the Supreme Court's "preference for closed over open and blanket primaries implicitly rests upon the 'responsible party' notion of parties and party membership" (2003, 86).

The analysis conducted here suggests responsible parties are more likely to conduct youth-centered activities. We might also conclude that these parties would be more likely to undertake a broad range of social functions—the types of programs that better link new voters to the political process more generally. Eliminating open primaries will not guarantee that party leaders will pursue more responsible goals, but it will reduce the willingness of candidates to break with their party in order to win a nomination.

The forces that push a local committee or a party leader toward a rational or responsible approach are complex, and not every responsible party leader will embrace youth-centered programs. If, however, we see parties as a viable means for engaging young citizens, and if responsible parties are more inclined to head in this direction than are rational-efficient parties, then it would make sense to reconsider the costs and benefits of open primaries.

Public Funding for Local Parties

One of the important findings of this study is that local parties are starved for cash. Some 75 percent of the county party committees in the sample operated on less than $25,000 per year. A stunning 50 percent ran on less than $10,000 per year. One should also keep in mind that the sample was drawn from the most populated 1,000 counties in the nation (as noted in the Appendix), and that there are roughly 2,200 smaller counties. A fair estimate, then, is that a majority of local party committees operate on less than $5,000 per year.

This analysis also tells us that financial resources are strongly correlated to a party's willingness to engage in youth-centered activities—as well as with the success of these programs. Well-funded committees (those in the highest 25th percentile) are 50 percent more likely to reach out to young voters than are committees with few resources. A great deal of public funding (local, state, and federal) is spent on efforts to draw new voters into the process. Public service announcements and "how to vote" flyers, for example, are common but only modestly successful because they are not aimed at forging a relationship with the new voter. They provide information.

Policy makers are starting to understand the importance of party-based voter mobilization efforts. The Bipartisan Campaign Reform Act of 2002, also known as McCain/Feingold, included a provision designed to help parties perform grassroots activities. The Levin Amendment, which was upheld in *McConnell v. FCC* (2003, 540 U.S. 93), allows state and local party committees to accept soft money contributions of up to $10,000 for get-out-the-vote efforts. Party leaders have noted the importance of this provision. Yet affording parties a special exemption in finance law may not be sufficient. Local parties should be given public funds to undertake voter outreach programs. We may specify how this money is used, such as on youth-centered projects or general GOTV initiatives, or we may look to the invisible hand of electoral competition to structure expenditures. Either way, when local parties have greater resources, they are much more likely to reach out to nonvoters. Moreover, these funds may also encourage parties to cultivate long-term relationships with new voters, which also serves an important public good.

Nonpartisan Redistricting Commissions

One cannot overstate the weight of electoral competition on young voter turnout. In the 10 most contested states in the 2004 presidential election, for example, turnout for voters 18 to 30 averaged 53 percent, but in the least contested states it was just 45 percent (Donovan, Lopez, and Sagoff, 2005, 1). Many studies have found a positive relationship between competition in congressional races and turnout (see, e.g., Cox and Munger, 1989). Young citizens are rational and less likely to vote if they believe the costs of voting will have little bearing on the outcome. Our analysis suggests the same, but it also suggests party committees are more likely to reach out to young voters in highly competitive areas than in noncompetitive communities. We might not go so far as to suggest that party-based youth initiatives in competitive areas could be the root of higher youth turnout. At the very least, the evidence is clear that parties are more involved in these programs in competitive areas.

We also know that the level of competition in congressional and state legislative races has decreased in recent years. Gary Jacobson, for example, charts the number of competitive House races since 1982 and finds that in many of these years about 75 races were competitive. Since 1996, however, this figure has been about 50. In 2004, 37 districts, just 9 percent of House races, were competitive

(Jacobson, 2005, 167). The incumbent advantage is part of this change, but at the core of the issue is ever-sophisticated partisan redistricting. Gerrymandering is not new, of course, but with the aid of geopolitical software, state lawmakers are able to fine-tune district lines to virtually guarantee outcomes.

Not surprisingly, the call for nonpartisan redistricting is growing. Some 12 states now use nonpartisan commissions, the most recent to join the list being Alaska, Idaho, and Arizona. Iowa uses a system where nonpartisan legislative staff develop maps for state house and senate districts, as well as U.S. House districts, without any political or election data including the addresses of incumbents. This is an interesting possibility.

Nonpartisan redistricting procedures will not guarantee competitive elections in every community—not by a long shot. But the shrinking number of truly contested legislative seats is one of the most portentous issues of our day, and policy makers should confront this issue head on.

Modifications to the Electoral College

Staying with the importance of electoral competition, the electoral college throws a wet blanket on the urgency of voting in many states, especially for many young voters. Why vote if your state is a foregone conclusion and the winner of the state nets all of its electoral college votes? Indeed, only about a dozen states are considered "in play" in most presidential elections. But the drive to eliminate the electoral college has been tepid, even after the 2000 election, likely because of the hurdles in amending the Constitution and the fears of a national recount. States can allocate their electoral votes as they see fit, however, and there is movement to find alternative approaches. Maryland, for instance, recently passed a law that would award their electoral votes to the winner of the national popular vote, as long as other states do the same. The idea is that each state would appoint presidential electors pledged to the winner of the national popular vote. The outcome of presidential elections would be dependent on the nationwide popular vote, without amending the Constitution.

A national popular election would help voters in each state to feel that their ballot matters. A voter from New York would feel that her ballot was just as important as a voter from a swing state, such as Ohio. This would drive party operatives in every state to muster as many popular votes as possible, to create young voter mobilization programs, and to undertake long-term party building initiatives.

A Public Holiday to Celebrate Parties

Finally, state policy makers, and perhaps even national legislators, should consider creating a holiday to recognize the importance of political parties. This might seem strange to many citizens, which is precisely why such a celebration is necessary. Most Americans do not understand why parties matter and why they should consider greater involvement with these organizations. The late Ralph Goldman noted, "Americans commemorate innumerable occasions and causes, from Groundhog Day in February to Sadie Hawkins Day in November. A Political Parties Day . . . could become a salutary ritual" (1993, 38). Citizens would better appreciate why parties matter, which would lead to greater involvement.

The core supposition of this chapter is that the particular types of party committees are more likely to engage in youth-centered activities than are others. It was assumed that party committees with a sharp focus on policy and broad voter appeal would more likely engage in youth programs than would more pragmatic parties; that greater resources would allow party committees to do more work with young voters; and that higher electoral competition would sharpen young voters initiatives. In each case expectations were confirmed by the data.

The challenge, then, is to consider policy innovations that aid responsible parties, enhance party resources, and build electoral competition. The policy suggestions noted above should be part of a broad conversation about the role of mobilizing institutions in engaging young voters. The activist at the Wingspread conference was right when he suggested that the best way to draw young citizens into the political process for the long term is to enhance existing institutions rather than to create new ones. Political parties have been at the forefront of voter mobilization for nearly 200 years. Perhaps it is time to embrace these important organizations and seek changes that enhance their role in the political system.

Finally, it is worth noting that political parties are not the only public institution that can help young Americans better appreciate their role in a democratic society. As noted elsewhere in this volume, public schools and the media can also play a key role in the process. Optimistically, we might envision a virtuous circle, or a civic division of labor, where each institution confronts a different aspect of citizenship. Schools might underscore foundational knowledge, the media could highlight important and often complex issues, and parties might draw young citizens into the process.

Appendix

The telephone survey of local party leaders was conducted as follows: A random sample of Democratic and Republican local party chairs was drawn from the 1,000 most populated counties across the country. According to the 2000 Census, these counties contain 87 percent of the American population. So this sample covers the local parties most capable of influencing the electorate and thus the youth vote. The survey was conducted between October 1 and November 10, 2003, at the University of Akron Survey Research Center, producing a total of 403 Democratic and 402 Republican responses, with a cooperation rate of about 50 percent. The responses were found to deviate only slightly from the geographic and demographic characteristics of the original sample of counties; the data was weighted to correct for these modest differences. These results have a margin of error of plus or minus five percentage points of each party and plus or minus four percentage points for the sample as a whole. Each interview lasted roughly 30 minutes and included batteries on organization strength, party activities, and the political environment as well as extensive questions on youth mobilization. The survey data were then matched with U.S. Census data for all the counties, and for 455 counties the 2000 voting records aggregated by age were appended.

Notes

1. The criterion for selecting these 27 states was cost. There does not seem to be a systematic bias, and some states simply charge more than others for their voter data files.
2. Noncompetitive counties are defined as those where either Bush or Kerry netted at least 75 percent of the vote; modestly competitive are those areas where Bush or Kerry netted between 60 and 74 percent of the vote; and highly competitive areas are those where either Bush or Kerry received less than 60 percent of the vote.

References

Brooks, S. C., Farmer, R., and Pagonis, K. (2001). The effects of grassroots campaigning on political participation. Paper presented at the 2001 annual meeting of the Southern Political Science Association, Atlanta, November 8–10.

Cox, G. W., and Munger, M. C. (1989). Closeness, expenditures, and turnout in the 1982 House elections. *American Political Science Review, 83,* 217–30.

Donovan, C., Lopez, M. H., and Sagoff, J. (2005). Youth voter turnout in states during the 2004 presidential and 2002 midterm elections. College Park, MD: Center for Information and Research on Civic Learning and Engagement.

Franklin, M. N. (2004). *Voter turnout and the dynamics of electoral competition in established democracies since 1945.* New York: Cambridge University Press.

Frendreis, J., Gibson, J. L., and Vertz, L. (1990, March). The electoral relevance of local party organizations. *American Political Science Review, 84* (1), 226–35.

Frendreis, J., and Gitelson, A. (1999). Local parties in the 1990s: Spokes in a candidate-centered wheel. In J. C. Green and D. M. Shea (Eds.), *State of the parties* (3rd ed.). Lanham, MD: Rowman and Littlefield.

Goldman, R. (1993). Who speaks for political parties? Or Martin Van Buren, where are you when we need you? In D. M. Shea and J. C. Green (Eds.), *State of the parties* (25–41). Lanham, MD: Rowman and Littlefield.

Green, D. P., and Gerber, A. (2004). *Get out the vote: How to increase voter turnout.* Washington, DC: Brookings.

Jacobson, G. C. (2005). The Congress: The structural bias of Republican success. In M. Nelson (Ed.), *The elections of 2004.* Washington, DC: Congressional Quarterly.

Norrander, B. (1991). Explaining individual participation in presidential primaries. *Western Political Quarterly, 44,* 640–55.

Patterson, T. E. (2002). *The vanishing voter: Public involvement in an age of uncertainty.* New York: Knopf.

Peck, D. (2002, November). The shrinking electorate. *Atlantic Monthly*, 48–49.

Putnam, R. D. (2000). *Bowling alone: The collapse and revival of American community.* New York: Simon and Schuster.

Ryden, D. K. (2003). Out of the shadows and into the dark? The courts and political parties. In J. C. Green and R. Farmer (Eds.), *The state of the parties* (4th ed.) (79–94). Lanham, MD: Rowman and Littlefield.

Schattschneider, E. E. (1942). *Party government.* New York: Holt, Rinehart and Winston.

Shea, D. M., and Green, J. C. (Eds.). (2007). *Fountain of youth: Strategies and tactics for mobilizing America's young voters.* Lanham, MD: Rowman and Littlefield.

Silby, J. H. (1991). Beyond realignment and realignment theory: American political eras, 1789–1989. In B. Shafer (Ed.), *The end of realignment? Interpreting American electoral eras* (3–23). Madison: University of Wisconsin Press.

Wattenberg, M. P. (2007). *Is voting for young people?* New York: Pearson/Longman.

PART III

Policy Models from Other Nations

8

Youth Electoral Participation in Canada and Scandinavia

Henry Milner

Electoral Participation versus Civic Engagement

The chapters in this book discuss how best to prepare our youth for active citizenship, as well as ways to help, or facilitate, young people to keep abreast of current affairs, make their views known publicly, vote regularly, form interest groups, participate in political campaigns, and lobby elected officials. While other chapters assess American experience using American research data, this chapter examines approaches outside the United States.

Given that my academic life is divided between Canada and Scandinavia (Sweden and Finland in particular), I naturally focus on these countries. But there are good reasons beyond my own familiarity that lead to this choice. It is useful, when assessing American experience, to be able to draw comparisons with countries that share basic democratic values and structures but have proven especially effective in preparing youth for active citizenship. In previous works I have shown that the Scandinavian countries have led the way in making it possible for their citizens to be politically informed (Milner, 2002) and, though not equally so in all of Scandinavia, to vote regularly (Ersson and Milner, 2009). In describing the institutions and policies that promote what I term "civic literacy," the Scandinavian approach is found to be quite different from that found in the United States.

Most Western European countries, if usually less successfully, share the basic features of the Scandinavian approach. To bring the comparison closer to home, I look at my own country, Canada, which is closest to the United States geographically and shares much else besides. Canadians are most influenced by American approaches but also most sensitive to differences where they exist.

I begin by looking at what we know about youth political participation in Canada and Scandinavia set in comparative perspective. I focus on electoral participation because, for comparative purposes, it is the most straightforward and objective indicator, but also because of my own orientation toward youth political participation. I see electoral participation and "civic engagement" (i.e., involvement in voluntary associations and community projects) as distinct phenomena. Of course, these can overlap, as many individuals combine both, but it is in no sense automatic. Moreover, unlike electoral participation, there is no single operational definition of civic engagement. Thus there is no reason to assume that these two phenomena are interconnected at the aggregate level: a community high in civic engagement can be low in electoral participation, and vice versa.[1]

Specifically, since the very definition and thus operationalization of civic engagement is tied to expectations arising from national norms, cross-national comparisons are fraught with methodological hurdles. The voluntary nature of civic engagement of young people in the United States is less voluntary than you might think, given the fact that such activity is obligatory in many American schools and colleges and therefore likely to be overreported. A recent study of young people in four U.S. high schools found "a single theme about the meaning of civic engagement [that] appeared repeatedly: 'résumé padding.' . . . Young people of all class strata, races, and ethnic backgrounds told us that they needed 'something' to put on their résumés" (Friedland and Morimoto, 2006, 32). Such incentives are weaker in Europe and Canada. Typically, studies limited to the United States are not concerned with distinguishing civic engagement and electoral participation, but this cannot be the case here. For comparative analysis to be meaningful, the two phenomena must be treated separately.

Institutionalized Incentives and Electoral Participation

While individuals can "pad" on surveys asking if they voted, there is objective, internationally comparable turnout data to fall back on. Of course, institutionalized incentives are also a factor when it comes to electoral participation, but these are ones we can identify and, potentially, alter through policy choices. As a general rule, institutions that make elections more competitive motivate parties and candidates to make greater efforts to inform and mobilize potential voters.

The most straightforward institutional incentive is compulsory voting. The simplest means of boosting turnout among the young is fining those who fail, without justification, to cast a vote.[2] Yet, reluctant to take away the right not to vote, the countries considered in this chapter do not use compulsory voting and are not contemplating doing so. Given that people are free to spoil their ballots, a more compelling argument against compulsory voting is that it would result in poorer decision making by the electorate, since people would be forced to cast a ballot but not make any effort to inform themselves before doing so. This is a question recently investigated in another study (Milner, Loewen, and Hicks, 2007), but beyond the scope of this chapter.[3]

There are many specific institutional measures (we will encounter specific examples of many of these in the countries under consideration), such as Internet voting, mail-in ballots, new voting hours, and Sunday voting, that can and do affect electoral participation and can be applied in all democratic countries irrespective of institutional contexts. Even here, however, the institutional context in which electoral participation takes place puts the United States well outside the mainstream. There are two aspects to this. The first is registration. In the United States it is up to voters to register, and great efforts need to be undertaken to get young people to register. In Canada, Scandinavia, and most comparable countries, registration is passive; the citizen is automatically placed on the voters' list. Hence the great effort on and off American campuses to register young citizens is superfluous elsewhere. Note that when it comes to comparing turnout cross-nationally, this is now taken into consideration by international bodies that use age-eligible citizens rather than registered voters as denominators.

A second, perhaps even more important but usually less stressed difference is the role of the U.S. Constitution. The first amendment, as interpreted by the Supreme Court, prevents the setting of legally enforceable campaign spending limits on parties and candidates. This, combined with the high TV advertising costs of getting name recognition, raises entry costs. The advantage thus gained by incumbents combined with that resulting from the partisan drawing of electoral boundaries saps political competitiveness and thus reduces turnout.

Underlying this is a wider distinction between the United States and other democratic countries, a distinction too often not given the attention it deserves in explaining differences in electoral participation and strategies for boosting turnout, namely, in the nature of the institutions that administer elections. Elsewhere, electoral administration is nonpartisan and, at least for national elections, centralized. Hence rules apply equally and throughout, and when reforms are proposed, it is on the premise that once adopted they will be applied in the same way in every electoral district. The United States is exceptional in that no such single body exists. The American system subjects to partisan considerations many aspects of the electoral process, including the very act of getting (young) people registered and to the ballot box. Some candidates and parties benefit—and know they benefit—from low turnout among groups that are underrepresented at the ballot box, and these considerations enter the decision process, as is evidenced in measures enacted in a number of states to keep former felons from voting.[4]

A simple contrast can be drawn with the role and activities of Elections Canada, the impartial body that administers Canadian federal elections and informs citizens about all aspects of voting: eligibility, dates, candidates, district boundaries, ballots, polls, etc. As we shall see, in response to declining youth turnout, it has recently undertaken intense efforts to boost youth electoral participation. The reason it has been able to do so credibly and without political interference or backlash is because Elections Canada is nonpartisan and is known to be so. There can be no American counterpart to Elections Canada, since the Constitution gives electoral administration—even for federal elections—to the states. If we compare the United States with Sweden, the distinction is even greater because, beyond the impartial body that administers elections, a number of government agencies have been created to foster participation, and there is no questioning as to their nonpartisan capacity to play this role. One reason for this is that in Sweden all political parties are, as a rule, represented on the board of such, and this, in turn, reflects electoral institutions based on proportional representation, which makes cooperation among parties the norm in these matters.

The typical Scandinavian pattern is that of the central government creating mechanisms for identifying the problem, setting out policy guidelines, and involving local and regional councils and civil society organizations in their implementation. Such coordination is far more difficult to attain in Canada given its federal distribution of powers and lack of proportional representation. Still, Canada is closer to Scandinavia than to the United States. In concrete terms, from an American citizen's point of view, although there are many private agencies and foundations providing information about electoral participation comparable to that provided by Elections Canada, none can have the credibility or guaranteed central place in the process as a public body that exists for that purpose.

In sum, institutional differences matter: not only in the effects of existing institutions but also in the capacity to change them to attain desired objectives. The perceived and real danger of partisan considerations entering where they do not belong inhibits the United States from acting to promote democratic participation in ways that are standard in comparable democracies.[5] These distinctions must be kept in mind as we seek to learn from what is being done and contemplated elsewhere.

Turnout among the Young and Not-So-Young in Scandinavia and Canada

Having placed electoral participation in a wider institutional context, we can now turn from these objective factors to more subjective ones affecting turnout. The first is "the civic duty to vote." It is obvious that declining voter turnout reflects a decline in the sense of a civic duty to vote. The 2000 Canadian Election Survey reported that while 75 percent strongly agreed that it is every citizen's duty to vote in federal elections, and 32 percent said that they would feel very guilty if they didn't vote in a federal election, only 55 percent of young Canadians strongly agreed with the statement about duty, and only 18 percent said that not voting would make them feel very guilty (Blais, Gidengill, Nadeau, and Nevitte, 2002). A similar though less steep decline in Europe is reflected in data from the 2002–2003 European Social Survey, which asked how important it is for a good citizen to vote in elections, using an 11-point scale from "extremely unimportant" to "extremely important." As set out in the two last columns of Table 8.1, the overall average rating was over 7.6, whereas for first-time voters the average was just below 7.[6]

There is a connection between such attitudes and reported voting. Looking at the final row of Table 8.1, we see that average overall reported turnout was 80.3 percent, dropping to a worrisome 52.7 for first-time voters.[7] Limiting ourselves to Europe and leaving aside the new democracies of Eastern Europe and those countries with compulsory or quasi-compulsory voting, we find that absolutely, as well as in comparison with older citizens, voting among young Danes, Swedes, Dutch, Germans, and Austrians is high, while among British, Irish, Swiss, Spanish, and Portuguese youth, it is low.[8]

Keeping in mind that a certain percentage of people will report having voted when they did not do so and that this is related to a perceived duty to vote, we note in Table 8.1 a positive relationship between reported turnout and importance of voting. The correspondence is consistent among voters overall, while it is slightly less so among new voters, for whom variation in levels of reported turnout is much greater. In Sweden, Denmark, Austria, Germany, and Hungary, where new voters place the highest levels of importance on voting, reported turnout is high, while in Switzerland, Spain, Portugal, and Great Britain, where new voters place the lowest levels of importance on voting, turnout

Table 8.1: Reported voting rates and attitude toward voting for 2002–2003

Country	% of citizens who reported voting in last election	% of citizens who voted for first time in last election[a]	Mean rating on an 11-point low-to-high scale on importance of voting (all voters)	Mean rating on an 11-point low-to-high scale on importance of voting (first-time voters)[a]
Austria	88.5	74.6	8.1	7.5
Belgium	85.2	53.5	6.6	6.4
Czech Republic	65.9	61.4	6.2	5.9
Denmark	93.7	78.9	8.9	8.1
Finland	81.7	54.5	7.6	6.0
Germany	85.3	72.8	7.6	7.1
Greece	90.6	59.8	8.1	7.6
Hungary	80.9	69.2	8.3	7.9
Ireland	75.9	41.8	7.7	7.2
Italy	89.5	76.4	7.5	6.7
Netherlands	86.3	74.8	7.5	6.9
Norway	83.7	50.0	8.2	7.5
Poland	66.2	48.2	7.7	7.0
Portugal	72.5	41.3	7.1	6.4
Slovenia	80.2	42.0	6.7	5.9
Spain	77.7	27.4	6.4	5.0
Sweden	87.0	81.4	8.4	8.1
Switzerland	69.0	17.6	7.4	6.7
Great Britain	72.4	41.0	7.2	6.5
All respondents	80.3	52.7	7.6	7.0

Source: Based on data from the first round of the European Social Survey, 2002–2003 (*ess.nsd.uib.no*).

[a]Respondents born in 1980 or later who reported voting for the first time.

is low. Finland fits in here as well, given that it shows an especially steep generational drop in both indicators, while in Norway and Greece the drop is only on the reported-voting side.

Other data help us to delve further into this contrast among the Nordic countries. As displayed in Table 8.2, we can see that when we compare first-time voters with the electorate at large in national elections over a period of 30

Table 8.2: Differences (%) in turnout rates in national elections between first-time voters and the electorate at large

Election year	Norway	Sweden	Denmark	Finland
2002		–11		
2001	–24			
1999				–17
1998		–8	–6	
1997	–21			
1994		–5	–7	
1993	–14			
1991		–8		
1990			–4	
1989	–5			
1988		–6		
1987				–17
1985	–11	–5		
1984			–9	
1982		–4		
1981	–12			
1979		–5	–12	–9

Source: Ersson and Milner, 2009.

years, there are signs of a growing disparity in generational turnout rates beginning in the 1990s. But the phenomenon differs in intensity, being significant in Finland and Norway, small in Sweden, and virtually nonexistent in Denmark.

Comparing Levels of Political Knowledge

Clearly, especially when it comes to the recent generation of new voters, we cannot rely on civic duty to bring citizens to the polls. Instead, we need to place emphasis on the role of the other "subjective" factor, political knowledge. This development is discernible in data from Great Britain and Canada. Among those with low levels of political knowledge, in earlier generations far greater proportions voted out of a sense of civic duty than is the case with young people today. A British study found that overall 63 percent of those who stated they were "not at all interested in news about the election" nevertheless reported casting a vote; but among those ages 18–24 this was the case for only

16 percent (Electoral Commission, 2002, 29). Howe (2003) compared data from 1956 Gallup polls testing political knowledge with those from the political knowledge items in the 2000 Canadian Election Study.[9] Age differences turn out to be significantly more important in 2000, especially among those with no more than a high school education. Moreover, the problem is compounded, since the young are less informed about politics today than they were 45 years ago.[10]

The only international survey that allows us to place the political knowledge of young North Americans in comparative context supports this conclusion. The 2003 National Geographic–Roper Global Geographic Literacy Survey assessed 3,250 young adults in 10 countries.[11] Apart from questions asking the respondents to identify countries on a world map, there were questions testing their knowledge of international politics.[12] Out of 56 questions that were asked across the countries surveyed, young Americans on average answered 23 questions correctly (just above the last-place Mexicans), with young people in Canada (27) and Great Britain (28) faring almost as poorly. Sweden (with 40) and Germany (38) led, followed by Italy (38), France (34), and Japan (31). The United States, Canada, and the Great Britain are roughly similar, averaging overall in the low 40s in turnout levels of new voters, while Sweden, Germany, and Italy are among the highest of the ESS countries, averaging in the high 70s.

While too focused on international and geographic facts to suit our purposes, the overall pattern of responses to the Roper survey corresponds to my findings (Milner, 2002) that the northern European countries, and especially the Scandinavian ones, are high in civic literacy; that is, they are countries where the proportion of citizens sufficiently informed to vote meaningfully is relatively high. By contrast, the English-speaking countries tend to fall into the low civic literacy category. I have taken up this question in a recent Canadian survey (Milner, 2007) in which people ages 15–25 were overrepresented. Ten questions tested political knowledge, several of which had been used in 2002 as part of the ESS in Finland. In Table 8.3, the average scores for the common questions for both countries are set out. As we can see, there is a similar disparity to that seen in the Roper survey. Given the significantly greater generational differences in turnout and attitude toward voting in Finland (compared with Sweden and Denmark), it would be interesting to compare young Finns with their Canadian counterparts—something that we have not been able to do because the ESS data was not broken down by age.

The data from the above-mentioned Canadian study reveal that Canadians ages 15–25 score 10 percent lower in political knowledge than those over 25 (3.7 vs. 4.1 average right answers out of 10). This generational difference is in

Table 8.3: Percentage of correct answers to political test questions in Finland and Canada

	Finland	Canada
Name the minister of finance (Finland)	67	
Name one cabinet minister (Canada)		32
Name the second largest party in legislature	52	57
Demonstrate an understanding of progressive income tax[a]	52	36
Name the UN Security Council permanent members (average correct)	52	45
Which of the following best describes who is entitled to vote in federal elections: residents, taxpayers, legal residents, or citizens?	73	56
Average	60	45

[a] Obviously, a person with a low income will pay less in income tax than someone on a higher income. But do you think that a person with a low income pays a larger proportion of their earnings in income tax than someone on a high income, the same proportion, or a smaller proportion of their earnings in income tax?

the lower range of differences found by Grönlund (2003) using the responses to the three political knowledge questions in recent election surveys in 23 countries participating in the Comparative Studies of Electoral Systems (CSES).[13]

In comparison, in their average score on seven of the political knowledge questions in a parallel survey in the United States (see Lopez et al., 2006), Americans ages 15–25 scored more than 25 percent lower (2.1 vs. 2.9 average correct answers) in political knowledge than those over 25. We do not have comparative data for generational differences in political knowledge in earlier periods, but what we do know suggests that, at least in Canada, the divergence is greater today (Howe, 2003).

In sum, when it comes to informed voting by young people, we can point to something that looks like a generational vicious circle: the absence of a sense of civic duty to vote (among other factors) results in young people who are less inclined to seek the information needed to vote meaningfully while making the act of voting more dependent on an adequate level of political knowledge. Under these circumstances, for young people, not casting a vote can easily become a habit that in turn diminishes the already limited interest in politics. As we turn to the measures to address the problem, we are confronted with the reality that since restoring a sense of civic duty is akin to putting the genie back into the bottle, our strategy will unavoidably have to tackle the deficit in political knowledge. In so asserting, let me make it clear that this is not a matter of changing attitudes but of reducing the cost of political knowledge for young people by making it more readily accessible and in a form corresponding to their styles of communication.

The Problem Recognized

In the rest of this chapter, we look at efforts in Scandinavia and Canada to address declining youth political participation that have come as a response to the public recognition of this decline, emphasizing those measures that address the political knowledge dimension. To keep the discussion from being bogged down with detail, we focus on Sweden, which faces far less of a challenge than Canada, and Finland, which faces a serious challenge. Despite wide differences in the acuteness of the problem, as in Canada, Scandinavian authorities generally have identified addressing the "democratic deficit" as a public policy priority.

Until not long ago, Swedish turnout levels rivaled—even exceeded—those of Denmark through the mid-1990s, with percentages for Swedish parliamentary elections in the high 80s. However, turnout plummeted to 81.4 percent in the 1998 elections and almost slipped below 80 percent in 2002.[14] Part of the reason for the decline was an increase in generational turnout disparity to 11 percent, as illustrated in Table 8.2. Moreover, turnout in elections to the European Parliament started low at 41.6 percent in 1994, placing Sweden fourth lowest among the 15 members, falling to 38.8 in 1999 and 37.2 in 2004, lowest among the 15. In 1998, the government created a minister for democratic issues, naming Britta Leion to the post. It also set up the National Commission on Swedish Democracy, chaired by former minister of education Lars Goransson, with a mandate to analyze the "low" voter turnout, stimulate public discussion, and present proposals for boosting citizens' democratic participation. The Commission produced a large number of documents drawn from the contributions of leading experts presented at one of the scores of public seminars held throughout the country. It submitted its final report to Leion in February 2000.

The report was followed up, in the spring of 2000, with a two-year program entitled "Time for Democracy." The first major event was a national conference on democracy and citizen involvement to follow up on the final report of the Commission, which had been sent out along with invitations to 924 public agencies, local and county (regional) council authorities, and other organizations, as well as to 501 randomly chosen citizens. In addition, financial support for democracy development projects was made available under the auspices of a special parliamentary committee, the Committee on Local Democracy. In a later section we look at some of the concrete initiatives that emerged from this—efforts which apparently bore fruit, as turnout increased to 82 percent in the 2006 national election.

Turning to Canada, the election of 2000 drew public attention to a far more acute phenomenon than in Sweden, with turnout percentages plummeting from the mid-70s in the 1980s to barely 60 percent. It soon became clear that youth abstention was a key factor (Blais et al., 2002). The results led Elections Canada to commission a study that produced the extremely worrisome claim that only 22.4 percent of people ages 18–21 actually voted (Pammett and LeDuc, 2003, 20). The concern generated resulted in Elections Canada conducting an in-house analysis of turnout in the subsequent election,[15] using a random sample of 95,000 voters from polling divisions in every province and territory. The data revealed a turnout rate of 38.7 percent for those for whom June 2004 was the first federal general election in which they were eligible to vote.[16] Moreover, while turnout rose steadily with age, reaching 75 percent among people ages 58–67, the exception was those 21–25, who voted at a marginally lower rate (35.4 percent) than did the first-time voters. This suggests that the measures introduced or supported by Elections Canada to try to counter the decline by mobilizing new voters played a role here. The first reports from Elections Canada's replication of the study for the 2006 election suggests an increase to 43 percent among first-time voters, again likely in part attributable to the efforts undertaken to get out the youth vote—to which we now turn.

Measures to Increase Informed Political Participation among Young People

The School

I divide the discussion of measures to address youth decline in political participation into two sections. The first looks at school-based measures, civic education in particular; the second looks at non-school-based measures. There are two reasons for this categorization. The first is simply convenience: school-based measures by definition address young people whereas the other measures tend to address all potential voters. The second reason has to do with the approach taken here: if, as we argue, knowledge is crucial, then it is education—and civic education in particular—that addresses this dimension directly.

I first draw from the comparative literature—which is far from comprehensive—some general guidelines for policies related to civic education:

- *Targets*: The primary targets should be where civic literacy is low: young people for whom home support and social connectedness is weak.[17] Frequently these are potential dropouts, and the course needs to be offered at a time when they are still in school but close to voting age.
- *Stance and timing*: The courses should be presented as practical, not moralistic. A good analogy is drivers' education—the value of which is apparent to young people. When they reach a certain age, it becomes practical to learn the rules of the road; the same applies to the age of citizenship and voting. Hence civic education should be concentrated on those nearing voting age.
- *Overall approach*: The stress should be on knowledge and skills relevant to voting and other forms of political participation, as well as inducing the habits of attentiveness to relevant sources of information and skills required for acquiring and making use of that information. This is different from the mainstream American approach, which plays down (partisan) politics, stressing American history and the U.S. constitution in the civics classroom and community-based volunteer activities outside it. Studies suggest that this approach is ineffective in generating political interest and involvement.[18]
- *Content*: There is no one-size-fits-all formula. It is largely a matter of learning from, adapting, and refining what works in comparable civic education courses when it comes to meeting the combined objectives of imparting the required knowledge and inducing the habits of attentiveness. Despite the lack of systematic data, we can accomplish much by looking at best practices elsewhere, exchanging course material via the Internet, etc.
- *Inputs from the media and political actors*: For most young people, their only contact with politicians is through the media (TV ads and ratings-driven news clips). As a result, many potential young voters are "turned off" by what they see as the apparent inauthenticity of politicians who are put on the defensive by an adversarial media (see Milner, 2005b). If representatives of political parties were as a matter of course invited to visit civic education classes, large numbers of young people

could be exposed to another, potentially more authentic, side of those seeking their votes. This means countering the unwillingness, in the United States especially, to allow discussion of partisan politics in the classroom. In fact, such visits would make it more important and more natural for the teacher to strive for impartiality. A useful pedagogical device is to have the students prepare to role-play journalists at a press conference given by the guest and write a report for their newspaper on what they learned, using the event to gain an appreciation for the informational role of the media. The goal is not merely to accumulate information, but also to develop habits of attentiveness to—and the ability to pick up signals about—the political world. We are learning more about the kinds of electronic sources of information that are most promising and how news websites can be made more attractive and informative to young people without being overloaded with high-tech gadgetry (Sherr, 2005).[19] Web-based material, moreover, has the added advantage that it can be incorporated into modules of civics education courses irrespective of location.

- *Appropriate institutions*: Movement in this direction is enhanced by a complementary institutional context. Planning such visits is easier under fixed election dates (see Milner, 2005a) and proportional (PR) systems of elections. PR elections give small parties with distinct principle-based positions, such as Greens or libertarians, a better chance of having democratically elected—and therefore legitimate—spokespersons to represent them in the classroom.[20] Contacts with political figures can also be made by "virtual" visits through electronic means.

A knowledge-based approach extends beyond the classroom. Mock elections are being carried on in high schools in the United States, Canada, Sweden, and Norway (and, no doubt, in other countries). The first such organization, founded in 1988, was Kids Voting USA.[21] Parallel Canadian efforts supported by the relevant election offices coincided with the October 2003 Ontario provincial election, the 2004 and 2006 federal election, and the 2005 BC provincial election.[22]

Below I briefly describe the approach to civic education in Scandinavia and Canada. Given the diversity within each, it is difficult to generalize, but my overall impression is that the Scandinavian approach conforms more closely to these guidelines than that in Canada. Canada increasingly tends to take a "hands-off" approach to political issues, less than the United States but more than in Scandinavia, and keeps partisan politics away from the classroom, stressing history and constitution instead (Westheimer, Cook, Llewellyn, and Molina Girón, 2007).

Civic education in Scandinavia

There are important similarities among the Nordic countries when it comes to civic education, though Norway tends to be more centralized in its approach than the other three, which allow for greater variation at the local level.[23] Each explicitly recognizes the encouragement of citizenship as an objective of education, though this is expressed in different ways in each country. In Finland, the goal of education is to support the students' development as citizens, and this is set out in a separate regulation; in the other Nordic countries, these goals are incorporated into the documents setting out the general goals and purposes of schooling. Typically, rather than using the term "citizenship," the guidelines refer to the preparation of young people for active and meaningful participation in society.

Traditionally the Nordic approach stressed knowledge *about* citizenship—about the structures and processes of government and political life. More recently there has also been a stress on knowledge *for* citizenship, values, understandings, and skills linked to the development of attitudes of tolerance, solidarity, gender equality, etc., most notably in Sweden. Sweden also goes further, not only educating *about* but also *by* the principles of democracy. The Swedish curriculum states explicitly that it is not sufficient to impart knowledge of fundamental democratic values; it must also be carried out in such a way that students are able to gain experience in the planning and evaluation of their own educational life. Each school is expected to live up to these overall goals. For primary and lower secondary level pupils, the emphasis is on democracy in the school, while for upper secondary level students an important dimension is (involvement with) democracy beyond the school environment.

In each country, civic education is compulsory at the secondary level, though there is a fair degree of variation as to the number of hours among the four countries. There is some variation in the evaluation systems, though none use national examinations to assess performance in civic education. Finland provides a not atypical example of the Nordic educational structure. Compulsory school for those ages 7 to 15 comprises six grades of primary education and three of intermediate. Secondary (i.e., upper secondary) school is for those ages 16–18. Civic education (including an economics component) is a compulsory subject in grade 9 taken three hours weekly. Similarly, in upper secondary school, which normally takes three years, the student takes two compulsory courses: civic knowledge and economics. There are also two popular optional courses: public law and Europe and the EU.

Schools are expected to follow general guidelines as to subject content, teaching method, evaluation and inspection, teacher education and training, student participation, etc., though in the more decentralized systems in Sweden and Finland, municipalities, schools, teachers, and students have quite a bit of latitude over subject content, teaching methods, and time allocated to the different areas of civic education. This results in more varied outcomes, but also allows for greater integration into local decision making.

There are ongoing efforts to strengthen and modernize civic education. The Nordic countries are increasingly making use of websites as a civic education tool: to present examples of civic education, to provide information about innovative teaching and learning methods, and to summarize relevant reports and research. Sweden has been developing a set of diagnostic tests for the purposes of evaluation. One Norwegian program selects demonstration schools to create democratic learning environments to be used for observation visits, practice for student teachers, and teachers' in-service training. Another program uses an interactive questionnaire to allow thousands of students to evaluate their educational experience and their ability to affect it.

One interesting innovation is the establishment of sophisticated interactive centers, called Democracy Workshops or Mini-Parliaments, that offer students at the end of high school the opportunity to experience through role-playing the parliamentary committee decision making processes. These are described in the Appendix.

Civic education in Canada

The fact that education is a provincial responsibility makes the Canadian situation somewhat comparable with Scandinavia as a whole. (There is one key difference, namely, that in Canada, one level of government—federal—sets priorities for education, while another—provincial—is responsible for citizenship.) Educational requirements in Canada vary from province to province, including the rules regarding civic education. In every province, with the partial exception of Quebec, high school graduates are required to have successfully completed at least one social studies course.[24] An overview is provided by Canadian specialist Alan Sears in his posting on the IDEA civic education website.

> In all jurisdictions [in] Canada, social studies programs contain specific and detailed outcomes related to civic knowledge skills and values. . . . The idea of agency—that individual citizens can and should make a

> difference through active participation in public live [sic] at a number of levels—permeates prescribed outcomes for social studies across provinces. This is most evident in Alberta [the only Canadian jurisdiction with regular provincial testing in social studies] and British Columbia where active citizenship is mandated at every level of the curriculum. In the elementary social studies curriculum in BC, for example, each year students . . . [in] grades two and three . . . might "contact a representative of a local environmental group or of the provincial or federal environment ministry and discuss ways in which the class could practice global citizenship," to grade five where working in the context of studying their region "it is expected that students will: identify and clarify a problem, issue, or inquiry; gather and record a body of information from a variety of primary and secondary sources; develop alternative interpretation[s] from varied sources [and] design, implement, and assess strategies to address community problems or projects." This trend of engaging students in civic action in ever wider contexts is present throughout the elementary curriculum, culminating in attention to global issues at grades six and seven.[25]

Only the province of Ontario mandates a civics course as such. It is a half-course incorporated into the grade 10 curriculum and combined with a required Canadian and World Studies course. Somewhat reminiscent of Scandinavia, "Profile for Civics" explores what it means to be an informed participant in a democratic society. It is broken down into three units: Democracy—Issues and Ideas (15 hours), The Canadian Context (25 hours), and Global Perspectives (15 hours). The curriculum guidelines stress the historical and institutional approach, with emphasis on knowledge of government procedures, as well as teach Canadian civic virtues, especially tolerance of diversity and commitment to the democratic process (see Table 8.4).

In the fall of 2005, British Columbia introduced an optional course, "Civics Studies," as part of the grade 11 curriculum, with a substantial project in civic action at its core. This latter pattern is becoming more common. In New Brunswick, there is an optional Canadian political science course in grade 12, but it is not widely offered or taken (although a new grade 9 course was implemented in the fall of 2006 that focuses on Canadian identity). Quebec has no such course either in high school or in its CEGEP program, which replaces the last year of high school and the first year of university. Its project of revamping its high school history program into a social studies program encompassing a vague civic education mission has stirred much controversy.

Table 8.4: Overall expectations of Ontario high school course "Profile for Civics"

Informed citizenship

- Demonstrate an understanding of the reasons for democratic decision making
- Compare contrasting views of what it means to be a "citizen"
- Describe the main features of local, provincial, and federal governments in Canada and explain how these features work
- Explain the legal rights and responsibilities associated with Canadian citizenship
- Demonstrate an understanding of citizenship within a global context

Purposeful citizenship

- Examine beliefs and values underlying democratic citizenship, and explain how these beliefs and values guide citizens' actions
- Articulate clearly their personal sense of civic identity and purpose, and understand the diversity of beliefs and values of other individuals and groups in Canadian society
- Demonstrate an understanding of the challenges of governing communities or societies in which diverse value systems, multiple perspectives, and differing civic purposes coexist
- Demonstrate an understanding of a citizen's role in responding to non-democratic movements through personal and group actions
- Demonstrate an ability to research questions and issues of civic importance, and to think critically and creatively about these issues and questions

Active citizenship

- Demonstrate an ability to apply decision making and conflict-resolution procedures and skills to cases of civic importance
- Demonstrate an ability to collaborate effectively when participating in group inquiries and community activities
- Demonstrate a knowledge of different types of citizenship participation and involvement

Source: Ministry of Education, course profile, civics, grade 10, open April 2000, Ontario, *www.curriculum.org* (adapted from Lewis, 2007).

Although there is some sign of improvement and increased concern, when compared with the Nordic countries, there appears to still be much room for improvement in Canada along the lines suggested above in order to address the low levels of political knowledge among Canadians reaching voting age (Milner, 2007).

Beyond the School: Policies to Address Youth Voting Decline in Scandinavia

In this section we describe policies and specific measures that have emerged in recent years to enhance democratic participation in the countries under consideration.[26] Some are specifically targeted at young people, but most are not. Nevertheless, other things being equal, they affect the new generation at least as much as other generations.

Denmark is the only Nordic country, perhaps the only stable democratic country, where decline in turnout has been negligible. It has thus, understandably, not been overly concerned with getting people to vote. Generally, to the extent that concerns about a democratic deficit are voiced in Denmark, they focus on the EU rather than on Danish institutions. Nevertheless, there have been important modifications and innovations with a view to enhancing citizens' influence on the democratic process, especially at the local level. A major objective of the structural reform, which created larger municipalities and which came into effect on January 1, 2007, was to improve the capacity of local political institutions to make political decisions and, in so doing, establish a forum for meaningful citizen involvement. Another recent Danish initiative has been to have draft parliamentary bills placed on the Internet for citizen input.

One notable recent initiative focused on helping young people understand Danish political institutions. In August 2004, groups made up of a high school teacher and eight or nine pupils were invited to prepare a draft bill and submit it to Parliament. The Danish Parliament then selected 60 of the bills, and the selected groups each chose three delegates. Further discussion of the bills took place with the Internet playing a major role. Next, each of the 12 committees of the Danish Parliament received five of the bills. Meetings of a Youth Parliament attended by the 180 delegates then took place, some electronically and some at the Christiansborg Palace (the Danish Parliament buildings) with members of the 12 committees. (The general public was able to follow the committees' work on the Internet.) Each committee framed a question which was then posed orally to a minister during question time. The final meeting was held in April 2005, chaired by the Speaker of the Danish Parliament.

Youth Parliaments run along similar lines are prominent in the other Scandinavian countries. The sixth biennial one in Finland was organized in April 2008 for students ages 15 and 16 (in the last two years of comprehensive schooling).

In Sweden the "Time for Democracy" project, noted above, was initiated in spring 2000 and slated to last two years.[27] Grants were given to educational projects that aimed at stimulating greater participation in the democratic process, especially among those groups in the population where participation is low. Two areas were singled out for priority consideration: the diverse population of the big cities and young people. Of the 1,200 applications received, 142 grants were approved, the largest number going to municipalities, adult education associations, immigrant organizations, and disabled people's groups. The projects focused on strengthening local democracy and developing conditions for youth involvement and participation, IT-based democratic initiatives, new approaches to citizen education, and new forums for dialogue between politicians and citizens. Extra resources were made available to political parties to provide information targeting people of foreign extraction. Money was also allocated to voluntary organizations working to encourage citizens to participate politically, and a number of seminars and other activities were funded. One was the voters' magazine, *Röster*, which, according to those responsible for its distribution, was used quite widely by social studies/civic education teachers. Though Sweden is comparatively advanced in the number of women who are politically active, special efforts continue to promote equal participation of men and women. A new scheme was introduced under which financial compensation could be claimed for childcare costs if one of the parents participated in local politics. Another program entitled people with disabilities to receive financial support for the costs incurred in their participatory activities as a result of their disability.

Young people and certain other groups have also been underrepresented in political activity. To address this, parallel efforts were made to remove obstacles in the way of young people, non-Swedish citizens (immigrants who are not Swedish citizens can vote in municipal elections), people with low incomes and little education, elderly people, citizens born in another country, and people with disabilities standing as candidates, especially at the local level. Parties were given extra funds to recruit and prepare candidates from these backgrounds. Moreover, research projects, including pilot projects, were initiated in the use of sign language and digitalized information so that those requiring it are able to carry out their tasks on the same terms as other councilors. The various initiatives were coordinated by the Swedish Association of Local Authorities and the Federation of Swedish County [Regional] Councils, which jointly organized seminars, lectures, and Internet discussions to keep up on ongoing developments.

"Ambassadors" were appointed and trained to act as information officers and election motivators among immigrant groups. In 2002, the turnout increased in the housing areas targeted by these ambassadors.[28] To broaden such activities, the organization in charge—the Swedish Integration Board—continues to seek out teachers and facilitators who speak the relevant languages.

In January 2002, Sweden adopted the "Democracy in the New Century" Act to encourage citizens to participate politically during and between elections. To implement this, there were a number of amendments to the Elections Act to simplify and facilitate voting, including the creation of a new single-purpose agency (Valmyndigheten) to run elections. Changes included increasing opportunities to vote by mail for voters residing abroad, allowing officials at polling stations to issue duplicate voting cards, and streamlining postal voting in cooperation with the national postal service. In the election following these modifications, more ballot papers reached voters on time, and voters could find more and better information about the voting process in a number of languages on the website of the Valmyndigheten. Turnout, which had declined from 86 percent in 1994 to 81 percent in 1998 and 80 percent in 2002, rose to 82 percent in 2006.

These efforts are continuing. To make it easier for citizens to influence the political process, a series of proposals are being implemented, in cooperation with various government bodies, political parties, and voluntary organizations. To enhance the ability of existing organizations to play this role and to encourage the forming of new organizations for this purpose, the government has made special funds available and set up a commission to investigate how to raise the quantity and quality of public space available for public gatherings. As a result, consultative councils and/or youth councils set up for this purpose now exist in most municipalities.

An additional objective concerns greater transparency in the financial administration of political parties and their election campaigns. The specific goal is to allow the citizens to be able to inspect the financial affairs of political parties (as they can with all public bodies). A wider objective is to enhance the legitimacy of party politics and inhibit corruption. One aspect of these various activities is the organization of "deliberation forums" to learn more about what makes people participate or not participate in society and especially in the political process.

The latest phase of the government's effort was launched in February 2006 and continues until 2009. Known as "Participating Sweden," it primarily seeks to learn from an evaluation of existing programs and experiences, with a view to improvement and continuity. The overall goal remains the same, enhancing political participation, but there is added emphasis on fighting discrimination and promoting the human rights of minorities. For the years 2006–2008, five municipalities were granted funds to develop and test different methods of fostering the involvement of those who do not usually participate in the political process between elections. In addition, 12 communities (all with low turnout in the latest election) have been granted money to work, in cooperation with local NGOs, to raise both the awareness of upcoming elections and the general knowledge of the political system in Sweden. In addition, a network was set up for newly elected representatives with foreign backgrounds to work with their counterparts with Swedish backgrounds.

Perhaps the most innovative aspect of these various initiatives has been the introduction of Citizens' Initiatives. As of July 1, 2002, municipal assemblies have been free to introduce citizens' proposals, that is, the right of residents (including adolescents and noncitizens) to raise matters in the municipal assembly. An evaluation in 2004 found that in the first 18 months, 125 municipal councils took action in this area, while in another 100 the idea was being considered. A total of 981 citizens' proposals were tabled in the municipal and county councils covered by the study. The proposals were usually concerned with service-related issues and were handled in the same way as ordinary motions and did not entail appreciably heavier workloads. Approximately 10 percent of the 296 proposals that had come before the councils were approved.

One particular youth-focused initiative was Skolval (School Vote), similar to the Canadian Youth Vote (see below). Election committees are formed to represent the various parties, and students serve as "campaign directors," with candidates invited to the school to debate the issues.[29] The first Skolval was in the 2002 election in which 91,744 students voted out of a potential 267,476 (only 34.3 percent participated). In 2006, of the 404,917 potential voters (the number of participating schools had increased), turnout jumped to 86.66 percent. Ballots were identical to the official ones and were counted in the same fashion as the national vote. The results were reported by the media, by total, by region, and by individual school—in the newspapers but also on TV during the coverage of the actual election results. There has also been some consideration of opening the vote to 16-year-olds—an initiative taken in at least one municipality, Eskiltuna in the greater Stockholm region.

Finland has taken a course similar to Sweden's in response to a more worrisome experience with declining turnout. Finnish turnout hit a low of just over 65 percent in the parliamentary elections of 1999 (rising slightly in the last two elections), and only 74.1 percent turned out in its last presidential election in 2006. (Note that Finns have a comparatively high level of confidence in the institutions in their country, as suggested in Table 8.3, as well as relatively high levels of knowledge about them.) A multifaceted response was initiated in 2003, known as the citizen participation program, targeting, as in Sweden, those groups with especially low levels of participation. This program touched on various aspects directly and indirectly linked to political participation, including the voting system, bureaucratic responsiveness, the use of electronic feedback systems, education and civic education at various levels, teacher training, and municipal democracy. The goals were made as precise as possible, and research continues to be carried out to measure whether these objectives are being attained using indicators such as the level of knowledge of public affairs shown by young people as well as their turnout levels. One goal is to ensure that neither young people nor any other identifiable groups attain less than 50 percent voter turnout.

With the drop in voter turnout most acute among young citizens, civic education especially is being rethought at all levels, up to and including university and adult education and teacher training. The initiative goes beyond the school, since the program is based on the belief that civil society is a training school for effective democratic participation. Voluntary associations of all kinds have been brought into the process and given support to address the relevant specific groups, especially young people and immigrants. One interesting dimension takes the form of organized visits between teachers, local officials, and elected politicians.

Finland, the land of Nokia, is well known for being on the vanguard in the use of electronic communications technology. This is evident in the use of electronic technology for voting and citizen-government communication to complement the referenda and popular initiatives that are becoming more frequent. The Ministry of Justice's ongoing project, "Your opinion.fi," seeks to improve the public sector feedback system. Related to this are efforts of the Interior Ministry to strengthen local democracy through a Municipal Democracy Audit, the goal of which is for ordinary citizens to have a greater influence on local politics, so that the local self-government system can develop mechanisms to counter the trend toward declining citizen involvement.

Policies to Address Youth Voting Decline in Canada

Like in Scandinavia, but unlike in the United States, the initiative in Canada has been taken in public institutions. At the center has been Elections Canada, the independent body that administers federal elections. Elections Canada, which plays an important role in fostering democracy internationally, has a mandate in Canada to actively promote voter participation through the media and otherwise. It also provides information about how to stand as a candidate and is involved in international projects fostering democracy. But since 2000, in response to the especially low turnout that year, the concentration has been on efforts, directed primarily at young people, to foster turnout.[30]

Most of the programs were put into effect in and around the 2004 election. One effort was to get first-time voters on the National Register of Electors. Some 77 percent of them were on the list for the 2004 election. In addition, Elections Canada took initiatives to foster citizens' awareness and interest in elections, such as devising and publicizing crosswords containing democratic words such as *vote*, *assembly*, and *elections*, and introducing a Trivia game on the Internet that involved questions about Parliament and elections. In specifically addressing young people, Elections Canada has sponsored or worked with other organizations to raise awareness among young people. Examples include the following:

- *"Cable in the Classroom"*: This is a program for students in grades 10–12. A contest was held for students to create public service announcements telling their peers why democracy is important and why it is important to vote. Some 108 entries were received.
- *Rush the Vote*: This is an organization that aims to increase youth voter turnout and political awareness through "edutainment."[31] Musical events at which performers encourage voting and democratic involvement were given support. Concerts were held in Ottawa, Toronto, and Edmonton.
- *Parallel elections*: In 2004 and 2006, Elections Canada launched Youth Vote, a joint initiative with Student Vote to provide students below voting age with the opportunity to experience the federal electoral process through a parallel election in their schools, with the results being broadcast on television, posted on the Internet, and published in newspapers across the country.[32]
- *Poster contests*: For the 2004 election, in partnership with four student associations—the Canadian Federation of Students, the Fédération étudiante universitaire du Québec, the New Brunswick Student Alliance, and the Canadian Alliance of Student Associations—a poster was displayed on campuses across Canada. A total of 3,200 posters were sent to these associations for distribution to their 119 member associations.

- *Education kits*: Elections Canada also provided support for a youth voter education kit as part of Youth Vote 2004 and 2006, an education and media initiative launched by the Dominion Institute.

Elections Canada has been working in partnership with the Historica Foundation to develop a new YouthLinks education module on citizenship and voting. YouthLinks is a free on-line education program that links high school students in Canada and abroad and operates in some 400 high schools across Canada. A new module, "Voices," was launched in late fall 2004 as a practical teaching tool on elections and the democratic process. These efforts are reflected on Elections Canada's homepage, which provides relevant information in an accessible format. The homepage is designed with young people in mind. When last consulted in the weeks before the October 14, 2008, Canadian federal election, it featured youth-focused FAQs about voting. The permanent part of the homepage opens up with links to election basics, members of Parliament and candidates, and learning resources. The latter is divided into three areas: (1) General Resources, which offers information designed for everyone, from reports and publications to facts and figures about elections, (2) Resources for Students, which provides information on organizing elections in high school, junior college, and university, and (3) Resources for Teachers, which offers games and activities to help make learning about elections enjoyable. This section is broken down by age group, each linked to materials to aid in the task. On the website, the following links and descriptions allow the user to interact with the program:

- Younger students, from kindergarten through grade 4, can try the Choosing Our Mascot election simulation.
- The School Elections Officer Guide gives step-by-step instructions for student council elections adaptable for grades 5 to 12.
- The Election Simulation helps students organize an election simulation in the classroom, adaptable for grades 5 to 12.
- There are election supplies, such as tally sheets and sample ballot paper.
- Order teacher resources.
- Explore other resources in the teacher links page.

The final section, "Get Involved," provides links to the basic information about voting and the electoral system, about how to become a candidate and start a political career, etc. It also provides guides to various youth organizations and lists events, games, and other useful links.

Apart from the organization behind the student vote project, both federally and in several provinces, perhaps the most important youth organization is the Democracy Project, supported by the Dominion Institute and other public and private funds. Its most significant activity is a series of surveys carried on by a related organization, Innovative Research, on issues related to youth political participation. For example, a survey during the 2006 federal election asked respondents what they thought about Canada's democracy, how to improve it, and how to get more young people to vote. Also during the election campaign, some 63 all-candidates debates were organized at high schools and universities.

Another activity in recent months was the organization of a contest (by sending in a video) to participate in a televised debate among Canadians ages 18 to 25 who believe they have the qualifications and aptitude to be the "Next Great Prime Minister." This took place in an *American Idol* type of format with former prime ministers as judges.

We do not know the extent to which these measures account for what appears to be a turnaround in electoral participation with the decline from 75 percent in the 1980s halted in 2004 with 61 percent of eligible voters turning out as in 2000, the number rising to 65 percent in 2006. But clearly they made a difference.

Conclusion

In contrast with the United States, in both Canada and Scandinavia encouraging youth electoral participation is accepted as a political priority to be coordinated, if not implemented, and evaluated by government agencies. Nevertheless, there are three important differences, at least in emphasis. First, when it comes to civic education, there is more reluctance in Canada to involve the students in discussion of current political issues and to invite politicians and parties into the (virtual) classroom. There is also an important difference in targeting. There is more of an effort to target young people known to be low in civic literacy and political participation, that is, those for whom home support and social connectedness are weak—the potential academic and political dropouts. This difference extends beyond civic education. For young people, as for the population as a whole, the Nordic countries seem more willing and able to target—with programs designed to correspond to their particular situation—those whose access to the means of political participation is weakest. This is an expression of what I have characterized (Milner, 2002) as nonmaterial redistribution, a distinctive characteristic of Nordic welfare states.

The third difference has to do with the role of the various levels of government and of political parties. An important role is played by a government agency, Elections Canada, whose coordinating activities are essentially confined to the voluntary sector. In Scandinavia, we see an array of programs developed at the center and implemented through local governments, political parties, government agencies at different levels, and voluntary organizations.

While such an approach may not be applicable to the United States, given the real and perceived dangers of partisanship built into its institutions and political culture, Canada would stand to benefit if it were to take a more Scandinavian approach.

Appendix: The Scandinavian Democracy Workshops

Traditionally students have taken tours of Parliament combined with lectures informing them about what goes on there. In the context of recent efforts to foster active youth political involvement, it was felt that this was inadequate: that the students tended to see this as a tour of a building, like a visit to a museum. To this end, the parliaments of Sweden, Norway, and Denmark created and funded interactive centers, called Democracy Workshops or Mini-Parliaments, that offer students in the last two years of compulsory school (typically ages 15 and 16) the opportunity to experience, through role-playing, the parliamentary committee decision making processes. Schools schedule class visits to the center, and subsidies are provided for travel costs. In Sweden, population 9 million, some 12,000 students visited the center between the opening in fall 2006 and early April 2008. The centers are specially designed areas to simulate miniature parliaments. The space is divided up to include places for party caucus meetings, areas set up to resemble committee rooms, and a larger area for plenary meetings. In Oslo, press conference rooms are set up to allow for televised debates.

While details vary, the general program and design of the centers are similar. Groups of 16–35 students come to the special center. Trained animators (who also work as parliamentary press or information officers) guide the students through a half-day role-play that attempts to simulate a key aspect of the work and the hectic life of a member of Parliament. After an introduction, the students are brought into the Democracy Workshop (or Mini-Parliament Experience). Each is assigned a card with the first name of an individual MP (and thus party) and placed in a committee that will deal with one or two issues.

For example, in Sweden, one committee considered whether punishments for graffiti should be increased, and the other discussed whether boxing should be outlawed. Both of these matters had come up in Parliament. In Norway, students have looked at legislative bills relating to whether upper secondary school students should receive wage payments, whether the government should establish ethnic housing project zones, whether domestic animals should be fenced in, and whether there should be compulsory identity chips. The students first get a chance to express their own opinions, then they are asked to express those of the person they are playing. The card gives information about the party to which the student's role character is a member, as well as the person's gender, age, professional background, etc. In the Swedish game, the five parties are fictitious, but their names and positions are based on those of the main existing parties.

The game begins when students in each committee go to their parties' caucus rooms (small, specially designed booths) and, basing their judgments on the roles and parties to which they have been assigned, consider the positions they should take on the legislative issue under consideration. The size of the party groups varies so as to reflect the real political situation. Students are guided in their deliberations by instructions provided to them via a computer screen in each booth and by the animator. In the party booths, students have access to newspaper articles and excerpts from TV and radio coverage. Their deliberations are interrupted by telephone calls and computer screen messages from "interested persons," including lobbyists, constituents, and party activists, thus exposing them to the efforts to influence the MPs. In the Norwegian role-play, a press conference scenario is also incorporated into the game.

Discussions on the bills are carried out alternatively in the party groups and in the all-party committee meetings. This means that the students not only have to arrive at a common party position but must work with other parties to form alliances or compromises in order to reach a majority position in the committee. And they need to keep in mind that the proposals will need to pass in the plenary, composed of all the students present.

Thus the bills drafted by each committee come to the floor at the plenary session at the end, and after speeches are made for and against, a vote is taken. This plenary session takes place in a mock-up of the Parliament itself, overseen by the animator acting as Speaker of the House. In some of the scenarios the prime minister, a spokesperson for the governing party/coalition, asks for a vote of confidence, and the members must reevaluate their views and take a stand on whether they want to support the government or bring it down.

At the end of the session, students are released from their party role-playing, no longer taking positions based on the role cards that they were given. At this point they are asked to vote as themselves on the issue and to reflect on whether their decisions have changed over the course of the simulation.

Judging by evaluations made by students and the civics teachers who coordinate their participation, these interactive role-playing scenarios have helped students understand the processes behind the passage of bills and the role of MPs as real human beings subject to the influences and constraints of parties as well as that of "interested persons." The use of a committee/caucus structure gives the students hands-on experience in making alliances and arriving at compromises. The most straightforward lesson drawn from the exercise is that a vote in Parliament constitutes the culmination of a long but nevertheless comprehensible legislative process.

Notes

1. Using World Values Survey data, I found no statistically meaningful relationship between the average number of memberships in voluntary associations and voter turnout (Milner, 2002, 31).
2. Print (2006) cites a study of young Australians (16–18) who were asked whether they planned to vote (voting is compulsory in Australia): 86 percent said yes, but that number dropped to only 50 percent when they were asked whether they would still vote if it were not compulsory.
3. This study took the form of an experiment, testing whether young people would make more of an effort to inform themselves if there were a financial penalty for not doing so. No statistically meaningful indication could be found (Milner, Loewen, and Hicks, 2007).
4. I know of no other democratic country where this exists. See "Felons and the right to vote," editorial, New York Times, July 11, 2004.
5. The reasons for this are complex and beyond the scope of this chapter, but they are linked to the United States' founding, which threw off not only a specific regime but the very notion of a "state" beyond the organized activities of the citizens.
6. The data for France were not available when these figures were tabulated. I wish to thank Svante Ersson of Umeå University for these calculations.
7. Since many were too young to vote in the last election, the *N* is quite small.
8. The 1999 International IDEA youth voter participation study based on figures in the mid-1990s identifies the same patterns (IDEA, 1999).
9. The 1956 Gallop surveys showed respondents a list of 10 prominent political figures, of which 2 were Canadian, and asked them to identify the country and position of each, as well as a list of Canada's 10 provincial premiers and asked them to identify their province. The 2000 CES included an unprecedented number of knowledge items: the names of the leaders of the Liberals, PC, Alliance, and NDP, the name of the federal finance minister, and the name of one's provincial premier.
10. In 1956, the difference in reported turnout levels between the groups at the upper and lower ends of the knowledge scale was 17 percentage points; moreover, for the youngest age group (21–29), the difference was actually lower—only 12 points. In the 2000 election study, the overall gap in turnout between the knowledgeable and ignorant had risen to 32 points, but now the

relationship to age was reversed. The 43-point gap that separates the most and least knowledgeable respondents ages 18–29 declines with increasing age to 13 percent among those 50 and older. "Nowadays . . . it is only older Canadians who will vote simply out of duty," he concludes. "Younger Canadians think differently; without some knowledge to make the voting decision comprehensible and meaningful, they prefer to abstain. . . . They know less about politics and . . . their impoverished knowledge is more likely to affect whether or not they vote" (Howe, 2003, 81).

11. I exclude the results of the Civic Education Study, which tested nearly 90,000 14-year-old students in 28 countries and 50,000 students ages 17–19 in 16 countries on political knowledge, skills, and attitudes (Torney-Purta et al., 2001). Not only was Canada not included, but the questions are problematic, since rather than testing political knowledge as such, they test understanding of the logic of democracy and the functioning of its institutions.
12. Examples of such questions include "The Taliban and al Qaeda movements were both based in which country?" "Which of the following organizations endorses the euro as the common currency for its members?" and "Which two countries have had a long-standing conflict over the region of Kashmir?"
13. Holding education constant, Grönlund finds that for those who did not finish secondary education, the average score on the three or more CSES political knowledge questions was .40 for people ages 18–35, just under .50 for those ages 34–55, and .53 for those 55 and older. For those who had completed secondary or vocational school, the disparity was essentially the same, with the youngest group's score rising to .53. Only when we get to those with university degrees is the disparity reduced—by roughly half—with the youngest group averaging .65 right answers (Grönlund, 2003).
14. This data is provided by IDEA International (*www.idea.int/vt/*).
15. Available at *www.elections.ca/loi/report_e.pdf.*
16. Reported in Elections Canada, Electoral Insight, February 2005. Given methodological differences, we cannot definitively state that more voted in 2004.
17. For example, in the (difficult) NAEP test of proficiency in civics (NCES 1999: 100), 32 percent of the 77 percent of students who reported discussing school studies with their parents at least once or twice a week scored satisfactory or better compared with 16 percent of those (23 percent) who never or hardly ever had such discussions.
18. See Stroupe and Sabato, 2004. See also Hunter and Brisbin, 2000; Andolina, Keeter, Zukin, and Jenkins, 2002; Henzey, 2003; and Beem, 2005.
19. An example is found in a multimedia "e-book" about the 2002 California gubernatorial election. Compiled on a CD, the e-book presented an exhaustive and easily searchable database about the two major candidates, Democrat Gray Davis and Republican Bill Simon, including televised advertisements, interviews with broadcast news sources, excerpts from the party platforms, and the audio of their one public debate (Iyengar and Jackman, 2004).
20. This representativeness also tends to make the entire political system more

legitimate in the eyes of the young people and promotes youth turnout. See IDEA, 1999.

21. Kids Voting USA now assists teachers in 39 states to help students gather information about candidates and issues, so that on election day the students cast their ballots in special booths (the younger ones going to the polls with their parents). The votes are then counted and publicly reported. One follow-up study of those who participated found that while it did not directly affect turnout three years later, in 2004 it did "animate the family as a setting for political discussion and media use, habits that eventually lead to voting. . . . Parents got caught up in their children's enthusiasm for politics" (McDevitt and Kiousis, 2006, 3).
22. The chief electoral officer reported, "Community relations officers for youth identified neighbourhoods with high concentrations of students for special registration drives, assisted in locating polls in places easily accessible to youth, and informed the community and youth leaders about registration and voting." Elections Canada, Electoral Insight—July 2003.
23. The information in this section comes from two main sources. The first is a synthesis of a detailed report: Rolf Mikkelsen, "Education for democratic citizenship: Policy-making and implementation in the northern European region," Council of Europe. The second is found in submissions to the International IDEA database on civic education (*civiced.idea.int/public/viewSurvey.jsp?sId=4032005*) for Canada (by Alan Sears), Sweden (Niklas Eklund), and Finland (Arja Virta).
24. Quebec is in the process of restructuring its history program to incorporate civic education.
25. See *civiced.idea.int/public/viewSurveyResponse.jsp?srId=4348117.*
26. The information in this section comes from two sources: (1) Secretariat, Council of the Baltic Sea States, Strömsborg, "Study on citizens' participation in the Baltic Sea region by the CBSS Working Group on Democratic Institutions," presented at the sixth Baltic Sea States Summit, Reykjavik, 2006, available at *www.cbss.st/summits/reykjavik2006/reports/*, and (2) Eva Wisse, for the UK Ministry of the Interior and Kingdom Relations Department of Constitutional Matters and Legislation, "Promoting democracy: An international exploration of policy and implementation practice," available at *www.minbzk.nl/contents/pages/55271/promotingdemocracy.pdf.*
27. For additional information, see the Swedish Ministry of Justice Fact Sheet, December 2004, Democracy Policy, available at *www.britishcouncil.org/brussels-power-inquiry-democracy-policy.pdf.*
28. One specific project encouraged Somali women to get involved in politics through study groups, seminars, and a program on local television. Women of different ages from the same background were able to exchange ideas that might not have been heard had the debate been held in a larger setting.
29. See *www.regeringen.se/sb/d/6148/a/55918.*
30. Chief electoral officer's keynote speech, CRIC seminar, Ottawa, October 1, 2004, available at *www.elections.ca.*

31. Rush the Vote is linked to the 501(c)(3) nonprofit U.S. organization Rock the Vote.
32. In 2004, 1,175 high schools participated in Student Vote from every province and territory, with 265,000 students casting a ballot, representing 267 of 308 electoral districts. In 2006, 2,504 schools participated from every province and territory, with 468,000 students casting a ballot, representing 284 electoral districts. See *www.studentvote.ca/fed07/index.php*. Student Vote has run mock-vote programs in three provincial elections. The first was in 2003 in Ontario, when 825 schools participated, including 72 percent of all secondary schools, and 335,000 students cast ballots, representing all 103 electoral districts. The second, in Alberta in 2004, took place in 386 schools, with 65,960 students casting ballots, representing 80 out of 83 electoral districts. The third was in British Columbia in 2005 with 359 schools and 66,404 students, representing 78 out of 79 electoral districts.

References

Andolina, M., Keeter, S., Zukin, C., and Jenkins, K. (2002). *The civic and political health of the nation: A generational portrait.* College Park, MD: NACE.

Beem, C. (2005). From the horse's mouth: A dialogue between politicians and college students. CIRCLE Working Paper 27, *www.civicyouth.org.*

Blais, A., Gidengill, E., Nadeau, R., and Nevitte, N. (2002). *Anatomy of a liberal victory: Making sense of the vote in the 2000 Canadian election.* Peterborough: Broadview.

Electoral Commission: UK. (2002). *Voter engagement and young people.* London: Electoral Commission.

Ersson, S., and Milner, H. (2009). Political participation in Scandinavia. In G. Gustafsson, C. Kite, and K. Lundmark (Eds.), *The Nordic countries in the New Europe: Institutions, politics, and policy.* Oslo: Universitetsforlaget, in press.

Friedland, L. A., and Morimoto, S. (2006). The lifeworlds of young people and civic engagement. In Peter Levine and James Youniss (Eds.), *Youth civic engagement: An institutional turn* (pp. 37–39). CIRCLE Working Paper 45. Available at *www.civicyouth.org.*

Grönlund, K. (2003). Knowledge and turnout: A comparative analysis. Paper presented at the 2003 ECPR conference, Marburg, Germany, September.

Henzey, D. (2003). North Carolina Civic Index: A benchmark study impacts state-level policy. *National Civic Review, 92* (1).

Howe, P. (2003). Where have all the voters gone? *Inroads, 12* (fall).

Hunter, S., and Brisbin, R. A., Jr. (2000). The impact of service learning on democratic and civic values. *PS: Political Science and Politics, 33* (3), 623–26.

IDEA. (1999). *Youth voter participation: Involving today's young in tomorrow's democracy.* Stockholm: IDEA.

Iyengar, S., and Jackman, S. (2004). Technology and politics: Incentives for youth participation. CIRCLE, *www.civicyouth.org.*

Lewis, J. P. (2007). Why civics? Adopting policy causal stories for citizenship education in Ontario. Paper presented at the 2007 CPSA meetinge, Saskatoon, Canada, June.

Lopez, M. H., Levine, P., Both, D., Kiesa, A., Kirby, E., and Marcelo, K. (2006). The 2006 civic and political health of the nation: A detailed look at how youth participate in politics and communities. CIRCLE, *www.civicyouth.org.*

McDevitt, M., and Kiousis, S. (2006). Experiments in political socialization: Kids voting USA as a model for civic education reform. CIRCLE Working Paper 49. Available at *www.civicyouth.org.*

Milner, H. (2002). *Civic literacy: How informed citizens make democracy work.* Hanover: University Press of New England.

Milner, H. (2005a). Do we need to fix our system of unfixed election dates? *Policy Matters*, December.

Milner, H. (2005b). The phenomenon of political drop-outs: Canada in comparative perspective. *Choices.*

Milner, H. (2007). The political knowledge and political participation of young Canadians and Americans. Paper presented at the Congress of the Canadian Political Science Association, Saskatoon, June.

Milner, H., Loewen, P., and Hicks, B. (2007). Compulsory voting and informed youth. *Policy Matters.* Montreal: IRPP, forthcoming.

NCES (National Center for Educational Statistics). (1999). *NAEP 1998 Civics Report Card for the Nation.* Washington, DC: Department of Education.

Pammett, J., and LeDuc, L. (2003). *Explaining the turnout decline in Canadian federal elections: A new survey of non-voters.* Ottawa: Elections Canada.

Print, M. (2006). Socializing young Australians to participate in compulsory voting. Paper presented at the World Congress of the International Political Science Association, Fukuoka, Japan, July.

Sherr, S. (2005). News for a new generation: Can it be fun and functional? CIRCLE Working Paper 29, March 2005.

Stroupe, K. S., and Sabato, L. J. (2004). @Politics: The missing link of responsible civic education. CIRCLE, *www.civicyouth.org.*

Torney-Purta, J., Lehmann, R., Oswald, H., and Schulz, W. (2001). *Citizenship and education in 28 countries: Civic knowledge at age 14.* Amsterdam: Eburon-IEA.

Westheimer, J., Cook, S., Llewellyn, K., and Molina Girón, A. (2007). *The state and potential of civic learning in Canada.* Democratic Dialogue occasional paper series, *DemocraticDialogue.com.*

9

Civic Education in Europe

Comparative Policy Perspectives from the Netherlands, Belgium, and France

Marc Hooghe and Ellen Claes

In recent years, various policy initiatives have been implemented to strengthen the importance of civic education in European countries. The Council of Europe even proclaimed 2005 to be the "European Year of Citizenship through Education," in an effort to harmonize the efforts of its member states. The Council also claimed that European liberal democracies share a specific political culture that would benefit from a harmonized approach to civic education. In reality, however, European countries tend to hold on to their own national legacies and the specific national characteristics of their education system. In general, little attention is given to the process of European unification in the curricula for civic education (Quintelier and Dejaeghere, 2008). In most countries, national political institutions and the specific national culture remain the most important reference frame for civic education. Although various authors have emphasized the need to establish a European form of citizenship and belonging, in practice we see little progress toward this goal in the field of civic education (Torney-Purta, Schwille, and Amadeo, 1999).

What European countries do have in common, however, is that they too have emphasized the importance of civic education in recent years, partly as a reaction to the growing concern about an alleged erosion of citizenship norms among young people. While some countries have implemented specific new courses on political education, in other education systems decision makers have opted for a broader formulation of educational goals that are not connected to any specific course. A further complicating factor is that while governments usually have a direct impact on the curriculum of public schools, this is not necessarily the case for private schools enjoying a larger degree of autonomy.

In this chapter we try to develop a comparative perspective by documenting the recent development of civic education in the Netherlands, Belgium, and France.

Citizenship Education in a Unified Europe

The process of European unification creates a unique setting for civic education. Since the 1950s, European unification has been implemented mainly as a top-down initiative, where political leaders and business elites have taken the lead to develop an ever closer union between the member states. Since the 1990s, however, concern has grown about a perceived lack of legitimacy of the European institutions. Turnout during elections for the European Parliament has declined dramatically and in some countries barely exceeds 30 percent of the electorate. Referenda on constitutional reform usually show a strong degree of Euroskepticism or even downright hostility toward the European Union among the population. The latest three referenda on European institutions—in France, the Netherlands, and Ireland—all resulted in a resounding defeat for the supporters of European unification.

One of the main reasons for this lack of legitimacy is the democratic deficit of the European Union: despite the direct elections for the members of the European Parliament, European citizens can exert only a limited impact on the decision making process within the European Union. Despite various reforms, most of the power still resides with the Council of Ministers, where the national governments have the final say. Since the 1990s, the European Union has tried to install more direct rights for European citizens, but ten years later, a deep Euroskepticism still prevails.

One of the basic problems for the efforts to promote European citizenship is that there is no such thing as a common European identity or citizenry. Various surveys demonstrate that the "sense of belonging" to a common European political sphere is limited in most of the member states. Linguistic, economic, and cultural cleavages within the European Union imply that a national sense of identity exists in most member countries. Various authors, therefore, have claimed that the real challenge is to develop a sense of European citizenship beyond the borders of the traditional nation-states (Delanty, 2007). The challenge of European citizenship is that unity and diversity need to be reconciled: the 27 member states start from diverging cultural and religious backgrounds, and language barriers often prevent the development of a joint European identity.

Although the European Union itself produces various educational materials on the functioning of the European institutions, one cannot help but notice that the reaction of educational systems and teachers is lukewarm. Although civic education is often invoked as a way to "create" a sense of European citizenship and to address the lack of legitimacy of the European Union, in practice it remains difficult to convince pupils of the democratic character of the European institutions. Despite the fact that the impact of European decision making is of increasing importance for the member states, civic education texts usually start from their own national context and in most cases they hardly venture into explaining European politics.

In practice, therefore, national identities still are of paramount importance. At best, the European Union plays a secondary role in civic education in employing the concept of multilevel government. Within that framework, the European Union is considered as just an extra level to be added to the already existing institutional framework. It makes little sense to try to paint an overall picture of civic education in Europe, since this would require a portrait of the situation in 27 countries. In this chapter, we will illustrate the many ways in which European education systems have come to promote civicness in their high schools.

Citizenship Education Policies in the Netherlands

The Netherlands offer a very specific setting for the study of civic education. The country prides itself on a long tradition of tolerant and liberal citizenship, dating back to the Dutch revolution in the sixteenth century. This citizenship concept emphasizes tolerance in accommodating opposing views in society. In recent years, however, the country has also been in the grip of a general concern about the decline of civility and moral norms. The recent murders of a political leader and an author with critical views on Islam have brought the question of multiculturalism strongly to the front in the intellectual and political debate: do the Netherlands still have a strong tolerant culture, and if so, how can this culture be transmitted to new groups within society?

A Distinct Civic Education Course

Before 1963, there was not a unified educational system with nationwide curricula and test requirements in the Netherlands. Various competing school systems had been established, each with a large degree of autonomy. Protestant and Catholic churches actually supported this proliferation, as it granted them a say in the way they could run their own schools. In 1963, the Dutch state imposed a general institutional framework for secondary education, including a compulsory civic education course. Although the 1963 law introduced a specific course that focuses on citizenship issues, there was no clear-cut and generally accepted content available for the course (Hooghoff, 1990). Teachers, teacher trainers, and textbook authors had to develop their own interpretation of the law, and they had to develop the content of this new course. In practice, however, this meant that almost every teacher developed his or her own interpretation of the topic, despite the calls for more guidance. In response to this concern, the Dutch minister of education established a special committee for curriculum development in 1965. This committee developed a model that can be described as a kind of "social education," highlighting the way societies build common values and practices. The course was still very traditionally organized, with an emphasis on acquiring cognitive skills. Political institutions were considered as just one of the various elements that help to explain the functioning of society in general (Dekker, 1999).

By the late 1970s, the content of this course was further developed, incorporating elements of social and political education. It now includes such topics as education and development, social environment, work and leisure, technology and society, state and society, and international relations. The curriculum further specifies that these topics have to be dealt with by using various perspectives, with an emphasis on political, social, economic, cultural, and comparative angles (Dekker, 1999). The result is that this course became more structured, but in practice it could still be regarded as a general introduction to life in Dutch society. Political aspects received only a limited amount of attention in the overall course design.

The consolidation of the content of this course, however, was not just a top-down process. Even more important was the initiative of a nationwide association of teachers in social studies. This association reached out to teachers all over the country and actively claimed ownership of this new course. The association organized various workshops and offered publications to its members, resulting in the development of a general curriculum for the civics course in 1981. While the ministry of education in the Netherlands refrained from imposing the use of this curriculum, it did set out clear "educational goals" for civic and social education that have to be met by every school in the Netherlands. In practice, following the standard curriculum is the only way to meet these educational goals (Hooghoff, 1990). Since 1990, civic education has been a regular A-level subject in all Dutch schools and part of the compulsory education of Dutch high school students (Dekker, 1999; Spiecker and Steutel, 1995).

The way in which the course was introduced is typical of Dutch decision making overall. The course was not introduced unilaterally by the minister of education, but came into being as the result of an ongoing interaction process between the minister, education officials, education experts, and the teachers themselves, by means of their national association. Including all these voices inevitably led to lengthy negotiations. The result, however, was that the civic course was effectively being taught in all schools in a rather uniform manner. The sense of "ownership" among the teachers proved to be an important element in explaining the general acceptance of the course (Leenders, Veugelers, and De Kat, 2008).

In 1997, the position of civic education again came under attack in Dutch schools. The minister of education was concerned about the fact that Dutch schools did not concentrate their efforts on the "core" tasks of the education process (i.e., languages and mathematics), and that the curriculum was overburdened by all kinds of "auxiliary" courses. The minister proclaimed a "back to basics" course, curbing the time spent on all courses that were not considered essential (Schnabel et al., 2007). As is customary in the Netherlands, the idea was taken up by a number of advisory committees that spent six years arriving at a final recommendation. The basic idea of the committees was indeed to limit the time spent on civic education by combining it with history. The main advice committee argued that a good understanding of contemporary society could only be reached by studying the historical processes that have led to the creation of current social structures, and that therefore both courses could easily be combined. In practice, however, this would mean that both history and civic education would receive less attention in the curriculum, which resulted in fierce opposition by the teachers' associations.

In the end, the views of the association prevailed, and civic education remained a separate course. Recent changes in the curriculum have emphasized civic skills instead of cognitive goals for the course. Parliamentary democracy and the welfare state receive ample attention, while the curriculum also emphasizes the multicultural character of contemporary Dutch society. A better understanding between the various communities and acquiring the skills to bridge cultural differences are explicit goals in the current curriculum. Civic education is still a comprehensive course for all students in the Netherlands, but schools can also add activities to the course.

Increasingly, however, the focus has shifted. Back in the 1990s, the main challenge seemed to be that civic education should prepare all pupils for life within a multicultural society. In the more recent debate, a recurring theme is that ethnic minorities stand to benefit from civic education. It is assumed that children from ethnic minorities do not always share the basic cultural and ethical orientations of Dutch society and that they should be socialized into Dutch social and political culture. Partly, this concern reflects the result of recent research: it has indeed been shown that children from a minority background do not always share the liberal democratic ideals that are inherent in the Dutch political system. Especially within families that have only recently arrived from authoritarian countries like Somalia or Iraq, more traditional notions still seem to predominate (Leeman, 2008). To some extent, however, the debate is also misguided, since it is assumed that native Dutch children are no longer in need of any civic education because they have received sufficient training in culture and morality at home. While empirical research clearly shows that this assumption is not warranted in numerous cases, civic education often is narrowed down to "civic education for ethnic minorities."

Reflections on Civic Education in the Netherlands

Despite some government initiatives to limit the time spent on civic education, the Netherlands now have had a compulsory and distinct civic education course for well over four decades. It is of course a perennial question whether civic education should be included in general courses or should be taught as a separate topic. The Dutch case demonstrates that having a separate course can have important consequences. Since civic education is a distinct course, teachers can claim ownership, and they also feel responsible for its future. The Dutch Association of Teachers in Civic Education has become a key player. First of all, it has helped to develop a standard curriculum for the course. This by itself is important, because in the Netherlands, like in numerous other countries, it would have been very difficult for the government to actually impose such a curriculum. Such a government initiative would have fueled concern that the political system would have too much influence on the curriculum, especially in a socially sensitive topic like civic education. The fact, however, that the teachers themselves were heavily involved in developing the curriculum alleviated this concern. The association also showed its strength by simply keeping the course on the program. While the minister of education tried to reduce the number of hours spent on civic education, the association successfully fought against these plans. One could interpret this as a form of corporatist decision making: indeed, the teachers themselves have a clear professional stake in keeping civic education on the books. A more positive interpretation, however, could be that the active involvement of the teachers led to a general acceptance of the course and to a strengthening of the quality of the curriculum. In line with the Dutch tradition, the content of the course is not imposed by the government but is the result of an active dialogue with society as a whole. Involving the association offers a kind of middle-ground solution: it allows the development of a national uniform curriculum, without fueling concerns about a mighty state apparatus that could use civic education to gain undue influence on citizens' minds: civic education can also function in a bottom-up manner. The downside of this elaborate decision making process is that it can go on for decades. Ministers of education in the Netherlands do not have all that many opportunities to change educational structures during their four-year terms.

Belgium: Two Communities

Despite the fact that Belgium is a small country, with regard to education it is effectively two communities that have little in common. Education is not a federal responsibility in Belgium, but it falls fully into the realm of the two autonomous communities. The only remaining authority of the federal government is to impose the age of compulsory schooling (until 18 in Belgium). This large degree of autonomy for the communities also has some unwanted side-effects. In 1999, for example, the French Community of Belgium decided to participate in the comparative Civic Education Study, while the Dutch Community decided that this was not a priority. As a result, we do not have nation-wide figures on the effects of civic education for the entire country, and the Belgian data only reflect the situation in the French Community.

Since the 1988 constitutional reform, both communities have developed a distinct political culture and style of decision making. The Dutch Community (population ca. 6 million) seems to mirror Dutch political culture: there is a strong emphasis on corporatist decision making with an active and lengthy consultation of all stakeholders. A specific element of the Dutch-language educational system in Belgium is that almost 75 percent of all students are enrolled in Catholic schools. The association of Catholic schools, therefore, enjoys a very strong bargaining position in the educational process. This limits what the education ministry can do. Just like in the Netherlands, therefore, the ministry refrains from imposing a standard curriculum, but it can proclaim educational goals that have to be met. The schools, however, remain free to determine exactly how they want to meet these goals.

Within the French Community (population ca. 4 million) a more centralist approach dominates. First of all, the percentage of pupils in public schools is higher in the French-speaking Community, allowing the ministry a more direct say in the way schools are run. Also with regard to curriculum development and other elements, the French Community is much less inclined to grant a large degree of autonomy to the schools.

Given the strong autonomy of both communities, civic education in the Dutch- and French-language communities of Belgium will be dealt with separately.

Civic Education in the Dutch Community

Within the Dutch-speaking Community, the perennial struggle over who can control education is continued. The Catholic schools are embedded in Flemish society, and they have always resisted imposing strict curriculum requirements on schools, as they argue that every school should be allowed to develop its own distinct educational project. The new Flemish authorities, on the other hand, wanted to impose uniform quality norms for all schools in the region. The compromise was that in 1991 the Flemish Parliament established "final attainment goals" for all schools in the region. Schools have the legal duty to strive to reach these goals, but they remain free to decide how. Most of the goals are tied to a specific course within the curriculum (mathematics, languages, geography, etc.), but the Flemish Parliament also enlisted a number of "cross-cutting" or overarching goals, involving health education, environmental education, and civic education. It is argued that these topics are so important to the future daily life of the pupils that, in some way or another, it is expected that all teachers and all topics will contribute to attaining these goals. These cross-curricular goals, furthermore, are meant to emphasize the place of the school system as a living environment for pupils, preparing them for life in society as a whole.

The most important "overarching education goal" is civicness: it is expected that pupils will voluntarily take responsibility for their own good and for the common good. These goals are not cognitive: the notion of "civicness" is rather attitudinal, as it is expected that pupils will learn to incorporate a social perspective into their daily actions. This attitude can help adolescents to become more actively engaged in society. The policy document claims that the education goals will "help young people to become *active* citizens who participate in social life in a constructive and critical manner." The ministry acknowledges, however, that full citizenship is not just a future intention, but should also be practiced in the school system itself (De Coninck, Maes, Sleurs, and Van Moensel, 2002). In 2004, therefore, the Flemish minister of education decided that every school in the region would have to install a participatory council, including representatives from the pupils, teachers, parents, and various groups. Although some Catholic schools opposed this obligation, in practice they had no other option than to oblige the new legislation (Claes and Hooghe, 2006).

Although the Flemish government refrained from proposing a full-fledged curriculum to reach the education goals with regard to civicness, the ministry offered a number of "suggestions" on the kind of perspectives that could be employed (Siongers, 2001). First, it is stressed that the legal concept of citizenship should be taught. In this framework, attention is focused on human rights agreements and basic liberties like freedom of speech or religion. A special point of attention is the International Treaty on the Rights of Children. Second, a political perspective is being employed. It is stressed that citizens are endowed with inalienable political rights and that they can participate in a direct manner in the political decision making process. Voting rights are a central element in this perspective, but it is also emphasized that there is a trade-off between political rights and social duties toward obeying a democratically established law. Third, the ministry focuses on social relations between individual members of society, invoking attitudes and values like solidarity, loyalty, and commitment. Bringing in this dimension is meant to demonstrate that attaining a civilized and inclusive society is dependent on having a strong moral commitment among the citizens. Just as in the Netherlands, multicultural citizenship is a strong focus of attention. Pupils are urged to reflect on the common cultural horizon of the Belgian population and in what manner cultural differences can be accommodated. Finally, an economic perspective is introduced, paying attention to the role that markets play in ensuring an inclusive society (Dejaeghere, 2005).

This broad framework is further specified for every grade and every school track. Specific goals for a grade can range from a precise listing of rules that have to be followed to guarantee participatory democracy in the school itself, to a broad discussion on what globalization means for current citizenship concepts. Thus far, these education goals have been changed only once, in 2006–2008, and in Flanders this meant a lengthy process of negotiations with all stakeholders, including the powerful association of Catholic schools.

Project Driven Approach

While the Flemish government does not impose a strict format for civic education, it does offer schools the possibility of implementing projects on civic education that are fully developed by the department itself. Even in these projects, however, extreme care is being taken not to prescribe every single element or to relate it too narrowly to the overarching education goals. It is stated again and again that this is an element of individual creativity of the teacher and of the autonomy of the school, and that therefore the ministry does not want to limit the freedom of the school to develop its own school project.

Support for school projects, however, still can be substantial. Every year, a competition is organized for large-scale school projects that fit within the framework of citizenship education. If selected by the ministry, the project is fully funded, allowing the school to mobilize resources. The autonomy of the school is fully respected: every school has to decide whether or not to participate in this annual contest.

Another project is based on class visits to the building of the Flemish regional parliament. Schools that opt for such a visit receive fully developed packages to introduce the visit and to get the pupils acquainted with democratic decision making procedures. During their visit, pupils can participate in a mock-session of a parliamentary committee and a plenary assembly. Here, the format basically is one size fits all, as all schools receive the same program if they participate in this guided tour.

Reflection on Civic Education in Flanders

Contrary to what happened in the Netherlands, the Flemish government did not choose to install a specific course in civic education. It only required that schools and teachers try to attain national goals for education by their own methods. The advantage of such an approach is that the autonomy of the schools is fully respected and the individual creativity of teachers is encouraged. The downside, however, is that in practice there is an enormous variation in the time and energy that schools spend on civic education. Some have even argued that in practice this leads to a "civic education for the happy few": for elite schools it is easy to develop all kinds of curricular and extracurricular activities for their pupils, whereas fewer initiatives are being taken in schools in impoverished neighborhoods. This is a troubling finding, as we know from previous research that in these underprivileged neighborhoods one can observe a lack of political participation and civic engagement.

Another important form of criticism is that the Flemish ministry of education does not spell out the relation between attitudes and activity. The overall education goal is that the democratic attitudes of the pupils will be influenced, and it is hoped that, in some way or another, this will lead to higher participation rates of the pupils. No mechanism, however, is offered to make this transition possible. In practice, civic education in Flanders remains largely focused on cognitive skills, while "hands-on" forms of civic education, like community service, are almost completely absent. Partly this is the result of a very formalistic approach to education: in secondary schools in Flanders, pupils have to be in school for 32 hours a week. Schools are not allowed to impose any additional obligations on the pupils beyond these 32 hours. In practice this means that community projects and forms of volunteering are made almost impossible. The ambitions of most schools remain limited to the 32 hours that pupils actually spend in the school buildings, and there are few efforts to reach out to society in general.

Another element that is missing from the Flemish approach is that there is no specific teacher training for civic education. The overarching attainment goals indeed imply that all teachers should contribute in some way or another to reaching toward these goals, and this obligation is shared by teachers for languages, history, and other courses. In the teacher training for these topics, however, civic education is hardly dealt with. On the other hand, very few students are inclined to follow a special teacher training course on civic education, as this is not being offered as a regular course, and so employment opportunities are limited. The sense of ownership that we encountered among the Dutch civics teachers is therefore completely absent in the Flemish case.

Civic Education in the French Community of Belgium

The French Community also decided not to opt for a distinct civic education course. Rather, it relies on specific projects that are meant to engage both pupils and teachers. These projects are being developed by a special coordination service with the rather impressive name "Démocratie ou barbarie" (Democracy or Barbarism). The projects of this service are strongly normative: the aim is to develop support for pacifism, justice, and solidarity. The projects are aimed at fighting racism and exclusion.

The Decree of 24 July 1997 establishes the framework for civic education in the French Community. Civic education should aim to "prepare young people to become responsible citizens who are capable of contributing to a democratic, social, pluralistic, and open society" (Article 6§3). This goal should be reached by offering democratic lessons in various courses. Pupils should understand the evolution of democratic institutions, and they should develop a sense of responsibility toward society in general and also to the environment. It is also stressed that democratic school structures, including participatory councils, are an important tool for developing citizenship skills.

Projects are seen as an important way to reach the goal of democratic citizenship. The ministry of education offers information on human rights, democratic values, justice, international institutions, and political systems, and the teachers and pupils are strongly encouraged to find further information on these topics. In practice, therefore, cognitive skills seem to receive most emphasis in these projects.

It has to be acknowledged that civic education in the French Community is much more internationally oriented than it is in the Flemish Community.

It is stressed again and again that the establishment of an international legal framework is one of the most important ways to protect human rights and to promote a democratic society.

The downside of the project-based approach is that there is little monitoring on how schools effectively use these projects. Schools can choose projects for themselves, and from our own research in French Community schools, we can conclude that there is a very wide range of activity in this regard. Some schools simply order one or two textbooks from the ministry, allowing their pupils to read them. Other schools are intensively engaged in one of these projects, developing various activities. In practice, therefore, we do not know for the moment what is the actual impact of these projects on the pupils enrolled in French Community schools in Belgium.

Civic Education in France

Since the nineteenth century, public schools in France have been expected to contribute to the formation of citizenship norms and a strong French identity. The education system was seen as one of the pillars of French society. Emphasis was placed on patriotism, but also on encouraging the "Republican ideals" of brotherhood and equality among all human beings. In practice, civic education was confined mainly to courses on history and philosophy, with a strong emphasis on cognitive skills (Audigier, 1991; Ruget, 2006).

During the 1960s, civic education disappeared in most French schools, as the emphasis on patriotic values was considered obsolete. From the early 1970s on, little attention was given to the topic, much to the concern of consecutive conservative governments and ministers of education. During the reign of the Socialist president François Mitterrand (1981–95), little changed in this respect. Mitterrand and the ministers of education serving under him emphasized that French schools should adapt to new changing social reality by reaching out to students from a poorer background and to students from different cultures. When the conservative president Jacques Chirac took office in 1995, however, he reestablished the importance of the moral education of pupils. What started in a number of project schools was gradually expanded toward the entire school system, with specific courses for vocational schools (Rexwinkel and Veldhuis, 2007). Most French pupils now receive two hours of "civic, legal, and social education" every week. The topics are wide-ranging, but often they concentrate on the way that legislation helps to ensure the rights of citizens and to provide equal opportunities for all. At the same time it is emphasized that traditional notions of citizenship are being challenged by large-scale structural transformation, especially by the increasing ethnic diversity in French society (Tutiaux-Guillon, 2002; Bergounioux, 2007). As is usual in France, the content of this course is laid out in full detail by the ministry of education. The program for the final year of secondary school, for example, stipulates that attention should be paid to questions of equality, liberty, sovereignty, justice, the common interest, security, and social responsibility. Teachers have a strong incentive to follow these guidelines, since the final exams in France are organized nationwide. If one wants to prepare one's students for these exams, one has few other options than to follow quite rigorously the guidelines from the ministry of education (Bergounioux, 2007). These exams also make it difficult to describe the goals of this course. Officially they are meant to encourage "republican values" among the pupils. But since it is difficult to judge values or attitudes in centrally organized exams, in practice cognitive skills again receive most attention.

France, therefore, offers a perfect counterexample to Belgium: there is a specific course on civic education, and schools all over the country follow exactly the same curriculum. By itself, the documents provided by the ministry offer a comprehensive account of social and political life in France. Nevertheless, one can also observe that there is no specific teacher training for this course, so in practice not all teachers will feel sufficiently prepared. The central exams used to evaluate French schools also have a downside. The elite schools tend to prepare their pupils in the best possible manner for these exams, as a good grade is essential if one wants to prolong studies at a good university or *Grande école.* For schools that are lowly ranked, there are few incentives to opt for such an elaborate preparation, since they know that their pupils will perform poorly anyhow. In practice, these centrally organized exams tend to reproduce inequality within French society.

Discussion

This brief overview of civic education in three countries already makes clear that there is no such thing as a unified European approach toward civic education. In most European countries there is a clear tendency to pay more attention to civics courses, but every education system seems to pursue its own distinct policy. With regard to content, there is little emphasis on the process of European unification, and most courses clearly start from the framework of the nation-state. In general, it is quite striking that the way civic education is being implemented often mirrors specific features of the political system of the country. While the French approach is heavily centralized, with a nationally enforced program, the Dutch system relies on interactive decision making and a large degree of autonomy for the schools.

The example of the Netherlands, Belgium, and France also demonstrates that there is no ideal solution to the question of how civic education can best be taught. Opting for a distinct course could entail the risk that all other teachers and the school system in general no longer feel obliged to pay any attention to the topic. This is a very negative trend, as we know from research that the presence of an open classroom and school climate plays a crucial role in the development of democratic citizenship. There is little point in having two hours a week of civic education if the rest of the school environment does not function in a democratic manner. However, proclaiming that civic education should be an integral part of "all courses" has its downside, too: the end result might as well be that nobody feels responsible and that no attention will be given to civic education. In this chapter, we do not wish to take sides, but we would like to mention an element that is often missing in this kind of discussion: the sense of "ownership" among civic education teachers. In the Netherlands, the association of civic education teachers has played a crucial role in developing the course and in safeguarding the place of civic education in the curriculum. In other countries, where there is no specific course on civic education, such a sense of ownership is absent, and a civic education is much more vulnerable to interference from the central political authorities. A strong community of civic education teachers therefore seems an important focus in discussing the future of civic education.

A point that is often absent from the discussion on civic education is the importance of teacher training. In numerous countries, civic education is given by teachers who are not prepared. No matter how the course is being taught, it is crucial that the teacher is adequately trained and feels responsible for the topic. It will be difficult to establish this sense of ownership, however, if civic education is not seen as a distinct topic in the curriculum. The Dutch example proves the importance of adequate teacher training. Not only should it lead to better teaching experiences, but it can also lead to the effect that a group of teachers feels responsible for the content of the course. In the Dutch case, the association of teachers responsible for civic education was even successful in keeping the course in the curriculum, despite the initial preference of the minister of education to diminish the time spent on civic education.

If we look at the historical development of civic education courses in Western Europe, we see that usually right-wing or conservative politicians have tried to promote the course. The main exception might be the Labor government of former British prime minister Tony Blair, which reinvigorated civic education in the 1990s, but in general it can be noted that more conservative politicians have had a stronger interest in the topic than more leftist parties. Apparently a dominating idea is that civic education should be regarded as a conservative issue, aimed at promoting traditional norms of civility and patriotism among pupils. Maybe conservative politicians are also more easily or more frequently alarmed about an alleged erosion of norms and values in Western societies. From a sociological perspective, one might place question marks with this one-sided concern. Any social system needs at least a minimal consensus on shared norms and values in order to be able to function, and there is no reason why liberal and conservative politics should not agree. Partisan bickering can only endanger the legitimacy of civic education as a stable element of the curriculum.

If one is to criticize European policies on civic education, a major argument could be that innovation, all in all, has been rather limited. Experiments with community service and other kinds of service learning are completely absent in the countries that we studied. Citizenship education seems to have a place in the curriculum, but it often gets lost in the weekly planning of school activities. Schools in Europe remain bureaucratically organized, and usually school buildings are completely deserted after 4 p.m. Dewey emphasized that democratic schools should be embedded in a democratic society and that they should cooperate in an active manner with other social actors. In practice, European schools seldom reach this ideal. All too often, civic education in European schools remains isolated from the outside world, aside from a one-day visit to city hall or to a parliament building. Given the lack of good evaluation studies, one can wonder, therefore, about the long-term effectiveness of these civic education efforts.

References

Audigier, F. (1991). Enseigner la société, transmettre des valuers [Teaching society and building values]. *Revue française de pédagogie, 94,* 37–48.

Bergounioux, A. (2007). L'education civique au collège et au lycée [Civic education in secondary schools]. *Education et Formations, 76,* 85–89.

Claes, E., and Hooghe M. (2006). Het Vlaamse Participatiedecreet (2004) en de "Democratische school" [The Flemish decree on participation and the democratic school]. *Tijdschrift voor Onderwijsrecht en -beleid, 6,* 557–65.

De Coninck, C., Maes, B., Sleurs, W., and Van Moensel, C. (2002). *Over de Grenzen. Vakoverschrijdende Eindtermen in de tweede en de derde graad van het secundaire onderwijs* [Beyond the limits: Educational attainment goals in secondary education]. Brussels: Ministry of the Flemish Community.

Dejaeghere, A. (2005). *Learning and living democracy: Flemish Community of Belgium.* Strasbourg: Council of Europe.

Dekker, H. (1999). Citizenship conceptions and competencies in the subject matter 'society' in Dutch schools. In J. Torney-Purta, J. Schwille, and J. A. Amadeo (Eds.), *Civic education across countries* (437–62). Amsterdam: IEA.

Delanty, G. (2007). European citizenship: A critical assessment. *Citizenship Studies, 11* (3), 64–72.

Hooghoff, H. (1990). Toward a curriculum for social and political education in the Netherlands. *Educational Leadership, 48* (3), 23–26.

Leeman, Y. (2008). Education and diversity in the Netherlands. *European Educational Research Journal, 7* (1), 50–59.

Leenders, H., Veugelers, W., and De Kat, E. (2008). Teachers' views on citizenship education in secondary education in the Netherlands. *Cambridge Journal of Education, 38* (2), 155–70.

Quintelier, E., and Dejaeghere, Y. (2008). Does European citizenship increase tolerance in young people? *European Union Politics, 9* (3), 339–62.

Rexwinkel, R., and Veldhuis, R. (2007). *Maatschappijleer over de Grens.* Amsterdam: Instituut voor Publiek en Politiek.

Ruget, V. (2006). The renewal of civic education in France and in America: Comparative perspectives. *Social Science Journal, 43* (1), 19–34.

Siongers, J. (2001). *Vakoverschrijdende thema's in het secundair onderwijs: Op zoek naar een maatschappelijke consensus* [Attainment goals in secondary education]. Brussels: Free University of Brussels.

Spiecker, B., and Steutel, J. (1995). Political liberalism, civic education, and the Dutch government. *Journal of Moral Education, 24* (4), 383–94.

Schnabel, P., et al. (Eds.). (2007). *Het vak maatschappijwetenschappen. Voorstel examenprogramma* [Civic education: Proposal for a central program]. Enschede: Stichting Leerplanontwikkeling.

Torney-Purta, J., Schwille, J., and Amadeo, J. A. (Eds.). (1999). *Civic education across countries: Twenty-four national case studies from the IEA Civic Education Project,* Amsterdam: IEA.

Tutiaux-Guillon, N. (2002). Civic, legal, and social education in French secondary school: Questions about a new subject. Accessed at *www.sowi-onlinejournal.de/2002–2/france_Tutiaux.htm.*

10

Strengthening Education for Citizenship and Democracy in England

A Progress Report

David Kerr and Elizabeth Cleaver

Setting the Context

The past two decades have witnessed a fundamental review of the concept of citizenship and what it involves in communities in the United Kingdom, in Europe, and globally.[1] This review has encompassed countries and communities at local, national, and regional levels, as well as supranational organizations such as UNESCO, the European Commission, and the Council of Europe. A central feature of debates about public education and educational policies has been the increasing stress on the importance of citizenship education. This has led UNESCO at an International Bureau of Education conference in 2004 to identify "education for active and responsible citizenship" as a priority for action in order to improve the scope and quality of education for all young people. Meanwhile, the Council of Europe launched its Education for Democratic Citizenship and Human Rights Education (EDC/HRE) project in 1997, leading to the designation of 2005 as the European Year of Citizenship through Education around the slogan "learning and living democracy." The EDC project has just entered its third phase with a focus on strengthening policy formation, sustaining networks, and providing training for practitioners. Not to be outdone, the European Commission (EC) has identified the development of European citizenship as a priority area for the European Union (EU), and has launched a major active citizenship program, Europe for Citizens (2007–2013), to stimulate opportunities for active citizenship in civil society and in non-formal settings. The EC is also working on a scoping study to provide indicators for active citizenship, as part of the 2000 Lisbon Objectives (Hoskins et al., 2006; Hoskins, Villalba, and Van Nijlen, 2007). At the Lisbon meeting, active citizenship and social inclusion were identified among the key competences in lifelong learning that all people in Europe would need to develop if Europe were to respond successfully to globalization and the shift to knowledge-based economies (European Commission, 2006). Finally, a further sign of the considerable interest in citizenship education is the recent launch of the 2007 IEA International Civic and Citizenship Education Study (ICCS) to investigate how young people are prepared for their role as citizens in schools and local communities. The study has already attracted almost 40 participating countries and has plans to develop innovative regional modules to address particular citizenship-related issues in Europe, Latin America, and potentially Asia (Kerr and Lopes, 2008; Reimers, 2008). England participated in the previous IEA CIVED study and has signed up to participate in the new ICCS study, along with Northern Ireland (Torney-Purta, Lehmann, Oswald, and Schulz, 2001; Kerr, Lines, Blenkinsop, and Schagen, 2002).[2]

This fundamental review of the concept of citizenship has been brought about by the need to respond to rapid changes in modern societies. The pace of change is having significant influence on the nature of relationships in modern society at a number of levels, including those between individuals, community groups, states, nations, regions, and economic and political blocs. This period of unprecedented and seemingly relentless change has succeeded in shifting and straining the traditional, stable boundaries of citizenship in many societies (Young, 1990; Kymlicka, 2001; Cogan, 2000). A series of major events across the world, such as the fall of the Berlin Wall, bombings in the United States, Bali, Madrid, and London, the war in Iraq, and the populist revolutions in Georgia and Ukraine, have resulted in important social and political changes that have, in turn, triggered considerable discussion and debate. These discussions have raged within and across national, academic, professional, and practitioner boundaries. The particular issues that have triggered heated debate in the context of the United Kingdom and England include declining voter turnout, the war on terror, political extremism, and the rapid movement of peoples across Europe. As a consequence, discussion has become centered on issues of political and civic engagement, identity, belonging, security, integration, and community cohesion.

The cumulative effect has caused experts and policy makers to reflect anew on the role of citizenship education in the curricula of public educational systems and, in particular, on its influence in the development of democratic, political culture in society (Crick, 2000; Beck, 2000; Audigier, 1998, 1999,

2000; Hahn, 1998; Ichilov, 1998; Arnot and Dillabough, 2000; Carnegie and CIRCLE, 2003; Levine, 2007). As a result of such reflection, discussions about citizenship education in public education have become enjoined with wider debates about approaches to issues such as human rights, equality, tolerance, and social justice (Callan, 1997; Feinberg, 1998; Gutmann, 1999; Macedo, 2000). Citizenship education has become strongly linked to discussions about the pressure of changes on the nature of relationships between differing groups in society as well as those between the individual and the state. Indeed, the pressure has become so great that it has triggered a fundamental review of the concepts and practices that underpin citizenship.

The review has focused on four issues concerning citizenship:

- *Diversity, inclusion, and cohesion*—of living in socially and culturally diverse communities and of successfully integrating existing and new citizens to ensure that these communities remain socially cohesive.
- *Location and identity*—of the nation-state no longer being the "traditional location" of citizenship and identity and the possibility of other locations across countries, including notions of "European," "international," "transnational," or "cosmopolitan" citizenship, as well as within countries such as the issue of "Basque" identity in Spain and the current debates in the United Kingdom around "British" identity and values as opposed to "English," "Welsh," and "Scottish" identity.
- *Social rights*—of changes in the social dimension of citizenship brought by the impact of an increasingly global economy.
- *Participation*—of engagement and participation in democratic society at local, national, regional, and international levels.

All four issues have been present in the review of citizenship in England over the past decade, although the emphasis given to them has shifted in line with changing political and societal concerns. The last issue, that of participation, was the catalyst that kick-started the review of education for citizenship and democracy in England. It has remained an underlying concern ever since. Indeed, participation is of particular relevance in many countries in Europe, including England, at the moment, with growing concerns about the lack of interest and involvement of young people in public and political life, what has been termed a "democratic deficit" (Jowell and Park, 1998; Putnam, 2000; Curtice and Seyd, 2004).

This issue of a "democratic deficit" has been given added focus in the United Kingdom following the May 2005 general election. The overall turnout was just over 61 percent of the electorate, a slight improvement on the 2001 figure, but still the third lowest turnout since 1857 (Electoral Commission, 2005). More worryingly, the lowest turnout was of those ages 18 to 24, at 37 percent, down 2 percent from turnout in the 2001 general election. There was a 4 percent decrease in the number of males ages 18 to 24 voting in 2005 compared with 2001. Indeed, young people were half as likely to vote as older people. The figures for turnout across age groups suggest a "staircase effect," with the highest turnout among those voters age 65 and older at 75 percent, dropping steadily with each age group. This has raised concerns that the "staircase effect" may be replaced in time, unless action is taken, by a "conveyor belt effect," with a leveling off of participation rates as older voters die off. This scenario was put more starkly in a recent report from the Electoral Commission: "Some people are now out of the habit of voting. . . . Younger age groups are much less likely to see voting as a civic duty than older age groups . . . suggesting the beginning of a cohort effect, i.e., a generation apparently carrying forward their non-voting as they get older" (Electoral Commission, 2006, 10).

There was also a marked social imbalance in voting patterns with higher income groups twice as likely to vote as those from lower income groups (Electoral Commission and Hansard Society, 2006). This has led to a recognition among researchers, policy makers, and linking organizations of the need to "reconnect" people with politics, political issues, and political processes and to reshape the relationships between politicians, political institutions, and the public. There has been considerable activity to "reconnect" people with politics in England over the past decade. Part of the proposed action is to introduce citizenship education in schools and colleges, educate students about the roles and responsibilities of being citizens, give them active and meaningful participative experiences in and beyond schools, and inculcate them with a disposition to participate in civic and political life. In other words, to establish a strong connection for children and young people with citizenship and participation from an early age, which will serve to keep them actively connected and engaged as they mature.

Reshaping citizenship has also led to the reformulation of citizenship education; the two go hand in hand (Kerr, 2001). This has been the case in England, Scotland, and Northern Ireland (Learning and Teaching Scotland, 2000; Advisory Group, 1998; Smith, 2003) and in Europe (Birzea et al., 2004; Kerr et al., 2004b; Kerr, 2004; Mikkelsen, 2004; Pol, 2004; Losito, 2004; Froumin, 2004). It is no coincidence that effective citizenship education has been included as a fundamental goal of education systems in the curriculum reviews that are under way in many countries. Schools, curricula, and teachers have been given a significant role in helping actively to prepare young people for engaging with and participating in modern society.

Policy Background and Actions

Citizenship education has moved rapidly up the policy agenda in the past decade in the United Kingdom. It began with a focus on the role of education in building secure and lasting foundations for civic and political participation. As with countries in Europe, citizenship education is being reviewed and revised as part of overall reforms of education systems (Kerr, Smith, and Twine, 2008). What is interesting is the impact that history, culture, and societal and educational context have on current policy developments. Though all the UK countries are united in their overall goals for citizenship education as part of the curriculum, the frameworks they use vary considerably:

- In England, citizenship was introduced as a new statutory subject in schools in September 2002.
- In Northern Ireland, local and global citizenship has been a new statutory subject in schools since 2007.
- In Scotland, values and citizenship is one of the five national priorities for education.
- In Wales, citizenship is part of the statutory provision for personal and social education.

There have been two particular complementary waves of policy action in England concerning citizenship education. Each has had a differing catalyst and focal point. The first wave ran from the election of a new Labour government in 1997 and peaked around 2002. Its catalyst was concern about the growing "democratic deficit" and its particular focus on renewing and strengthening citizenship education in schools, building out to other educational institutions and settings The second wave ran from around 2001 to the present, peaking around 2004. Its catalyst was a concern with community cohesion for those already living in communities and for those newly arrived from other parts of Europe and the world. The focus of the second wave was on strengthening citizenship in community settings, in partnership with educational institutions. Both policy waves have been affected by the aftermath of the London bombings in 2005 and the shock and bewilderment that they had been planned and carried out by British-born and educated citizens. This has brought a renewed impetus for and emphasis on citizenship education. Indeed, since 2005 there has been a refocused policy drive on the role of education for citizenship and democracy, both in schools and in community settings, in addressing issues of identity and diversity and educating for cohesion, alongside strengthening civic and political engagement. These two policy waves are now reviewed in turn.

Strengthening Citizenship Education in and beyond Schools

In England, the revision of citizenship education began with the election of a new Labour government in 1997. It has centered on the work of the government-appointed Advisory Group on Education for Citizenship and the Teaching of Democracy in Schools, chaired by Professor (now Sir) Bernard Crick (Kerr, 1999a, 1999b; Crick, 2000). The Crick Group (as it is more commonly known) was invited to set out the aims and purposes of citizenship education and the teaching of democracy in schools and a framework for how it could be successfully delivered, both within and outside the formal school curriculum and through links between the school and the wider community.

Citizenship education in schools

The explanation as to why the Crick Group was set up lies in a complex interplay of factors, some deep-seated and others more immediate. Perhaps, above all, the main reason was that by the late 1990s there was broad support in England, from within and outside the education system, for a review of this area. The time was right, and the conditions necessary to sustain a review were in place: there was growing concern, in particular, about the rapidly changing relationships between the individual and the government and the decline in traditional forms of civic cohesion, and there were increasing calls for action to address the signs of alienation and cynicism among young people about public life and participation. Such signs are apparent in a number of industrialized nations, though there is some debate as to whether they are a natural feature of the life cycle—engagement increasing with age—or a more permanent phenomenon (Jowell and Park, 1998; Wilkinson and Mulgan, 1995; Putnam, 2000).

The final catalyst for action was the existence of a strong political will. This had not always been present in past policy approaches, particularly in the early 1990s, and it goes some way in explaining their failure. The political will came not just from the new secretary of state for education and employment, David Blunkett, a longtime supporter of the area, but also from the new Labour government supported by the other major parties. The political will, combined with growing public and professional calls for action, paved the way for the establishment of the Crick Group.

This advisory group set out to strengthen citizenship education and, in so doing, defined "effective education for citizenship" as three aspects that are to be developed progressively through a young person's education and training experiences, from preschool to adulthood (Advisory Group, 1998, 11–13):

- *Social and moral responsibility*: "children learning from the very beginning self-confidence and socially and morally responsible behaviour both in and beyond the classroom, both towards those in authority and towards each other." This component acts as an essential precondition for the other two.
- *Community involvement*: "learning about and becoming helpfully involved in the life and concerns of their communities, including learning through community involvement and service to the community." This, of course, is by no means limited to children's time in school.
- *Political literacy*: "pupils learning about, and how to make themselves effective in, public life through knowledge, skills, and values." Here the term *public life* is used in its broadest sense to encompass realistic knowledge of, and preparation for, conflict resolution and decision making at the local, national, European, or global level.

The Crick Group sought to establish a flexible yet rigorous framework that would encourage schools and colleges to develop active citizenship education in ways that best suited their needs, context, and strengths. Within the framework the onus would be on institutions, in partnership with their local communities, to develop meaningful citizenship education practice and experiences for all young people.

The definition of citizenship education put forward by the Crick Group deliberately resonates with the past. They took into consideration the definitions of citizenship education offered in the late 1980s and early 1990s by the Conservative government, which championed the individualism of the free market and placed an emphasis on the importance of civic obligation or "active citizenship" (Hurd, 1988; MacGregor, 1990). The Conservative government urged individuals to fulfill their civic responsibilities rather than leave it to the government to carry them out. It backed up the call with policies that encouraged greater private ownership and the privacy of consumer rights in all areas of life, including education.

The new Labour government, which came to power in May 1997, championed a different approach. This was a definition associated with the communitarian movement with a particular emphasis on "civic morality." This is part of the wider philosophy of "new Labour" based on the civic responsibilities of the individual in active partnership with the state. The Labour government is urging individuals to act as caring people aware of the needs and views of others and motivated to contribute positively to wider society. This is part of what is commonly referred to as the "Third Way" (Giddens, 1998).

The Crick Group's final report contained a bold statement that the central aim of strengthening citizenship education is to effect "no less than a change in the political culture of this country both nationally and locally: for people to think of themselves as active citizens, willing, able, and equipped to have an influence in public life and with the critical capacities to weigh evidence before speaking and acting; to build on and to extend radically to young people the best in existing traditions of community involvement and public service, and to make them individually confident in finding new forms of involvement and action among themselves" (Advisory Group, 1998, 7).

The Advisory Group's report was well received, and following the revision of the National Curriculum, citizenship education was incorporated for the first time in the school curriculum for ages 5–16 (Qualifications and Curriculum Authority, 1999). Citizenship is now part of a nonstatutory framework for personal, social, and health education (PSHE) and citizenship at key stages 1 and 2 (ages 5–11) and a new statutory foundation subject at key stages 3 and 4 (11–16). Schools in England have been legally required to deliver citizenship education since September 2002.

The Citizenship Order at key stages 3 and 4 defines the importance of citizenship as a new foundation subject in England as to give

> pupils the knowledge, skills, and understanding to play an effective role in society at local, national, and international levels. It helps them to become informed, thoughtful, and responsible citizens who are aware of their duties and rights. It promotes their spiritual, moral, social, and cultural development, making them more self-confident and responsible both in and beyond the classroom. It encourages pupils to play a helpful part in the life of their schools, neighborhoods, communities, and the wider world. It also teaches them about our economy and democratic institutions and values; encourages respect for different national, religious, and ethnic identities; and develops pupils' ability to reflect on issues and take part in discussions. (QCA, 1999, 12)

The Citizenship Order has programs of study for citizenship and an attainment target based on three elements:

- knowledge and understanding about becoming informed citizens;
- developing skills of inquiry and approach;
- developing skills of participation and responsible action.

It is intended that these three elements are interrelated in order that teaching should ensure that knowledge and understanding about becoming informed citizens are acquired and applied when developing skills of inquiry and communication and participation and responsible action.

The Citizenship Order differs from those in other national curriculum subjects in being deliberately "light touch." It sets out a barebones but rigorous framework for what is to be taught and learned but then leaves it up to the professional judgment of those in schools—leaders, coordinators, and teachers—working in partnership with local communities to decide how best to approach the framework. Approaches will be dependent on factors such as school ethos and culture, staff interest and experience, local community context, and the background and interests of students. There is no official directive for how all schools and colleges should approach citizenship.

The following sets out the program of study for citizenship at key stage 4 (ages 14–16 in two years of schooling).

1. Knowledge and understanding about becoming informed citizens
Pupils should be taught about

- the legal and human rights and responsibilities underpinning society and how they relate to citizens, including the role and operation of the criminal and civil justice systems;
- the origins and implications of the diverse national, regional, religious, and ethnic identities in the United Kingdom and the need for mutual respect and understanding;
- the work of parliament, the government, and the courts in making and shaping the law;
- the importance of playing an active part in democratic and electoral processes;
- how the economy functions, including the role of business and financial services;
- the opportunities for individuals and voluntary groups to bring about social change locally, nationally, in Europe, and internationally;
- the importance of a free press and the media's role in society, including the Internet, in providing information and affecting opinion;
- the rights and responsibilities of consumers, employers, and employees;

- the United Kingdom's relations in Europe, including the European Union, and relations with the Commonwealth and the United Nations;
- the wider issues and challenges of global interdependence and responsibility, including sustainable development and Local Agenda 21.

2. Developing skills of inquiry and communication
Pupils should be taught to

- research a topical political, spiritual, moral, social, or cultural issue, problem, or event by analyzing information from different sources, including ICT-based sources, showing an awareness of the use and abuse of statistics;
- express, justify, and defend orally and in writing a personal opinion about such issues, problems, or events;
- contribute to group and exploratory class discussions and take part in formal debates.

3. Developing skills of participation and responsible action
Pupils should be taught to

- use their imagination to consider other people's experiences and be able to think about, express, explain, and critically evaluate views that are not their own;
- negotiate, decide, and take part responsibly in school and community-based activities;
- reflect on the process of participating. (QCA, 1999, 15–16)

Citizenship in other education settings
The introduction of statutory citizenship in secondary schools has been further strengthened by a parallel drive to widen the reach of citizenship education to encompass other education and training phases beyond schools. This is seen as vital in laying the foundations for lifelong citizenship education. It caters particularly to young people when they complete formal education at 16 and move into other education and training settings and/or into the world of work. This drive saw the establishment of a second Crick panel to propose action on citizenship education for people ages 16-19. Following the second Crick report (Further Education Funding Council, 2000), a series of pilot development projects was started in 2001 to explore what an entitlement to citizenship education might look like for all people ages 16–19. The pilot projects were successful, leading to a widened national program and the establishment of the

Post-16 Citizenship Support Program (Craig, Kerr, Wade, and Taylor, 2005).[3] As its name suggests, it seeks to support those in post-16 settings, whether in schools, colleges, or the workplace, including principals, teachers/tutors, and young people, in developing, disseminating, and sustaining best practice in citizenship across all areas of 16–19 education and training. The success of the post-16 program has seen growing interest among higher education institutions in citizenship education. A number of HE institutions now offer HE students some form of citizenship entitlement, either in the HE institution or through links with local communities.

Citizenship Education in and beyond Communities

The policy process has moved on considerably since the statutory introduction of citizenship into schools in 2002. It has been marked by a second policy wave with a focus on civil renewal in communities. This entails getting everyone, including children and teenagers, more involved in decision making in relation to the institutions (such as schools) in the communities in which they live. There has been a particular push to renew local communities and to strengthen their links with and contribution to the wider national community. This push has seen policy initiatives aimed, first, at those citizens already living in communities and, second, at assisting immigrants who wish to embark on their journey to citizenship.

The reason for this second policy thrust on citizenship education in and beyond communities lies in a complex mixture of personalities and circumstances. Having been behind the introduction of citizenship education in schools, during his time as secretary of state for education and employment, David Blunkett was then promoted by the prime minister, Tony Blair, to become the new home secretary in 2001. Once installed at the Home Office, he set about renewing and strengthening citizenship education within and beyond communities. He was assisted in this push by a number of developments:

- growing recognition of the challenges to diversity and inclusion resulting from the rapid movement of peoples within the UK alongside an increasing influx of peoples from other parts of Europe and the world into the United Kingdom.
- particular concern, from all political parties, to address issues of identity, integration, and community cohesion created by the race riots in northern England in 2001. The riots saw fighting between Asian and white youths and the burning of buildings and vehicles.

- underlying pressure to renew and reinforce the bonds between citizens and civic and political institutions, beginning with encouraging people to participate more in their local communities.

These developments created the broad political and social platform for action. The solution to these challenges was seen by the government, with backing from other political parties and political commentators, as creating partnerships between the government and citizens at all levels; bringing communities closer together in order to foster integration and cohesion; and strengthening citizens' knowledge and skills so they can become more active in political and civic society. This was translated via a two-pronged policy approach that saw a concentration on promoting civil renewal and active citizenship in communities for everyone, matched by a specific and separate focus on addressing the needs of new entrants to the United Kingdom.

Although the policy thrust on citizenship education in and beyond communities around civil renewal was launched by David Blunkett at the Home Office, it quickly spread to other government departments. It has since been championed by a range of ministers and government departments, prospering in spite of Blunkett's high-profile resignation from the Home Office in 2004.[4] It has also permeated general education policy, in particular, thereby linking citizenship education in schools with its promotion in and beyond communities. The policy thrust was given renewed vigor and direction in the aftermath of the London bombings in 2005. Once the initial horror had abated, it was replaced by a widespread concern for addressing the circumstances that had led to British citizens killing fellow citizens. This concern has been translated into a specific focus on the role of education for citizenship, in schools and communities, in addressing issues of identity, diversity, integration, and educating for cohesion in the United Kingdom. This role is to be developed alongside the existing role of citizenship education in strengthening and deepening civic and political participation across society. The policy thrusts on civil renewal in communities and citizenship education for new entrants to the United Kingdom are each reviewed in turn.

Civil renewal in communities

The Home Office policy initiative on citizenship education in and beyond communities has been centered around the concept of civil renewal (Blunkett, 2003a, 2003b). Civil renewal is at the heart of the Labour government's vision of life in modern communities. It takes place where people become actively engaged in the well-being of their communities and are able to define the problems they face and tackle them together with help from the government and public bodies. The Home Office viewed civil renewal as comprising three essential ingredients:

- *Active citizenship*: people who take responsibility for tackling problems in their own communities
- *Strengthened communities*: communities who can form and sustain their own organizations, bringing people together to deal with their common concerns
- *Partnerships in meeting public needs*: public bodies that involve local people in improving the planning and delivery of public services

The new policy emphasis on individuals, strengthening and linking communities, consultation, and partnerships has also permeated general education policy. The launch of the Children Bill (Great Britain, Parliament, 2004) aims to put children and families at the heart of policy, with services built around those who use them (such as children) rather than those who deliver them. The Children Bill has been followed by a flurry of policy initiatives and statements to bring service providers, including government departments, into line with the new agenda. The Department for Education and Skills (DfES) has been particularly active in this respect over the past few years by doing the following:[5]

- Issuing *Working Together* (DfES, 2004) guidelines to all schools that outline the ways in which children and young people can be involved in and consulted on many school issues.
- Launching a *Five-Year Strategy for Teaching and Learning* (DfES, 2006), which includes the key principles of "greater personalisation and choice" and "building partnerships" with volunteers and voluntary organisations.
- Committing to deliver the *Every Child Matters* (HM Government, 2004) strategy through five outcomes in schools, one of which is "pupils making a positive contribution to the life of the school and community."
- Planning a 10-year strategy, *Aiming High for Young People*, to transform leisure-time opportunities, activities and support services for young people in England. This includes a commitment to providing active citizenship opportunities, building community cohesion, and giving young people and communities opportunities to have real influence over local services that affect their everyday lives (HM Treasury/DCSF, 2007).

Although the term "citizenship education" is not mentioned specifically in these policy statements and reforms, being superseded by terms such as "active citizenship," "personalized learning," "community cohesion," and "community capacity," it is writ large in the processes by which the intended outcomes of these policy initiatives are to be achieved in practice. The current policy agenda suggests that there will be increased consultation with children and teenagers in the coming years and greater encouragement and incentives for them to become actively involved in the processes of change at all levels of the education system as well as in their local communities.

As a sign of its continued commitment in this area, and soon after its general election victory in May 2005, the government launched *Together We Can: The Government Action Plan for Civil Renewal* (Home Office, 2005). *Together We Can* sets out eight key public policy areas and 62 action points to be carried out across 12 government departments in order to strengthen citizens' engagement in delivering success across those policies. The action plan will be regularly reviewed. The eight key public policy areas include the following:

1. Ensuring that children and teenagers have their say
2. Strengthening our democracy
3. Revitalizing neighborhoods
4. Increasing community cohesion and racial equality
5. Building safer communities
6. Reducing crime and creating greater confidence in the criminal justice system
7. Improving our health and giving voice to vulnerable people
8. Contributing to sustainable development locally and globally

These eight policy areas are broad, and the recent outrages in London have given added focus and impetus to a number of these areas. However, there is a clear acknowledgment in the action plan of the particular contribution that citizenship education will make in relation to the first two key policy areas.

Citizenship education for new entrants to the United Kingdom

Alongside the promotion of citizenship education for all, in schools and communities, there has been a specific and separate policy initiative to address the citizenship education needs of new entrants to the United Kingdom. This initiative was first promoted by government in a white paper entitled *Secure Borders, Safe Haven* with the intention of raising the status of becoming a British citizen and offering more help to new entrants. The government sought, in the words of the home secretary, David Blunkett, "to make gaining British citizenship meaningful and celebratory rather than simply a bureaucratic process" (Home Office, 2004, preface). This was translated in the Nationality, Immigration, and Asylum Act 2002 into a requirement that residents seeking British citizenship be tested to show sufficient knowledge of the English language, to have sufficient knowledge about life in the United Kingdom, and to take a citizenship oath and pledge at a civic ceremony. An independent group, chaired once more by Bernard Crick, was established in 2003 to advise the government on the development of language and political literacy courses as well as the assessment of new entrants to the United Kingdom.

The Life in the UK Advisory Group, as it became known, in its report entitled *The New and the Old* (Home Office, 2003) recommended

- that a flexible language requirement be developed with a citizenship program and a handbook on living in the United Kingdom;
- that those with poor language skills be required to complete an ESOL (English for students of other languages) course of "language-with-civic-content" and to demonstrate progress in order to gain a certificate;
- that those with higher level language skills should be able to qualify for naturalization after successfully passing a citizenship test;
- that citizenship ceremonies be established at a local level to celebrate the success of those who had met the language and knowledge requirements in order to help them to integrate into their new communities;
- that an implementation and assessment authority be set up to take the recommendations forward.

The new requirements that applicants for naturalization have to show sufficient knowledge of the English language and of life in the United Kingdom went into effect in 2005. Similar requirements were introduced in 2007 for those looking to settle in the United Kingdom but not take British citizenship.

Recommendations from the Life in the UK Advisory Group included

- the development of a 45-minute, computer-based, multiple-choice citizenship test.
- the establishment of an Advisory Board for Naturalization and Integration (ABNI) to implement the Life in the UK recommendations.

- the publication of a handbook entitled *Life in the United Kingdom: A Journey to Citizenship*, filled with basic history, how Great Britain is governed, and the laws and sources of help and information concerning employment, housing, education, and other everyday needs (Home Office, 2004). An updated version of the handbook was produced three years later (Home Office, 2007).
- the commencement of citizenship ceremonies in local communities, often in town halls and council offices. The first ceremony in London saw Prince Charles present successful entrants with certificates. To date, more than 200,000 people have attended citizenship ceremonies.

Certainly, the initiative has succeeded in raising the status and profile of citizenship for new entrants to the United Kingdom, both those seeking British citizenship and those looking to settle in the United Kingdom. However, it is questionable how far it has permeated the consciousness of existing British citizens and connected to their everyday lives.

The aftermath of the London bombings has succeeded in bringing greater connectivity in policy and practice between the two policy thrusts on citizenship education, namely, that of developing citizenship education in and beyond schools and that of promoting civil renewal in and beyond communities. The growing connection, both implicit and explicit, between citizenship education and civil renewal (and community cohesion in particular) has been most recently acknowledged in three policy documents: *Diversity and Citizenship Curriculum Review* (DfES, 2007; Maylor and Read et al., 2007); the 2007 report of the Commission on Integration and Cohesion; and *Guidance on the Duty to Promote Community Cohesion* (DCSF, 2007).

The diversity and citizenship curriculum review, led by former head teacher (now Sir) Keith Ajegbo, had the aim of reviewing the teaching of ethnic, religious, and cultural diversity across the curriculum to age 19. The review's main recommendations include a strengthening of pupil voice, an audit of education for diversity in the curriculum, increased teacher training, and greater use of local contexts and a whole-school exploration of identities, diversity, and citizenship around the question "Who do we think we are?" Within this process, citizenship education is given a central role. In particular, the review recommends that a fourth strand of citizenship be developed, entitled *Identity and Diversity: Living Together in the UK*, and that a review of resources to support this strand is carried out. These recommendations have been adopted by the government, and a revised National Curriculum for Citizenship, due to be implemented as part of a wider review of the English National Curriculum in 2008, will embrace this fourth strand.

At much the same time, the Commission on Integration and Cohesion was gathering evidence at a local level. Based on new evidence and consultation responses, the report recommends

- a clear statement of integration and cohesion policy;
- an ambitious response to the Ajegbo report on citizenship education;
- a new program of voluntary service for young people expressly linked to local citizenship.

It also recommends that the outcomes of the youth strand of the Department for Children, Schools and Families/HM Treasury/Children and Young People's Review, *Aiming High for Young People* (HM Treasury/DCSF, 2007), consider ways of spreading good practice about how to work with young people on integration and cohesion.

Finally, in light of these wide-ranging recommendations, and to facilitate good practice, the Department for Children, Schools, and Families (DCSF replacing DfES) and the Department for Communities and Local Government (DCLG) published *Guidance on the Duty to Promote Community Cohesion* (DCSF, 2007), which explains community cohesion and how schools can contribute to this process, highlighting examples of good work already under way in the sector.

The Future of Citizenship Education in England

In September 2007, a new national secondary curriculum was introduced. Its purpose is to enable schools to "raise standards and help all their learners meet the life challenges of our fast-changing world" (Qualifications and Curriculum Authority, 2007a). Schools will be required to implement the new curriculum in a year on year rolling program, beginning with Year 7 (ages 11 and 12) in September 2008.

This new program allows schools to design their own "locally determined curriculum that matches the ethos of the school, the needs and capabilities of its community of learners and the local context" (Qualifications and Curriculum Authority, 2007b, 5). The emphasis is on flexibility of delivery, the development of skills and concepts alongside knowledge, and the integration and linking of learning experiences across both the curriculum and the whole school. Perhaps most significant for citizenship education, however, are the three newly defined aims of the new secondary curriculum, which state that the curriculum should enable all young people to become "successful learners who enjoy learning, make progress, and achieve; confident individuals who are able to live safe, healthy, and fulfilling lives; and responsible citizens who make a positive contribution to society" (QCA, 2007b, 6). By following the new curriculum at Key Stage 4 (ages 14–16), schools will be expected to teach students about the following concepts (Qualifications and Curriculum Authority, 2007c):

Democracy and justice

- Participating actively in different kinds of decision making and voting in order to influence public life
- Weighing up what is fair and unfair in different situations, understanding that justice is fundamental to a democratic society, and exploring the role of law in maintaining order and resolving conflict
- Considering how democracy, justice, diversity, toleration, respect, and freedom are valued by people with different beliefs, backgrounds, and traditions within a changing democratic society
- Understanding and exploring the roles of citizens and parliament in holding government and those in power to account

Rights and responsibilities

- Exploring different kinds of rights and obligations and how these affect both individuals and communities
- Understanding that individuals, organizations, and governments have responsibilities to ensure that rights are balanced, supported, and protected
- Investigating ways in which rights can compete and conflict, and understanding that hard decisions have to be made to try to balance these

Identities and diversity: Living together in the UK

- Appreciating that identities are complex, can change over time, and are informed by different understandings of what it means to be a citizen
- Exploring the diverse national, regional, ethnic, and religious cultures, groups, and communities in the United Kingdom and the connections between them
- Considering the interconnections between the United Kingdom and Europe and the wider world

- Exploring community cohesion and the different forces that bring about change in communities over time

It is this latter strand which dramatically alters the focus of the citizenship curriculum and makes explicit its role in educating for community cohesion as recommended by the *Diversity and Citizenship Curriculum Review* (DfES, 2007).

However, findings from the *Citizenship Education Longitudinal Study* (*CELS*) (Cleaver, Ireland, Kerr, and Lopes, 2005; Ireland et al., 2006; Kerr et al., 2004a; Kerr et al., 2007) suggest that if the new curriculum for citizenship education with its new focus on community cohesion and the new overarching aim of the new National Curriculum to enable young people to become responsible citizens are to succeed, a number of issues need to be addressed. The emerging lessons from the study of citizenship education in England are discussed below. We hold that these lessons are not only important for the continuing success of citizenship education in England but also may prove helpful to those with responsibility for designing and implementing citizenship education in other countries.

Emerging Lessons

The introduction of the new statutory subject, Citizenship, in 2002 marked the beginning rather than the end of the policy process in England. Indeed, citizenship education has continued to attract considerable interest and activity from policy makers, practitioners, researchers, and commentators. So what are the emerging lessons from the experience of introducing citizenship education in England? These lessons largely concern citizenship education in schools and colleges because this is the aspect that is most developed, with a growing body of policy, practice, and research evidence. It is too early to draw conclusions about the progress of civil renewal in communities, the separate initiative on citizenship education for new entrants, and current attempts to educate for community cohesion through the new National Curriculum. That will require another chapter at a later date.

Up until now, most of the interest has been with emerging definitions and curriculum approaches to citizenship in schools and colleges, particularly given the lack of a tradition of citizenship in the curriculum. How well has citizenship education been understood by senior managers and teachers? How is it being delivered in schools and colleges? What are the emerging issues and challenges for schools, colleges, and teachers? How can these issues and challenges be overcome? Such questions have dominated the literature (Kerr et al., 2004a; Kerr and Cleaver, 2004; Gearon, 2003; Deakin Crick, Coates, Taylor, and Ritchie, 2004).

The emerging lessons can be grouped into three categories: those connected with the policy process and the policy formulation; those arising from the drive to turn policy into effective practice in schools, colleges, and communities; and those emerging from the growing evidence base about citizenship education in England.

Lessons Emerging from the Policy Process

The experiences in England have underlined a number of important lessons concerning the political process surrounding the review of citizenship and citizenship education. The first lesson is the need to have a strong political will to act as a catalyst for action. It is doubtful whether the citizenship initiative in English schools and communities would have progressed without the personal and political commitment of David Blunkett. The second lesson is to have that political will reinforced by general support at public, professional, and political levels for action in relation to citizenship education. This broad support for action legitimated the political remit in England. The third lesson is to establish a clear remit for any group reviewing citizenship and citizenship education and to ensure that the membership of that group is broad-based. The original Crick Group benefited from having a clear remit and timescale for action. Although set up under a Labour government, the membership was deliberately broad, containing those with political expertise alongside those with public and professional expertise in education and communities. Having the Speaker of the House of Commons as the Crick Group's patron confirmed the support of the leaders of all the political parties and preempted accusations of political or party bias. The same held true for the second and third advisory groups on 16–19 citizenship and "Life in the UK." The fourth lesson is to set out a clear definition of citizenship education and a forward-looking vision of its aims and goals, set within a lifelong learning perspective. It is vital that this definition is sufficiently flexible to be able to address fresh challenges to citizenship in society, such as those concerning diversity, identity, and community cohesion brought in the aftermath of the London bombings. The goal of changing the political culture in England has been particularly powerful and enduring. The fifth lesson is to maintain and broaden the political will across government and political parties. Begun through education citizenship, admittedly in a number of guises, it now permeates all aspects of government across government departments, while retaining cross-party interest and support. The sixth and final lesson, and perhaps the most valuable, is to recognize that the policy process is the beginning rather than the end. Policy needs to be continually reviewed and adapted and to be supported by a clear implementation strategy in order to begin to lay the foundations for replication and sustainability.

Lessons Emerging from Attempts to Turn Policy into Practice

Perhaps the most important lesson that has emerged from the implementation of citizenship education in and beyond English schools is the recognition that the report from the Crick Group and the new curriculum, Order for Citizenship, are not sufficient to encourage the development of effective citizenship education in schools and beyond. Instead, there needs to be a systematic and concerted strategy to bridge the potential implementation gap between policy and practice and to lay the foundation for the development of effective practice.

Policy makers and support agencies are working hard to meet the considerable development needs of managers and practitioners as they introduce and build the new subject of citizenship. These development needs have led to four strategic streams of activity.

Providing detailed advice and guidance on citizenship

This approach includes the following activities:

- Producing schemes of work for each educational stage from primary schools through to 16–19 education and training that offer teaching and learning activities, ideas for developing student participation, and a teachers guide (Qualifications and Curriculum Authority, 2001a, 2001b, 2002, 2004; Quality Improvement Agency, 2006).
- Producing a framework for the inspection of citizenship as part of arrangements for school self-evaluation, and encouraging schools to monitor and report on their progress (DfES, 2003).
- Setting up a new dedicated website for citizenship with resources, case studies, training activities, and information.[6]

Funding the production of resources

This approach includes the following activities:

- Commissioning mapping exercises of existing resources mapped against the topics and areas in the nonstatutory guidance for citizenship in primary schools and the new statutory Citizenship Order in secondary schools (Kerr, Blenkinsop, and Dartnall, 2000).

- Commissioning a critical review of educational resources concerning the new strand of identity and diversity in the new Citizenship curriculum (Huddleston, 2007).
- Using the findings from the mapping exercise to fund a series of curriculum development projects involving the leading nongovernment organizations to produce resources to fill in the gaps in relation to the new Citizenship Order. These resources have been made available to schools and teachers.

Encouraging professional training

This approach includes the following activities:

- Developing initial teacher training courses in citizenship. In England these have been set up by the Training and Development Agency (TDA) in higher education institutions across the country. More than 200 new citizenship teachers are trained each year.
- Setting up a new subject association. The Association for Citizenship Teaching (ACT) has been established to meet the needs of all those interested in citizenship education, mirroring associations that support other long-standing curriculum subjects.
- Creating "specialist" teacher posts in citizenship.

Setting up a strong research and evidence base for citizenship education

In the national case study of England, as part of the IEA Civic Education Study, Kerr (1999a) drew attention to the "huge gaps that currently exist in the knowledge and research base which underpins this area in England" (9). With citizenship education moving rapidly from a policy proposal to a real school subject, there was a need to strengthen this base. Accordingly, DfES commissioned the National Foundation for Educational Research (NFER) to undertake the Citizenship Education Longitudinal Study (CELS), which is evaluating citizenship education for eight years. This is tracking a cohort of over 18,000 young people who entered secondary school in September 2002 and, as such, were the first students to have a continuous statutory entitlement to citizenship education until age 18, to ascertain the effects of citizenship education on students' knowledge, understanding, attitudes, and behaviors.[7] It also commissioned NFER to carry out a three-year national evaluation of the post-16 citizenship pilot development program from 2001 to 2004.

Lessons Emerging from Research and Evaluation

The research and evidence base for citizenship education in schools, colleges, and communities is being strengthened all the time, and many of the previous gaps are rapidly being filled (Cleaver et al., 2005; Craig et al., 2005; Ireland et al., 2006; Kerr and Cleaver, 2004; Kerr et al., 2004a; Kerr et al., 2007; Office for Standards in Education, 2005, 2006; Qualifications and Curriculum Authority, 2003; Whiteley, 2005). As a result, consensus is emerging about the definition of citizenship education that schools and colleges are working with, how they are approaching this new subject, and the challenges they are encountering in attempting to transform policy into effective practice. This evidence base is providing a growing sense of realism about the current state of citizenship education in England. Moreover, in the final two years of the CELS, the study will be able to track schools' early reactions to and experiences of implementing the new curriculum at key stages 3 and 4.

An implementation gap

It is now recognized that an implementation gap exists between the vision of policy makers, as laid out by the Crick Group and in various curriculum frameworks for citizenship education, and the ability of those in schools and colleges to understand, act upon, and own that vision in practice. This implementation gap is not just at national level but also at individual school and college levels. CELS reveals differences in attitudes toward citizenship delivery. School leaders are the most positive about citizenship practices in the school or college with regard to what is planned; teachers are less positive about what is actually delivered; and students are the least positive about what is actually received. There will probably always be a gap between what is planned, how it is delivered, and how it is received, but the challenge is narrowing the gap to an acceptable level. One of the major findings of the Council of Europe's All-European Study on EDC Policies (Birzea et al., 2004) was of a similar "implementation gap" between intended policy and actual practice in this area in Europe. It will take time to close this gap in England and Europe—a situation that other nations may wish to take note of. Notwithstanding such a recognition, citizenship education in England has not stalled.

An evolving definition of citizenship education

Citizenship is evolving away from the three strands in the Crick Group report—social and moral responsibility, community involvement, and political literacy—to a growing conceptualization of citizenship in schools as comprising the new three citizenship *Cs*: citizenship in the *curriculum*—how it is delivered as a separate subject, through links with other subjects and through tutorials and collapsed timetable events; citizenship in the school *culture*—how it relates to wider democratic processes and practices in the whole institution, including opportunities for student participation through formal mechanisms, such as school councils, and informal daily practices; and citizenship through links with the wider *community*—how the school links with partners in the local community as well as those at national and international levels. Practitioners find it helpful to talk about the three *Cs* of citizenship, as they fit better with the reality of daily practice in schools and colleges. Moreover, this fits well with the recent focus on the role of schools in England in promoting community cohesion as set out in the *Diversity and Citizenship Curriculum Review* (DfES, 2007) and *Guidance on the Duty to Promote Community Cohesion* (DCSF, 2007).

Factors influencing the approach chosen

Our evidence suggests that a one-size-fits-all approach to citizenship education would not be helpful. A number of factors can affect how citizenship is explained in the school setting.

What is clear from the latest data from the CELS (Kerr et al., 2007) is the growing power and influence of school leaders in deciding on approaches to citizenship education. Two of our case-study schools have recently appointed a new school leader who has put his/her mark on how citizenship should be taught. Decisions about approaches to the delivery of citizenship are made by school leaders, often in consultation with internally appointed citizenship coordinators, in the majority of schools surveyed.

While it is hard to get at the reasons why particular delivery models are chosen, the typology outlined above and case-study visits undertaken with schools suggest that it is most likely a mixture of philosophy about and vision for citizenship combined with pragmatic decisions about how this vision/philosophy of citizenship fits best in relation to school-level challenges and factors. The typology reveals a range of visions and philosophies for citizenship. These are encapsulated in the various starting points or key drivers for citizenship in schools. They range from a narrow interpretation of citizenship as being curriculum based and driven, to a broader view that sees citizenship as encompassing participation and promoting student efficacy in and beyond schools, through drivers that are linked to the wider education policy agenda.

However, these starting points and drivers are often tempered by the challenges posed by school-level factors. These include

- finding time in an already crowded curriculum;
- raising citizenship's status, credibility, and identity alongside existing subjects;
- identifying appropriate staff to coordinate the subject;
- securing teachers who have appropriate expertise and enthusiasm;
- finding sufficient funding to develop/purchase appropriate resources;
- providing staff with relevant training and development;
- generating student enthusiasm for citizenship;
- deciding how to assess, record, and report student outcomes.

With these in mind, it is possible to highlight some factors that may prove helpful:

- A clear understanding of what is meant by citizenship education
- A supportive school ethos and values systems that dovetail with the goals of citizenship education
- Strong senior management support, with senior managers promoting citizenship education through active involvement in planning and delivery approaches in partnership with a strong, respected coordinator
- Equal status and value accorded to citizenship education alongside other curriculum subjects and areas of school experience
- Evidence of ongoing processes of reflection, planning, action, and review in relation to citizenship education
- Recognition of the need for staff training and development in order to build confidence and improve teaching and learning strategies and identification of training priorities
- Sufficient time and resources allocated to citizenship education in terms of curriculum space, teaching staff, teaching and learning resources, and staff training and development opportunities
- A dedicated teaching staff: the more confident and enthusiastic staff are about citizenship education, the more likely they are to develop effective practices and transmit that enthusiasm to students, teachers, and community representatives
- A recognition of gaps in teacher knowledge, understanding and skills in relation to citizenship education, and plans for staff training and development to address these issues
- Emerging assessment strategies for recognizing student achievement that are effective, realistic, and manageable

- Active involvement of students in the school/college as a community, through a range of structures and initiatives, such as school or class councils, peer mediation schemes, and extracurricular activities based on trust, respect, and dialogue
- Opportunities to learn about and experience citizenship education in a range of contexts, not just in the classroom but also through whole-school/college processes and activities involving the wider community

The result?

Despite the recognition that citizenship education in England is uneven and still evolving, a number of school and college approaches have emerged. Table 10.1 and Figure 10.1 outline these types (Kerr et al., 2007). What this typology of citizenship education illustrates is the broad range of ways in which citizenship education is delivered and experienced in English schools. Each school type has a strength or key driver in at least one aspect of citizenship, and none is weak in all.[8]

School type 1 provides a firm grounding of citizenship education in the curriculum but has less participation and inconsistent levels of student efficacy. The key driver for citizenship education is the curriculum.

School type 2 has a sound level of student efficacy in the school, but is weak on student participation in extracurricular activities and its delivery of

Table 10.1: Typology of four approaches to citizenship education in England

	School type			
	1	2	3	4
Student efficacy	Mixed	Average/ high	Low	Average/ high
Level of student participation	Low	Average/ low	Average/ high	High
Importance of CE in curriculum	High	Low	Average	Average/ high
Number of schools	55	52	30	78
Percentage of total	26	24	14	36

Source: Kerr et al., 2007.

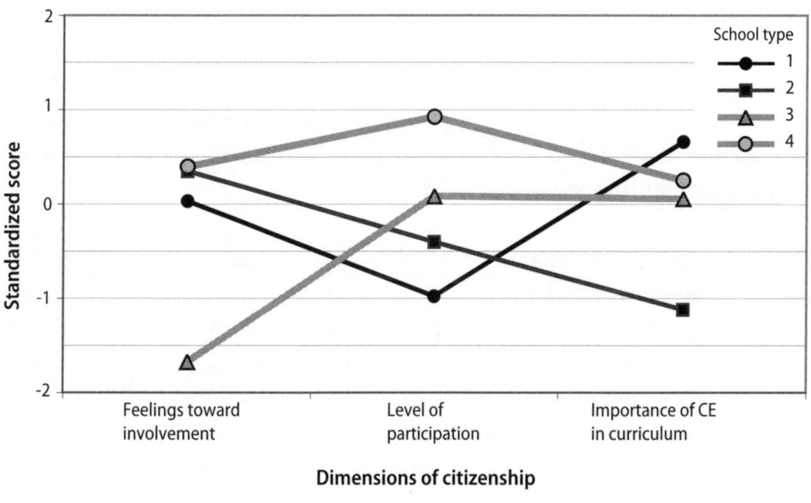

Figure 10.1: Four approaches to citizenship education in England

citizenship through the curriculum. The key driver for citizenship education is student efficacy.

School type 3 has higher than average levels of student participation, but its students feel low levels of efficacy, and the importance placed on citizenship as a curriculum subject is average. The key driver for citizenship education is participation.

Finally, in school type 4, students show high levels of efficacy and participation, and citizenship education is viewed as a strong and central subject within the curriculum. There are a number of key drivers for citizenship, including the curriculum, student efficacy, and participation. This school type is what some observers have defined as offering a "full service" or "citizenship-rich" delivery model (Breslin and Dufour, 2006), a model that comes closest to turning the vision of the Crick report (Advisory Group, 1998) for citizenship in schools into effective practice. It is encouraging to note that the largest single group of schools in our sample (36 percent) fits with this type.

The analysis in the latest report of the CELS (Kerr et al., 2007) reveals that there are three main modes of delivery of citizenship in the curriculum in the schools surveyed, namely, citizenship through modules in PSHE (used in almost two-thirds of schools); citizenship as a dedicated timetable slot (discrete delivery) (used in almost one-third of schools), and citizenship through a cross-curricular approach involving a range of subjects as well as tutorials and assemblies (used in almost half of schools). These modes of delivery have been chosen by schools for various reasons. These reasons, in turn, are influenced by a number of factors mentioned earlier. The revised typology highlights how these factors play out differently within and across schools. This helps to explain the current diversity of approaches to citizenship in secondary schools in England.

Ultimately, the development of citizenship education is not the result of one particular delivery model or mode being in place. Rather it is the outcome of a complex multilayering of factors, influences, and individuals. Although no single factor is dominant, the development of effective practice depends on the influence of key individuals in schools and colleges, notably school and college leaders and the citizenship coordinator. The attitudes and actions of these individuals will guide the progress of citizenship education in the coming years.

Narrowing the implementation gap

In terms of narrowing the implementation gap and tackling the challenges associated with it, the emerging findings from the research and evidence base are already being scrutinized and acted upon by policy makers, support agencies, and practitioners. This underlines the importance of making the findings from the research and evidence base readily available. There has been a particular push on meeting the training and development needs of teachers and in setting clearer indicators in terms of standards and expectations. For example:

- DCSF has supported a major initiative to promote greater CPD (continuing professional development) activity for teachers and schools in citizenship education. The initiative included three strands. First was the appointment of a national citizenship CPD coordinator and three regional coordinators. Second was the development of a practice-based citizenship CPD handbook (Huddleston and Kerr, 2006), and third was the launch of a pilot citizenship CPD certificate for those teaching and leading citizenship in schools and colleges.
- TDA (Training and Development Agency) is funding a major project, entitled *Citized*, to develop and share expertise among all those involved with citizenship in initial teacher education. With its new remit for CPD, there is likely to be increased collaboration between TDA and DCSF concerning citizenship CPD activities.
- QCA is focusing on improving understanding of what pupil and teacher assessment in citizenship means in practice through a series

of pilot projects as well as monitoring the progress of the new GCSE Citizenship Studies short courses at key stage 4.

Current Policy Developments and Progress to Date

There has been a further policy impetus on citizenship education and civil renewal since the accession of the new prime minister, Gordon Brown, in mid-2007. Although the direction of this policy push is clear, its impact cannot yet be measured because it is still unfolding. At the same time, preparations are under way to help schools to translate the ambition of the new National Curriculum and the new Citizenship curriculum into effective policies and practice.

Current Policy Developments

Citizenship education remains at the center of policy debates and policy implementation in the United Kingdom. Indeed, Brown's arrival has caused a flurry of policy initiatives that seek to build on existing developments in citizenship education and civil renewal but also emphasize particular dimensions and approaches. Brown came in talking about the need for what he termed "a new type of politics" (Brown, 2007). This "new type of politics" is founded on a belief that the modernization and renewal of the constitution and democratic institutions are key strategic challenges. Brown wants to address the continuing "democratic deficit," especially the current skewed political and civic participation, with young people and those from lower socioeconomic groups half as likely to participate as those in other groups. His overall strategy to tackle these issues includes

- making civic institutions more responsive and relevant;
- encouraging active citizenship at all levels of society and involving all groups, including children and young people;
- harnessing the power of new technology to facilitate greater civic participation and political involvement;
- announcing constitutional reform and reform of government institutions to provide increased opportunities and influence for people to be involved in decision making (both nationally and locally) and to strengthen government accountability.

To date, Brown has

- Published *The Governance of Britain* (Great Britain, Parliament, 2007). This green paper announced a range of actions including consultations on proposals for increasing participation in England including a formal petitioning process; requirements for citizens' juries; powers of redress to scrutinize and improve the delivery of local services; and powers to ballot on spending decisions. Some electoral reform is also possible. The paper also called for the establishment of a Youth Citizenship Commission to consider "how citizenship education can be connected to both a possible citizenship ceremony when young people reach adulthood and to the acquisition of voting rights." To do this, the Commission will address whether reducing the voting age would increase participation in the political process.
- Commissioned a Citizenship Review to be conducted by Lord Goldsmith. The terms of reference for the review include clarifying the legal rights and responsibilities associated with British citizenship; considering the different categories of British nationality; and exploring the role of citizens and residents in civic society, including voting, jury service, and other forms of civic participation.
- Set up a Governance of Britain Youth Citizenship Commission, chaired by a leading political scientist, Jonathan Tonge, and focusing on young people ages 11–19. The terms of reference include examining what citizenship means to young people; considering how to increase young people's participation in politics and how citizenship can be promoted through volunteering and community engagement; and leading a consultation on whether the voting age should be lowered to 16.
- Signaled a move to tackle migration and codify the steps that new entrants need to take for citizenship. In a recent speech, the prime minister spoke of the need to create a "citizenship contract" that explains an individual's rights and responsibilities. He also proposed tougher tests for citizenship in the future with clear responsibilities set out at each stage of the process for new entrants (Brown, 2008). Brown framed the comments around the twin notion of managed migration and "earned citizenship," of new entrants having to show that they have earned the chance to gain British citizenship and/or to settle in the United Kingdom.
- Talked about the need for a national debate about Britishness. In the light of the rapid changes in modern society, this included the need to debate the heritage and unique features that define the United

Kingdom and those who live in its countries and ensure that these are passed on to young people and new entrants.

Meanwhile, training is under way to prepare schools and teachers to unlock the potential of the new National Curriculum and the new Citizenship curriculum. This includes an emphasis on less prescription and more personalization of learning for children and young people, on less content and more skills development, and on less isolation of subjects and learning and more integration. In terms of citizenship education in schools and colleges, this emphasis is on developing citizenship-rich policies and practices that promote the three *C*s:

- *Citizenship in the school culture*: pervading the culture of the school through formal and informal opportunities, such as an effective school council.
- *Citizenship in the curriculum*: discrete time for citizenship with a specialist team of teachers and citizenship as an entitlement for all students. Citizenship enhances learning in other subjects, for example, a joint project with geography to campaign on a local regeneration development.
- *Citizenship in the community*: through numerous citizenship compelling learning experiences, with student voice and student action, for example, where students investigate local community safety and present recommendations to the local police.

This is a challenging and ambitious approach to the new National Curriculum and to Citizenship that, as the latest findings from the CELS underline, needs to recognize the different routes that schools and colleges have taken in approaching the initial statutory citizenship curriculum in 2002 and their differing rates of progress. Developing citizenship-rich policies will be much easier for some schools than for others.

Progress to Date: A Final Comment

While recent developments in citizenship education provide considerable food for thought, it is important that they are seen within the wider review of citizenship education that is taking place globally. Developments in England are a rapid response to the parallel and common challenge we ultimately face of how to develop the notion among young people that they, as individuals and in collaboration with others, can engage, participate, and make a difference in society. A true measure of citizenship education will be the extent to which it succeeds in building this notion of student efficacy for young people, particularly in school as highlighted in the IEA CIVED study (Torney-Purta et al., 2001; Kerr et al., 2002), as well as at home and in civil and political society at local, national, regional, and international levels. We believe it remains our most important parallel and common challenge for citizenship education. If we succeed, young people will help to redefine citizenship education in the process. However, this will not be an easy task, for as Kerry Kennedy (2003) reminds us, we have to consider the issue of "how to prepare young people for democracy in contexts that are quite different from those that have been known in the past."

This is a challenge not just in England but wherever citizenship education is reviewed, revised, and implemented. It is also important to understand that it is an ongoing challenge, not a one-off. Only time will tell how well we have responded to this challenge in England. The evidence will lie in the attitudes, actions, and behaviors of young people. Only then will we be able to judge how far the central aim of strengthening citizenship education, as set out by the Crick Group, to effect "no less than a change in the political culture of this country [England] both nationally and locally" has been achieved. All we can say, at present, is that a promising start has been made but that these are still early days for citizenship education.

Though green shoots of best practice in citizenship are emerging in schools and colleges in England, they are fragile and by no means universal. They still require careful nurturing with the right climate, drivers, and supports. We have certainly come a long way in a short space of time in England. However, we still have some way to go before we can say with any certainty that we have succeeded in strengthening and renewing education for citizenship and democracy. It will be interesting to monitor how far Gordon Brown succeeds in establishing "a new type of politics"; to see how the relationship develops between "earned citizenship" for new migrants and education for citizenship, what might be termed "learned citizenship" for all plays out in practice; and to evaluate how well schools come to grips with the ambition of the new National Curriculum and Citizenship curriculum with its new emphasis on educating for community cohesion and opportunities to develop locally determined curriculum.

It is perhaps fitting to leave the last word to Professor Jonathan Tonge, the chair of the new Youth Citizenship Commission, who notes in his acceptance of the position that "helping young citizens engage fully with their community and political system is one of the most important challenges in contemporary Britain." This sounds surprisingly similar to the sentiments expressed when the Crick Group was announced a decade earlier in 1998. It encapsulates the enduring challenge of developing education for citizenship in all countries and contexts and not just in England. The overall message is that while good progress has been made in citizenship education over the past decade, there is still much more left to achieve.

Notes

1. The United Kingdom (UK) comprises England, Northern Ireland, Scotland, and Wales.
2. Further details about the new IEA ICCS study can be accessed at *iccs.acer.edu.au/*.
3. Further details about post-16 citizenship can be accessed at *www.post16citizenship.org*.
4. Following the Labour government's election victory in 2005, the function of the Home Office was streamlined to tackle immigration, prisons, and internal and external security. A new, separate Department for Communities and Local Government (DCLG) was created alongside the Home Office to address local issues.
5. The Department for Education and Skills (DfES) has recently been replaced by two new government departments, in the changes brought by the new prime minister, Gordon Brown. These are the Department for Children, Schools, and Families (DCSF) and the Department for Innovation, Universities, and Science (DIUS).
6. There are a number of useful websites for citizenship set up by government departments and support agencies. They include *www.dcsf.gov.uk/citizenship*, *curriculum.qca.org.uk/citizenship*, and *www.post16citizenship.org*.
7. All outputs from the CELS study and further information can be found at *www.nfer.ac.uk/cels*.
8. It is important to remember that strengths and weaknesses are measured in relation to other schools in our sample. It may be desirable that even schools with high levels in each of the three dimensions continue to improve in them.

References

Advisory Group on Education for Citizenship and the Teaching of Democracy in Schools. (1998). *Education for citizenship and the teaching of democracy in schools* (Crick report). London: Qualifications and Curriculum Authority.

Arnot, M., and Dillabough, J.-A. (2000). *Challenging democracy: International perspectives on gender, education, and citizenship.* London: Routledge.

Audigier, F. (1998). *Basic concepts and core competences of education for democratic citizenship: An initial consolidated report.* Strasbourg: Council of Europe.

Audigier, F. (1999). *L'éducation à la citoyenneté.* Paris: INRP.

Beck, U. (2000). *What is globalisation?* London: Polity Press.

Birzea, C., Kerr, D, Mikkelsen, R., Pol, M., Froumin, I., Losito, B., and Sardoc,

M. (2004). *All-European study on education for democratic citizenship policies.* Strasbourg: Council of Europe.

Blunkett, D. (2003a). *Active citizens, strong communities: Progressing civil renewal.* London: Home Office.

Blunkett, D. (2003b). *Civil renewal: A new agenda.* London: CSV/Home Office.

Breslin, T., and Dufour, B. (Eds.). (2006). *Developing citizens: A comprehensive introduction to effective citizenship education in the secondary school.* London: Hodder Murray.

Brown. G. (2007). A new type of politics. Speech to the National Council of Voluntary Organisations, September 3. Available at *www.number-10.gov.uk/output/Page13008.asp.*

Brown, G. (2008). Managed migration and earned citizenship. Speech organized by IPPR at Camden Centre, London, February 20. Available at *www.number10.gov.uk/output/Page14624.asp.*

Callan, E. (1997). *Creating citizens: Political education in a liberal democracy.* Oxford: Oxford University Press.

Carnegie Corporation of New York and CIRCLE. (2003). *The civic mission of schools.* Washington, DC: Carnegie Foundation for the Advancement of Teaching and CIRCLE.

Cleaver, E., Ireland, E., Kerr, D., and Lopes, J. (2005). *Listening to young people: Citizenship education in England.* Citizenship Education Longitudinal Study, 3rd annual report. DfES research report 626. London: DfES.

Cogan, J. (2000). Developing tomorrow's citizens. *The School Field: International Journal of Theory and Research in Education, 11* (3 and 4).

Craig, R., Kerr, D., Wade, P., and Taylor, G. (2005). *Taking post-16 citizenship forward: Learning from the post-16 citizenship development projects.* DfES research report 604. London: DfES.

Crick, B. (2000). *Essays on citizenship.* London: Continuum.

Curtice, J., and Seyd, B. (2004). *Is there a crisis in political participation?* BSA 20th ed., NCSR. London: Sage.

Deakin Crick, R., Coates M., Taylor M., and Ritchie S. (2004) A systematic review of the impact of citizenship education on the provision of schooling. In *Research evidence in education library.* London: EPPI-Centre, Social Science Research Unit, Institute of Education, University of London.

Department for Children, Schools, and Families. (2007). *Guidance on the duty to promote community cohesion.* London: DfES.

Department for Communities and Local Government. (2007). *Commission on Integration and Cohesion: Our shared future.* London: DCLG.

Department for Education and Skills. (2003). *The school self-evaluation tool for citizenship education in secondary schools.* London: DfES.

Department for Education and Skills. (2004). *Working together: Giving children and young people a say.* London: DfES.

Department for Education and Skills. (2006, July). *Five-year strategic plan and 2006/07 annual plan.* National Primary and Secondary Strategies. London:

DfES. Available at *www.standards.dfes.gov.uk/secondary/keystage3/downloads/annualplan06_ns_sum.pdf.*

Department for Education and Skills. (2007). *Diversity and citizenship curriculum review* (Ajegbo report). London: DfES.

Electoral Commission. (2005). *Election 2005: Turnout. How many, who, and why?* London: Electoral Commission.

Electoral Commission. (2006). *Voting for change: Delivering democracy?* London: Electoral Commission.

Electoral Commission and Hansard Society. (2006). *An audit of political engagement 4.* London: Electoral Commission and Hansard Society.

European Commission. (2006). *Recommendation of the European Parliament and of the Council of 18 December 2006 on key competences for lifelong learning (2006/962/EC).* Brussels: European Commission.

Feinberg, W. (1998). *Common schools/uncommon identities: National unity and cultural difference.* New Haven: Yale University Press.

Froumin, I. (2004). *All-European study on policies for EDC: Regional study eastern European region.* Strasbourg: Council of Europe.

Further Education Funding Council. (2000). *Citizenship for 16–19-year-olds in education and training: Report of the advisory group to the secretary of state for education and employment.* Coventry: FEFC.

Gearon, L. (2003). *How do we learn to become good citizens? A professional user review of UK research undertaken for the British Educational Research Association.* Nottingham: BERA.

Giddens, A. (1998). *The third way: The renewal of social democracy.* London: Polity Press.

Great Britain. Parliament. House of Commons. (2004). *The children bill.* London: Stationery Office.

Great Britain. Parliament. House of Commons. (2007). *The governance of Britain.* London: Stationery Office.

Gutmann, A. (1999). *Democratic education* (2nd ed.). Princeton: Princeton University Press.

Hahn, C. L. (1998). *Becoming political: Comparative perspectives on citizenship education.* Albany: State University of New York Press.

HM Government. (2004). *Every child matters: Change for children.* Available at *www.everychildmatters.gov.uk/_files/F9E3F941DC8D4580539EE4C743E9371D.pdf.*

HM Treasury/Department for Children, Schools, and Families. (2007). *Aiming high for young people: A 10-year strategy for positive activities.* Available at *www.dfes.gov.uk/publications/tenyearyouthstrategy/docs/cyp_tenyearstrategy_260707.pdf.*

Home Office. (2003). *The new and the old: The report of the "Life in the United Kingdom" Advisory Group.* London: Home Office.

Home Office. (2004). *Life in the United Kingdom: A journey to citizenship.* London: Home Office.

Home Office. (2005). *Together we can: The government action plan for civil renewal.* London: Home Office.

Home Office. (2007). *Life in the United Kingdom: A journey to citizenship.* (2nd ed.). London: Home Office.

Hoskins, B., Jesinghaus, J., Mascherini, M., Munda, G., Nardo, M., Saisana, M., Van Nijlen, D., and Villalba, E. (2006). *Measuring active citizenship in Europe.* CRELL research paper 4. Ispra: Joint Research Centre/CRELL.

Hoskins, B., Villalba, E., and Van Nijlen, D. (2007). *Civic competence: A composite indicator to measure the ability to be an active citizen.* Discussion paper. Ispra: CRELL.

Huddleston. E., and Kerr, D. (Eds.). (2006). *Making sense of citizenship: A CPD handbook.* London: Hodder Murray.

Huddleston, E. (2007). *Identity, diversity, and citizenship: A critical review of educational resources.* London: Association for Citizenship Teaching/Citizenship Foundation.

Hurd, D. (1988, April 29). Citizenship in the Tory democracy. *New Statesman*, 14.

Ichilov, O. (Ed.). (1998). *Citizenship and citizenship education in a changing world.* London: Woburn Press.

International Association for the Evaluation of Educational Achievement. (2007). *International civic and citizenship education study: Assessment framework.* Amsterdam: IEA.

Ireland, E., Kerr, D., Lopes, J., Nelson, J., and Cleaver E. (2006). *Active citizenship and young people: Opportunities, experiences, and challenges in and beyond school.* DfES Research Report 732. London: DfES.

Jowell, R., and Park, A. (1998). *Young people, politics, and citizenship: A disengaged generation?* London: Citizenship Foundation.

Kennedy, K. (2003). Preparing young Australians for an uncertain future: New thinking about citizenship education. *Teaching Education, 14* (1), 53–67.

Kerr, D. (1999a). *Re-examining citizenship education: The case of England.* Slough: National Foundation for Educational Research.

Kerr, D. (1999b). *Citizenship education: An international comparison.* London: Qualifications and Curriculum Authority/National Foundation for Educational Research.

Kerr, D. (2001). Citizenship education and educational policy making. In J. Arthur, I. Davies, A. Wrenn, T. Haydn, and D. Kerr, *Citizenship through secondary history* (3–28) London: Routledge/Falmer.

Kerr, D., Blenkinsop, S., and Dartnall, L. (2000). Mapping citizenship education resources. Unpublished report. Slough: National Foundation for Educational Research.

Kerr, D., Lines, A., Blenkinsop, S., and Schagen, I. (2002). *What citizenship and education mean to 14-year-olds: England's results from the IEA citizenship education study.* London: DfES/ National Foundation for Educational Research.

Kerr, D. (2004). *All-European study on policies for EDC: Regional study western Europe region.* Strasbourg: Council of Europe.

Kerr, D., Ireland, E., Lopes, J., and Craig, R., with Cleaver, E. (2004a). *Making citizenship real: Citizenship Education Longitudinal Study, 2nd annual report. First longitudinal survey.* DfES research report 531. London: DfES.

Kerr, D., Mikkelsen, R., Pol, M., Froumin, I., Losito, B., and Sardoc, M. (2004b). *EDC policies in Europe: A synthesis of six regional studies.* Strasbourg: Council of Europe.

Kerr, D., and Cleaver, E. (2004). *Citizenship Education Longitudinal Study: Literature review—Citizenship education one year on—What does it mean? Emerging definitions and approaches in the first year of national curriculum citizenship in England.* DfES research report 532. London: DfES.

Kerr, D., Lopes, J., Nelson, J., White, K., Cleaver, E., and Benton, T. (2007). *Vision versus pragmatism: Citizenship in the secondary school curriculum in England.* DfES research report 845. London: DfES.

Kerr, D., and Lopes, J. (2008). Studying civic and citizenship education in the European context. Paper prepared for the annual meetings of the American Educational Research Association, New York, March 24–28.

Kerr, D., Smith, A., and Twine, C. (2008). Citizenship education in the UK. In J. Arthur, I. Davies, and C. Hahn (Eds.), *Handbook for citizenship education* (252–62). London: Routledge/Falmer.

Kymlicka, W. (2001). *Politics in the vernacular: Nationalism, multiculturalism, and citizenship.* Oxford: Oxford University Press.

Learning and Teaching Scotland. (2000). *Education for citizenship in Scotland: A paper for discussion and consultation.* Dundee: LTS.

Levine, P. (2007). *The future of democracy: Developing the next generation of American citizens.* Medford: Tufts University Press.

Losito, B. (2004). *All-European study on policies for EDC: Regional study southern Europe region.* Strasbourg: Council of Europe.

Macedo, S. J. (2000). *Diversity and distrust: Civic education in a multicultural democracy.* Cambridge: Harvard University Press.

MacGregor, J. (1990). Helping today's children become tomorrow's citizens. Speech at the Consultative Conference on Citizenship, Northampton, February 16.

Maylor, U., and Read, B., with Mendick, H., Ross, A., and Rollock, N. (2007). *Diversity and citizenship in the curriculum: Research review.* DfES Research Report 819. London: DfES.

Mikkelsen, R. (2004). *All-European study on policies for EDC: Regional study northern European region.* Strasbourg: Council of Europe.

Office for Standards in Education. (2005). *Citizenship in secondary schools: Evidence from OFSTED inspections (2003/04).* HMI Report 2335. London: OFSTED.

Office for Standards in Education. (2006). *Towards consensus? Citizenship in secondary schools.* HMI Report 2666. London: OFSTED.

Pol, M. (2004). *All-European study on policies for EDC: Regional study central European region.* Strasbourg: Council of Europe.

Putnam, R. (2000). *Bowling alone: Civic disengagement in America.* New York: Simon and Schuster.

Qualifications and Curriculum Authority. (1999). *Citizenship: Key stages 3–4.* London: DFEE/QCA.

Qualifications and Curriculum Authority. (2001a). *Citizenship: A scheme of work for key stage 3.* London: QCA.

Qualifications and Curriculum Authority. (2001b). *Citizenship at key stage 3: Getting involved—Extending opportunities for pupil participation.* London: QCA.

Qualifications and Curriculum Authority. (2002). *Citizenship: A scheme of work at key stages 1 and 2.* London: QCA.

Qualifications and Curriculum Authority. (2003). *Citizenship: 2002–2003 annual report by QCA's diversity and inclusion team.* London: QCA.

Qualifications and Curriculum Authority. (2004). *Play your part: Post-16 citizenship.* London: QCA.

Qualifications and Curriculum Authority. (2007a). New secondary curriculum. Available at *www.qca.org.uk/qca_11717.aspx.*

Qualifications and Curriculum Authority. (2007b). *The new secondary curriculum: What has changed and why?* London: QCA.

Qualifications and Curriculum Authority. (2007c). Citizenship program of study: Key stage 4. Available at *www.qca.org.uk/libraryAssets/media/Citizenship_KS4_PoS.pdf.*

Quality Improvement Agency. (2006). *Getting started with post-16 citizenship.* Coventry: QIA.

Reimers, F. (2008). Assessing citizenship skills in Latin America: The development of a regional module as part of the International Civic and Citizenship Education Study. Paper prepared for the annual meetings of the American Educational Research Association, New York, March 24–28.

Smith, A. (2003). Citizenship education in Northern Ireland: Beyond national identity? *Cambridge Journal of Education, 33* (1), 15–31.

Torney-Purta, J., Lehmann, R., Oswald, H., and Schulz, W. (2001). *Citizenship and education in 28 countries: Civic knowledge and participation at age 14.* Amsterdam: International Association for the Evaluation of Educational Achievement (IEA).

Whiteley, P. (2005). *Citizenship Education Longitudinal Study second literature review —Citizenship education—The political science perspective.* DFES research report 631. London: DfES.

Wilkinson, H., and Mulgan, G. (1995). *Freedom's children.* London: Demos.

Young, I. M. (1990). Polity and group difference: A critique of the ideal of universal citizenship. *Ethics, 99* (2), 58–68.

Conclusion

The Way Forward

Peter Levine and James Youniss

Although the chapters collected in this volume range widely across institutions, policies, and practices, they share several important principles. First, they understand "civic engagement" broadly. The activities and attitudes that the chapters treat as desirable include voting, volunteering, trusting other people, tolerating other people and their views, discussing issues, attending meetings, joining groups, and advocating for political change. One could reasonably ask whether even more outcomes should be added, such as military service, patriotic sentiments, religious attendance, civil disobedience, membership in online groups and games, or even "hacktivism" (the creation or use of illegal software for political purposes). A long and varied list requires a conceptual foundation—a principle of inclusion. But there can be no consensus about which activities constitute valuable "civic engagement." That is a matter that divides people depending on their views of basic social issues. One will be, for example, far more enthusiastic about protest and civil disobedience if one considers the current social order to be fundamentally unjust than if one admires it.

Instead of deciding which forms of civic engagement are desirable or appropriate, we might say that this is a question for citizens to decide, depending on their situations. George Washington and his contemporaries opted for violent revolution, Martin Luther King Jr. and his allies chose nonviolent resistance, and plenty of Americans have chosen everyday service or regular voting. Decisions about how to engage are for citizens to make, as are decisions about whether the government is an ally, an obstacle, or irrelevant to their particular causes. That is a "citizen-centered," rather than a government-centered, notion of politics (Gibson, 2007).

Still, responsible citizenship is not just in the eye of the beholder. It requires that we engage (rather than sit on the sidelines) and that we choose a course of action with good information, in dialogue with others. Individuals' perspectives and assumptions should be challenged by facts and rival opinions.

In short, one way to answer the question, "How should people engage?" is to say that they should deliberate about what to do. Deliberative democracy arises as a norm explicitly in Diana Hess's chapter and implicitly in several others. But these chapters are also about action, not only about talk. Deliberation alone is artificial and scholastic. Most people are not motivated to discuss public issues unless there is also an opportunity to change the world, and those who do talk without acting miss the chance to learn from personal experience. Excellent practices of civic education—from service-learning to youth organizing, from membership on city commissions to activism within political parties—combine deliberation with experience in ways that model excellent citizenship.

Thus we detect a common normative core in all the contributions to this book. They put citizens at the center of politics, as active and deliberative agents. This ideal is not incompatible with representative democracy, which assigns decisions to professional leaders who are chosen by the public in periodic elections. Henry Milner's chapter emphasizes the importance of teaching specifically about voting and other interactions with the government. Clearly, there must be a division of labor between representative institutions and the public; neither can solve every problem on its own. But representative institutions cannot work without a strong base of active and deliberative citizenship. We citizens will not know how to choose representatives who are good at deliberating unless we have personal experience with discussing and addressing common problems in diverse groups (Elkin, 2006, 177). Thus public participation is necessary, at least, as a complement to formal debate in legislatures.

In addition to taking a broad view of citizenship, the chapters in this book move from individual behavior to policy change. They recognize that it matters how citizens behave. People have civic agency; their activism is a powerful form of renewable energy. But the authors do not presume that we can lecture people into behaving as conscientious and active citizens—nor that a failure to engage is a sign of bad character.

Public engagement is a public good, in the strict sense that it benefits members of a community even if they do not themselves engage. By volunteering and joining and running associations, we make our communities safer, healthier, and more attractive for all. Notoriously, public goods are difficult to generate because of "free-rider" problems. People who calculate their individual self-interest are unlikely to contribute. Even voting (a relatively cheap and easy activity) does not pay off for the individual voter because too many other votes are also cast (Downs, 1957). Volunteering and political activism are more costly and difficult and therefore more difficult to sustain. Yet clearly communities are capable of generating public goods through voluntary action. Alexis de Tocqueville thought that Americans were especially good at that. Sustained civic engagement requires a combination of public norms and arguments, grassroots organizations that recruit and support members, and favorable policies.

Policies are favorable if they make engagement more rewarding or supply the skills, motivations, and information that people need to engage effectively. The authors of this book provide and defend a series of concrete policy recommendations to enhance civic engagement, targeted at youth because they are more malleable than adults and because the state has a recognized responsibility for their education. The proposed policies include

- school policies that support discussions of controversial issues, community service linked to academic study (service-learning), simulations of government and politics, extracurricular participation, and student voice in school governance;
- support for teachers to learn how to do these things well;
- municipal policies that involve youth in policymaking at various levels of city or county government, as part of a broader "pyramid" of participation that also includes service opportunities for youth;
- funding and other support for after-school and community-based programs that offer opportunities for service and for youth activism;
- reforms within political parties to encourage them to invest more in developing young members with real voice;
- political reforms to make legislative districts more competitive.

It will not be easy to achieve these changes. They are not in anyone's narrow self-interest. To be sure, individual children are better off when they have opportunities for service, activism, and leadership; they are more likely to flourish (Lerner, 2004). But that does not mean that it pays for a parent to work to expand service opportunities for all youth. Although some parents are committed activists, it is more common for families to influence schools by deciding where to enroll their own children. In turn, schools and school systems—and especially colleges and universities—feel intense pressure to attract students, especially those who have choices. In making decisions about enrollment, families seem most interested in obtaining skills that are valuable in the labor market. Published rankings of high schools and universities almost always emphasize test scores, not civic engagement.[1]

To make matters worse, some organizations and leaders actually stand to lose power if diverse young people become more engaged. Higher turnout, for example, means more voters who might opt not to reelect the incumbents, who won office when turnout was lower. Redistricting is an even more direct assault on incumbents' advantages.

These are cautions; they do not prove that it is impossible to achieve beneficial reform. If we could never overcome such challenges, there would be no system of universal education (for its original nineteenth-century rationale was to prepare young people to be active citizens). We would have no Land Grant state university system or network of community colleges. We would never have lowered barriers to voting or created national and community service programs such as the Civilian Conservation Corps or AmeriCorps. Such reforms are possible, but they require strategic thinking.

The chapters in this book should guide strategists by laying out some of the crucial questions. First, several authors (especially Kahne and Middaugh and Hart and Kirshner) argue that civic opportunities must be targeted at disadvantaged young people. Educational success correlates with civic participation: that is the "best documented finding in American political behavior research" (Nie, Junn, and Stehlik-Barry, 1996, 31). Public schools and other government-funded programs should try to compensate for this inequality by directing their resources to students who are on less successful academic tracks. Instead, they tend to reinforce disparities by reserving civic opportunities for the most academically successful students in the schools and communities with the best educational outcomes.

This is a problem, but it admits of several possible answers. One would be to write legislation that directs resources to poorer communities, schools, and students. For example, Title I high schools (those with low-income student bodies) might receive most of the new resources for teacher training that Hess and Kahne and Middaugh advocate. Poor neighborhoods might be given advantages in the competition for after-school funding advocated by Youniss and Levine and Hart and Kirshner.

That would be an efficient way to enhance equity, but it might prove politically unsustainable when highly educated and affluent adults lost interest in subsidizing the civic development of other people's children. The alternative is to write legislation to universalize a set of civic opportunities, so that they are understood as part of the package of educational experiences that *all* students must receive (along with basic education in reading and mathematics). This is a less efficient path to equity but perhaps a more politically realistic one. Its success will depend upon providing support for civic education on an equal basis, not just requiring the same courses in every school. In their discussion of French civic education, Hooghe and Claes show that a universal mandate actually heightens inequality because the poorly performing schools assume they will score badly on civics and put their resources elsewhere.

Another strategic choice is presented by the strong link between civic engagement and healthy human development or "flourishing." Because of that link, we could present civic experiences as tools to reduce teen pregnancy and drug abuse and to enhance students' performance in schools and jobs. That argument would be valid, and it might appeal to legislators and other powerful interests that are concerned with social problems and global economic competition. In the modern workplace, after all, economically valuable skills (such as teamwork and problem solving) are also democratic skills.

The drawback, however, is that civic programs can be watered down if they are designed and promoted mainly for their economic and health benefits. It appears, for example, that service-learning and extracurricular participation enhance students' success in school (Dávila and Mora, 2007a and 2007b). This is useful information, but it does not show that the experiences that would *maximize* students' identities as democratic citizens would also *maximize* their success in school. It might turn out that youth organizing (described by Hart and Kirshner) is particularly good for democratic development because it is open-ended, youth-led, and concerned with real issues of power. But other civic experiences, such as participation in sanctioned school organizations or community service, might have better academic outcomes.[2]

In the worst case, we might repeat the experience of Progressive Era educational reforms. John Dewey and his contemporaries (1916) promoted serious opportunities for democratic engagement and tried to "reorganize" American education "so that learning takes place in connection with the intelligent carrying forward of purposeful activities." Diane Ravitch (1983) wrote that Dewey saw this kind of educational reform as a "vital part" of a broader "social and political reform movement" that aimed to make political participation more meaningful and more equitable. Thus, while Dewey and his fellow progressives introduced new educational opportunities in schools, they also tried to reform politics by fighting corruption and discrimination. Unfortunately, the innovations that the progressives introduced into schools often lost their original connection to democratic reform. When their political purpose was forgotten or ignored, extracurricular activities and social studies classes became means to impart good behavior, academic skills, or "social hygiene." Soon, as Ravitch wrote, "the progressive education movement became institutionalized and professionalized, and its major themes accordingly changed. Shorn of its roots in politics and society, pedagogical progressivism came to be identified with the child-centered school; with a pretentious scientism; with social efficiency and social utility rather than social reform; and with a vigorous suspicion of 'bookish' learning." Today there is a serious risk that we could repeat the same pattern.

We recommend consciously seeking to provide challenging and authentic democratic experiences to youth who need those opportunities most, without forgetting the importance of a broad and sustainable constituency. Facing political reality, we should distribute opportunities widely (not target them only at poor students). We should cite both political and economic purposes and goals for civic education. Finally, we should form partnerships between civic educators and their organizations, on the one hand, and political movements that would benefit from broader participation, on the other. Civil rights groups, unions, environmental organizations, and insurgent political movements of the center, right, and left all have reasons to support civic opportunities that will generate new supporters for them in the next generation. Through a combination of coalition politics, idealistic public rhetoric, tangible evidence of economic and social benefits, and political reform, we can continue the legacy of the nineteenth-century public school movement and the Land Grant system, the original progressive reforms, the Civilian Conservation Corps, and the Freedom Schools of the civil rights movement. We can once again expand, strengthen, and broaden opportunities for young people to become citizens.

Notes

1. Exceptions include *Washington Monthly's College Guide* and Princeton Review's *Colleges with a Conscience*, but these represent a small part of the market.
2. We are not aware of any direct comparisons in the empirical literature.

References

Dávila, A., and Mora, M. T. (2007a). Civic engagement and high school academic progress: An analysis using NELS data. CIRCLE Working Paper 52.

Dávila, A., and Mora, M. T. (2007b). Do gender and ethnicity affect civic engagement and academic progress? CIRCLE Working Paper 53.

Dewey, J. (1916). *Democracy and education.* Carbondale: Southern Illinois University Press, 1985.

Downs, A. (1957). *An economic theory of democracy.* New York: Harper and Row.

Elkin, S. L. (2006). *Reconstructing the commercial republic: Constitutional design after Madison.* Chicago: University of Chicago Press.

Gibson, C. (2007). *Citizens at the center: A new approach to civic engagement.* Washington: Case Foundation, 2007.

Lerner, R. M. (2004). *Liberty: Thriving and civic engagement among America's youth.* Thousand Oaks, CA: Sage.

Nie, N. H., Junn, J., and Stehlik-Barry, K. (1996). *Education and democratic citizenship in America.* Chicago: University of Chicago Press.

Ravitch, D. (1983). *The troubled crusade.* New York: Basic Books.

Contributors

Ellen Claes is a Ph.D. candidate at the Catholic University of Leuven in Belgium. Her research focuses on civic education in Western Europe.

Elizabeth Cleaver is an Academic Practice Consultant at the University of Birmingham, UK. Prior to this appointment, she spent five years leading the government-funded Citizenship Education Longitudinal Study at the National Foundation for Educational Research, UK.

James G. Gimpel is Professor of Government at the University of Maryland, College Park. His research interests lie in the areas of political socialization, political behavior, and geographic variation in political attitudes and opinions. He was the principal investigator in a path-breaking study of variations in civic knowledge and engagement across local districts between Baltimore, MD, and Washington, DC, as described in *Cultivating Democracy: Civic Environments and Political Socialization in America* (Brookings Institution Press).

Daniel Hart is Professor of Psychology and Childhood Studies at Rutgers University, Camden. He has done extensive research on personality and civic development in adolescents, particularly those living in low-wealth urban environments. He has looked especially at the demographic makeup of neighborhoods and found a negative correlation between "child saturation" and civic knowledge.

Diana Hess is Associate Director of Curriculum and Instruction at the University of Wisconsin, Madison. Since 1998, she has studied what young people learn from deliberation of highly controversial political and legal issues in the classroom. She is currently the lead investigator of a five-year study that seeks to understand relationships between various approaches to democratic education in schools and political engagement among young people after they leave school.

Marc Hooghe is Professor of Political Science at the Catholic University of Leuven in Belgium. He has published widely on aspects of political socialization, social capital, and political culture and is currently working on a comparative study of youth civic engagement in Western Europe and Canada.

Joseph Kahne is Abbie Valley Professor of Education, Dean of the School of Education, and Director of the Civic Engagement Research Group at Mills College, Oakland, CA. He is currently conducting a longitudinal study of the impact of schools and digital media on civic and political development. His recent work dealing with digital media and civic opportunity gaps is available at *www.civicsurvey.org*.

David Kerr is Principal Research Officer at the National Foundation for Educational Research, UK, and Visiting Professor of Citizenship at Birbeck College, University of London. He directs the Citizenship Education Longitudinal Study and is Associate Director of the IEA International Civic and Citizenship Education Study.

Ben Kirshner is Assistant Professor of Educational Psychology and Adolescent Development at the University of Colorado, Boulder. His research examines how young people learn and grow through participation in civic activism, action research, and community-related after-school programs.

Peter Levine is Research Director of the Jonathan M. Tisch College of Citizenship and Public Service and Director of the Center for Information and Research on Civic Learning and Engagement (CIRCLE) at Tufts University. He is the former Chair of the Campaign for the Civic Mission of Schools and author of *The Future of Democracy: Developing the Next Generation of American Citizens* (Tufts University Press).

Ellen Middaugh is Senior Research Associate at Mills College and a doctoral candidate in Human Development in the Graduate School of Education at the University of California, Berkeley. She studies civic education in cultural and social contexts and is coauthor of the paper *Democracy for Some: The Civic Opportunity Gap* (CIRCLE).

Henry Milner is Visiting Professor at Umea University in Sweden, Research Fellow at the Université de Montréal and the Institute for Research in Public Policy, and co-publisher of *Inroads,* the Canadian journal of opinion and policy. He is the author of eight books on politics and society.

Shanna Pearson-Merkowitz is a Ph.D. candidate in the Department of Government at the University of Maryland, College Park. She studies and has published in the areas of political behavior, elections, political socialization, and ethnic minority politics.

Diana Marginean Schor is currently pursuing her Ph.D. in Social Policy with focus on youth civic engagement at Brandeis University. She brings to her studies a background in work for grassroots-level nonprofit organizations in Romania and the United States and has worked as a social development scientist for the World Bank.

Daniel M. Shea is Professor of Political Science and Director of the Center for Political Participation at Allegheny College, Meadville, PA. His research interests center mainly on political parties, elections, and the legislative process. His most recent coauthored book is *Living Democracy* (Prentice Hall).

Carmen Sirianni is Professor of Sociology and Social Policy at Brandeis University. He has served as Senior Advisor to the National Commission on Civic Renewal, Research Director of the Reinventing Citizenship Project, and Coordinator of a collaborative governance group within Barack Obama's 2008 Urban Policy Committee. He is also the author of the forthcoming book *Investing in Democracy: Engaging Citizens in Collaborative Governance* (Brookings Institution Press).

James Youniss is the James and Wylma R. Curtin Professor of Psychology at the Catholic University of America in Washington, DC. He has studied youth development for more than four decades, and his current work focuses on the resources and conditions that lead to civic engagement.

Index